SUPER HOROSCOPE
LEO
2013
JULY 21 - AUGUST 21

B
BERKLEY BOOKS, NEW YORK

THE BERKLEY PUBLISHING GROUP
Published by the Penguin Group
Penguin Group (USA) Inc.
375 Hudson Street, New York, New York 10014, USA
Penguin Group (Canada), 90 Eglinton Avenue East, Suite 700, Toronto, Ontario M4P 2Y3, Canada
(a division of Pearson Penguin Canada Inc.) • Penguin Books Ltd., 80 Strand, London WC2R 0RL,
England • Penguin Group Ireland, 25 St. Stephen's Green, Dublin 2, Ireland (a division of Penguin
Books Ltd.) • Penguin Group (Australia), 250 Camberwell Road, Camberwell, Victoria 3124, Australia
(a division of Pearson Australia Group Pty. Ltd.) • Penguin Books India Pvt. Ltd., 11 Community
Centre, Panchsheel Park, New Delhi—110 017, India • Penguin Group (NZ), 67 Apollo Drive,
Rosedale, Auckland 0632, New Zealand (a division of Pearson New Zealand Ltd.) • Penguin Books
(South Africa) (Pty.) Ltd., 24 Sturdee Avenue, Rosebank, Johannesburg 2196, South Africa

Penguin Books Ltd., Registered Offices: 80 Strand, London WC2R 0RL, England

The publishers regret that they cannot answer individual letters requesting personal horoscope information.

2013 SUPER HOROSCOPE LEO

PUBLISHING HISTORY
Berkley trade paperback edition / July 2012

Berkley trade paperback ISBN: 978-0-425-24637-5

Library of Congress Cataloging-in-Publication Data

ISSN: 1535-8968

PRINTED IN THE UNITED STATES OF AMERICA

10 9 8 7 6 5 4 3 2 1

ALWAYS LEARNING   PEARSON

Contents

THE CUSP-BORN LEO

Are you *really* a Leo? If your birthday falls during the fourth week of July, at the beginning of Leo, will you still retain the traits of Cancer, the sign of the Zodiac before Leo? And what if you were born late in August—are you more Virgo than Leo? Many people born at the edge, or cusp, of a sign have difficulty determining exactly what sign they are. If you are one of these people, here's how you can figure it out, once and for all.

Consult the cusp table on the facing page, then locate the year of your birth. The table will tell you the precise days on which the Sun entered and left your sign for the year of your birth. In that way you can determine if you are a true Leo—or whether you are a Cancer or Virgo—according to the variations in cusp dates from year to year (see also page 17).

If you were born at the beginning or end of Leo, yours is a lifetime reflecting a process of subtle transformation. Your life on Earth will symbolize a significant change in consciousness, for you are either about to enter a whole new way of living or are leaving one behind.

If you are a Leo, born during the fourth week of July, you may want to read the horoscope book for Cancer as well as Leo. Cancer holds the keys to many of your secret uncertainties and deep-rooted problems, and your secret needs and wishes. You are the spirit of independence and creativity, or want to be. Yet through Cancer you reveal your deep, but often hidden, need to have strong ties. You may be trying to leave dependencies behind, yet you find yourself drawn again and again to the past or to family responsibilities.

You reflect the birth of a new sign, a ripe, whole person, fully able to tap and realize all your potentials for love and creativity.

If you were born after the third week of August, you may want to read the horoscope book for Virgo as well, for through Virgo you learn to put all your talents as a lover or creator to work. Your love for life is infectious, and your zest and sunny disposition are an inspiration to everyone around you. You are capable of seriousness, discipline, and great diligence.

You are a lover—ardent, passionate, and determined that love will not elude you. Though you may try to avoid it, you will find yourself in work, health, or duty situations that demand less emotion and more mind. You are not afraid of taking a gamble and are reluctant to give up your love of enjoyment for work or studies. You can blend professionalism and propriety in perfect amounts. You are the natural mixture of creativity and discipline, able to feel and to analyze. You symbolize the warmth and fullness of a late summer day, a natural ripeness and maturity that is mellow and comfortable to be near.

THE CUSPS OF LEO

DATES SUN ENTERS LEO
(LEAVES CANCER)

July 23 every year from 1900 to 2015, except for the following:

July 22						
1928	1953	1968	1981	1992	2001	2010
32	56	69	84	93	2002	2011
36	57	72	85	94	2004	2012
40	60	73	86	96	2005	2013
44	61	76	88	97	2006	2014
48	64	77	89	98	2008	2015
52	65	80	90	2000	2009	

DATES SUN LEAVES LEO
(ENTERS VIRGO)

August 23 every year from 1900 to 2015, except for the following:

August 22				
1960	1980	1992	2001	2012
64	84	93	2004	2013
68	88	96	2005	
72	89	97	2008	
76		2000	2009	

THE ASCENDANT: LEO RISING

Could you be a "double" Leo? That is, could you have Leo as your Rising sign as well as your Sun sign? The tables on pages 8–9 will tell you Leos what your Rising sign happens to be. Just find the hour of your birth, then find the day of your birth, and you will see which sign of the Zodiac is your Ascendant, as the Rising sign is called. The Ascendant is called that because it is the sign rising on the eastern horizon at the time of your birth. For a more detailed discussion of the Rising sign and the twelve houses of the Zodiac, see pages 17–20.

The Ascendant, or Rising sign, is placed on the 1st house in a horoscope, of which there are twelve houses. The 1st house represents your response to the environment—your unique response. Call it identity, personality, ego, self-image, facade, come-on, body-mind-spirit—whatever term best conveys to you the meaning of the you that acts and reacts in the world. It is a you that is always changing, discovering a new you. Your identity started with birth and early environment, over which you had little conscious control, and continues to experience, to adjust, to express itself. The 1st house also represents how others see you. Has anyone ever guessed your sign to be your Rising sign? People may respond to that personality, that facade, that body type governed by your Rising sign.

Your Ascendant, or Rising sign, modifies your basic Sun sign personality, and it affects the way you act out the daily predictions for your Sun sign. If your Rising sign indeed is Leo, what follows is a description of its effect on your horoscope. If your Rising sign is not Leo, but some other sign of the Zodiac, you may wish to read the horoscope book for that sign as well.

With Leo on the Ascendant, that is, in the 1st house, the planet that rules Leo is therefore in the 1st house. That planet is the Sun. Here it may give you a special robustness—in appearance, in health, in spirit, in action—that you can count on long after your normal energy reserves have dried up. On the negative side, the Sun here may give you an overdose of pride or insolence. Such pride could make you quick to resent or retaliate when reason instead should be the response.

Leo in the 1st house accentuates every Leo trait, for the Rising sign has a strong influence in your horoscope. A flair for the dramatic will be especially evident in the fabric of your life. You like managing people and events as long as you can play center stage, or at least weave a powerful character part, for much of the time. You could create intrigue if it provides an opportunity for you to take a leading role. However much you like pulling strings, though, your frank and generous disposition rises above petty disputes. You abhor superficial alliances or cliques of any sort.

There may also be drama in your personal appearance and in your possessions and surroundings. You have been known to adorn yourself and your environment as much, maybe sometimes more, for the effect it will create as for the comfort it will give you and others. Your appearance itself, whether natural or affected, may well run to the true Leo type: high coloring, proud head, bold stance. You can use physical gestures as signals to people—to lure, to persuade, to threaten. And because love, especially to be loved, is a fundament of your ego, your body language acts instinctively to attract people to you.

Your search for identity will never be a solitary, introspective one. Public appreciation and power are important to you. You need constant interaction with and approval from people. You are likely to find the most satisfying ties with groups whose goals are humanitarian and ideological, whether the groups are social or political or educational. But before you do, you may discover in youth and early adulthood many facets of yourself through creations that are not so tightly bound to an organized group. And it is imperative for you to create—a work of art, a child, an intrigue, a love affair, a partnership, a principle.

Your need for people may reflect an inner insecurity. That self-image, which you experience as constantly changing, may not be actualized until you see it mirrored in people's responses; a positive one reinforces your natural enthusiasm, a negative one may induce self-pity. Your need for creation may also be tied to the building of an ego. You seek success, and are very likely to get your lion's share of it in your lifetime, through what you do, not through what you are. For what you do allows you to know and then to be who you are. You expect your creations and your things to bestow honor upon you; they are not merely natural or spontaneous expressions.

Above all, love and loyalty are the key words through which you with Leo Rising seek to root yourself in your environment. Love and loyalty motivate your simplest act, your grandest attempt. They, too, can be the cause of pain and loss. You are happiest when you love and are loved in return.

RISING SIGNS FOR LEO

Hour of Birth*	Date of Birth		
	July 22–27	**July 28–August 1**	**August 2–6**
Midnight	Taurus	Taurus	Gemini
1 AM	Gemini	Gemini	Gemini
2 AM	Gemini	Gemini	Cancer
3 AM	Cancer	Cancer	Cancer
4 AM	Cancer	Cancer	Cancer
5 AM	Leo	Leo	Leo
6 AM	Leo	Leo	Leo
7 AM	Leo	Leo; Virgo 8/1	Virgo
8 AM	Virgo	Virgo	Virgo
9 AM	Virgo	Virgo	Virgo
10 AM	Libra	Libra	Libra
11 AM	Libra	Libra	Libra
Noon	Libra	Libra; Scorpio 7/30	Scorpio
1 PM	Scorpio	Scorpio	Scorpio
2 PM	Scorpio	Scorpio	Scorpio
3 PM	Sagittarius	Sagittarius	Sagittarius
4 PM	Sagittarius	Sagittarius	Sagittarius
5 PM	Sagittarius	Capricorn	Capricorn
6 PM	Capricorn	Capricorn	Capricorn
7 PM	Capricorn; Aquarius 7/26	Aquarius	Aquarius
8 PM	Aquarius	Aquarius	Aquarius; Pisces 8/3
9 PM	Pisces	Pisces	Pisces
10 PM	Aries	Aries	Aries
11 PM	Aries; Taurus 7/26	Taurus	Taurus

*Hour of birth given here is for Standard Time in any time zone. If your hour of birth was recorded in Daylight Saving Time, subtract one hour from it and consult that hour in the table above. For example, if you were born at 6 AM D.S.T., see 5 AM above.

Hour of Birth*	Date of Birth		
	August 7–11	**August 12–17**	**August 18–24**
Midnight	Gemini	Gemini	Gemini
1 AM	Gemini	Gemini	Cancer
2 AM	Cancer	Cancer	Cancer
3 AM	Cancer	Cancer	Cancer; Leo 8/22
4 AM	Leo	Leo	Leo
5 AM	Leo	Leo	Leo
6 AM	Leo	Leo; Virgo 8/16	Virgo
7 AM	Virgo	Virgo	Virgo
8 AM	Virgo	Virgo	Virgo; Libra 8/22
9 AM	Libra	Libra	Libra
10 AM	Libra	Libra	Libra
11 AM	Libra	Libra; Scorpio 8/14	Scorpio
Noon	Scorpio	Scorpio	Scorpio
1 PM	Scorpio	Scorpio	Scorpio; Sagittarius 8/22
2 PM	Sagittarius	Sagittarius	Sagittarius
3 PM	Sagittarius	Sagittarius	Sagittarius
4 PM	Sagittarius	Capricorn	Capricorn
5 PM	Capricorn	Capricorn	Capricorn
6 PM	Capricorn	Aquarius	Aquarius
7 PM	Aquarius	Aquarius	Pisces
8 PM	Pisces	Pisces	Pisces; Aries 8/21
9 PM	Aries	Aries	Aries
10 PM	Aries; Taurus 8/11	Taurus	Taurus
11 PM	Taurus	Taurus	Gemini

*See note on facing page.

THE PLACE OF ASTROLOGY IN TODAY'S WORLD

Does astrology have a place in the fast-moving, ultra-scientific world we live in today? Can it be justified in a sophisticated society whose outriders are already preparing to step off the moon into the deep space of the planets themselves? Or is it just a hangover of ancient superstition, a psychological dummy for neurotics and dreamers of every historical age?

These are the kind of questions that any inquiring person can be expected to ask when they approach a subject like astrology which goes beyond, but never excludes, the materialistic side of life.

The simple, single answer is that astrology works. It works for many millions of people in the western world alone. In the United States there are 10 million followers and in Europe, an estimated 25 million. America has more than 4000 practicing astrologers, Europe nearly three times as many. Even down-under Australia has its hundreds of thousands of adherents. In the eastern countries, astrology has enormous followings, again, because it has been proved to work. In India, for example, brides and grooms for centuries have been chosen on the basis of their astrological compatibility.

Astrology today is more vital than ever before, more practicable because all over the world the media devotes much space and time to it, more valid because science itself is confirming the precepts of astrological knowledge with every new exciting step. The ordinary person who daily applies astrology intelligently does not have to wonder whether it is true nor believe in it blindly. He can see it working for himself. And, if he can use it—and this book is designed to help the reader to do just that—he can make living a far richer experience, and become a more developed personality and a better person.

Astrology and Relationships

Astrology is the science of relationships. It is not just a study of planetary influences on man and his environment. It is the study of man himself.

We are at the center of our personal universe, of all our relationships. And our happiness or sadness depends on how we act, how we relate to the people and things that surround us. The emotions that we generate have a distinct effect—for better or worse—on the world around us. Our friends and our enemies will confirm this.

Just look in the mirror the next time you are angry. In other words, each of us is a kind of sun or planet or star radiating our feelings on the environment around us. Our influence on our personal universe, whether loving, helpful, or destructive, varies with our changing moods, expressed through our individual character.

Our personal "radiations" are potent in the way they affect our moods and our ability to control them. But we usually are able to throw off our emotion in some sort of action—we have a good cry, walk it off, or tell someone our troubles—before it can build up too far and make us physically ill. Astrology helps us to understand the universal forces working on us, and through this understanding, we can become more properly adjusted to our surroundings so that we find ourselves coping where others may flounder.

The Challenge of Love

The challenge of love lies in recognizing the difference between infatuation, emotion, sex, and, sometimes, the intentional deceit of the other person. Mankind, with its record of broken marriages, despair, and disillusionment, is obviously not very good at making these distinctions.

Can astrology help?

Yes. In the same way that advance knowledge can usually help in any human situation. And there is probably no situation as human, as poignant, as pathetic and universal, as the failure of man's love.

Love, of course, is not just between man and woman. It involves love of children, parents, home, and friends. But the big problems usually involve the choice of partner.

Astrology has established degrees of compatibility that exist between people born under the various signs of the Zodiac. Because people are individuals, there are numerous variations and modifications. So the astrologer, when approached on mate and marriage matters, makes allowances for them. But the fact remains that some groups of people are suited for each other and some are not, and astrology has expressed this in terms of characteristics we all can study and use as a personal guide.

No matter how much enjoyment and pleasure we find in the different aspects of each other's character, if it is not an overall compatibility, the chances of our finding fulfillment or enduring happiness in each other are pretty hopeless. And astrology can help us to find someone compatible.

Astrology and Science

Closely related to our emotions is the "other side" of our personal universe, our physical welfare. Our body, of course, is largely influenced by things around us over which we have very little control. The phone rings, we hear it. The train runs late. We snag our stocking or cut our face shaving. Our body is under a constant bombardment of events that influence our daily lives to varying degrees.

The question that arises from all this is, what makes each of us act so that we have to involve other people and keep the ball of activity and evolution rolling? This is the question that both science and astrology are involved with. The scientists have attacked it from different angles: anthropology, the study of human evolution as body, mind and response to environment; anatomy, the study of bodily structure; psychology, the science of the human mind; and so on. These studies have produced very impressive classifications and valuable information, but because the approach to the problem is fragmented, so is the result. They remain "branches" of science. Science generally studies effects. It keeps turning up wonderful answers but no lasting solutions. Astrology, on the other hand, approaches the question from the broader viewpoint. Astrology began its inquiry with the totality of human experience and saw it as an effect. It then looked to find the cause, or at least the prime movers, and during thousands of years of observation of man and his *universal* environment came up with the extraordinary principle of planetary influence—or astrology, which, from the Greek, means the science of the stars.

Modern science, as we shall see, has confirmed much of astrology's foundations—most of it unintentionally, some of it reluctantly, but still, indisputably.

It is not difficult to imagine that there must be a connection between outer space and Earth. Even today, scientists are not too sure how our Earth was created, but it is generally agreed that it is only a tiny part of the universe. And as a part of the universe, people on Earth see and feel the influence of heavenly bodies in almost every aspect of our existence. There is no doubt that the Sun has the greatest influence on life on this planet. Without it there would be no life, for without it there would be no warmth, no division into day and night, no cycles of time or season at all. This is clear and easy to see. The influence of the Moon, on the other hand, is more subtle, though no less definite.

There are many ways in which the influence of the Moon manifests itself here on Earth, both on human and animal life. It is a well-known fact, for instance, that the large movements of water on our planet—that is the ebb and flow of the tides—are caused by the Moon's gravitational pull. Since this is so, it follows that these water movements do not occur only in the oceans, but that all bodies of water are affected, even down to the tiniest puddle.

The human body, too, which consists of about 70 percent water, falls within the scope of this lunar influence. For example the menstrual cycle of most women corresponds to the 28-day lunar month; the period of pregnancy in humans is 273 days, or equal to nine lunar months. Similarly, many illnesses reach a crisis at the change of the Moon, and statistics in many countries have shown that the crime rate is highest at the time of the Full Moon. Even human sexual desire has been associated with the phases of the Moon. But it is in the movement of the tides that we get the clearest demonstration of planetary influence, which leads to the irresistible correspondence between the so-called metaphysical and the physical.

Tide tables are prepared years in advance by calculating the future positions of the Moon. Science has known for a long time that the Moon is the main cause of tidal action. But only in the last few years has it begun to realize the possible extent of this influence on mankind. To begin with, the ocean tides do not rise and fall as we might imagine from our personal observations of them. The Moon as it orbits around Earth sets up a circular wave of attraction which pulls the oceans of the world after it, broadly in an east to west direction. This influence is like a phantom wave crest, a loop of power stretching from pole to pole which passes over and around the Earth like an invisible shadow. It travels with equal effect across the land masses and, as scientists were recently amazed to observe, caused oysters placed in the dark in the middle of the United States where there is no sea to open their shells to receive the nonexistent tide. If the land-locked oysters react to this invisible signal, what effect does it have on us who not so long ago in evolutionary time came out of the sea and still have its salt in our blood and sweat?

Less well known is the fact that the Moon is also the primary force behind the circulation of blood in human beings and animals, and the movement of sap in trees and plants. Agriculturists have established that the Moon has a distinct influence on crops, which explains why for centuries people have planted according to Moon cycles. The habits of many animals, too, are directed by the movement of the Moon. Migratory birds, for instance, depart only at or near the time of the Full Moon. And certain sea creatures, eels in particular, move only in accordance with certain phases of the Moon.

Know Thyself—Why?

In today's fast-changing world, everyone still longs to know what the future holds. It is the one thing that everyone has in common: rich and poor, famous and infamous, all are deeply concerned about tomorrow.

But the key to the future, as every historian knows, lies in the past. This is as true of individual people as it is of nations. You cannot understand your future without first understanding your past, which is simply another way of saying that you must first of all know yourself.

The motto "know thyself" seems obvious enough nowadays, but it was originally put forward as the foundation of wisdom by the ancient Greek philosophers. It was then adopted by the "mystery religions" of the ancient Middle East, Greece, Rome, and is still used in all genuine schools of mind training or mystical discipline, both in those of the East, based on yoga, and those of the West. So it is universally accepted now, and has been through the ages.

But how do you go about discovering what sort of person you are? The first step is usually classification into some sort of system of types. Astrology did this long before the birth of Christ. Psychology has also done it. So has modern medicine, in its way.

One system classifies people according to the source of the impulses they respond to most readily: the muscles, leading to direct bodily action; the digestive organs, resulting in emotion; or the brain and nerves, giving rise to thinking. Another such system says that character is determined by the endocrine glands, and gives us such labels as "pituitary," "thyroid," and "hyperthyroid" types. These different systems are neither contradictory nor mutually exclusive. In fact, they are very often different ways of saying the same thing.

Very popular, useful classifications were devised by Carl Jung, the eminent disciple of Freud. Jung observed among the different faculties of the mind, four which have a predominant influence on character. These four faculties exist in all of us without exception, but not in perfect balance. So when we say, for instance, that someone is a "thinking type," it means that in any situation he or she tries to be rational. Emotion, which may be the opposite of thinking, will be his or her weakest function. This thinking type can be sensible and reasonable, or calculating and unsympathetic. The emotional type, on the other hand, can often be recognized by exaggerated language—everything is either marvelous or terrible—and in extreme cases they even invent dramas and quarrels out of nothing just to make life more interesting.

The other two faculties are intuition and physical sensation. The sensation type does not only care for food and drink, nice clothes and furniture; he or she is also interested in all forms of physical experience. Many scientists are sensation types as are athletes and nature-lovers. Like sensation, intuition is a form of perception and we all possess it. But it works through that part of the mind which is not under conscious control—consequently it sees meanings and connections which are not obvious to thought or emotion. Inventors and original thinkers are always intuitive, but so, too, are superstitious people who see meanings where none exist.

Thus, sensation tells us what is going on in the world, feeling (that is, emotion) tells us how important it is to ourselves, thinking enables us to interpret it and work out what we should do about it, and intuition tells us what it means to ourselves and others. All four faculties are essential, and all are present in every one of us. But some people are guided chiefly by one, others by another. In addition, Jung also observed a division of the human personality into the extrovert and the introvert, which cuts across these four types.

A disadvantage of all these systems of classification is that one cannot tell very easily where to place oneself. Some people are reluctant to admit that they act to please their emotions. So they deceive themselves for years by trying to belong to whichever type they think is the "best." Of course, there is no best; each has its faults and each has its good points.

The advantage of the signs of the Zodiac is that they simplify classification. Not only that, but your date of birth is personal—it is unarguably yours. What better way to know yourself than by going back as far as possible to the very moment of your birth? And this is precisely what your horoscope is all about, as we shall see in the next section.

WHAT IS A HOROSCOPE?

If you had been able to take a picture of the skies at the moment of your birth, that photograph would be your horoscope. Lacking such a snapshot, it is still possible to recreate the picture—and this is at the basis of the astrologer's art. In other words, your horoscope is a representation of the skies with the planets in the exact positions they occupied at the time you were born.

The year of birth tells an astrologer the positions of the distant, slow-moving planets Jupiter, Saturn, Uranus, Neptune, and Pluto. The month of birth indicates the Sun sign, or birth sign as it is commonly called, as well as indicating the positions of the rapidly moving planets Venus, Mercury, and Mars. The day and time of birth will locate the position of our Moon. And the moment—the exact hour and minute—of birth determines the houses through what is called the Ascendant, or Rising sign.

With this information the astrologer consults various tables to calculate the specific positions of the Sun, Moon, and other planets relative to your birthplace at the moment you were born. Then he or she locates them by means of the Zodiac.

The Zodiac

The Zodiac is a band of stars (constellations) in the skies, centered on the Sun's apparent path around the Earth, and is divided into twelve equal segments, or signs. What we are actually dividing up is the Earth's path around the Sun. But from our point of view here on Earth, it seems as if the Sun is making a great circle around our planet in the sky, so we say it is the Sun's apparent path. This twelvefold division, the Zodiac, is a reference system for the astrologer. At any given moment the planets—and in astrology both the Sun and Moon are considered to be planets—can all be located at a specific point along this path.

Now where in all this are you, the subject of the horoscope? Your character is largely determined by the sign the Sun is in. So that is where the astrologer looks first in your horoscope, at your Sun sign.

The Sun Sign and the Cusp

There are twelve signs in the Zodiac, and the Sun spends approximately one month in each sign. But because of the motion of the Earth around the Sun—the Sun's apparent motion—the dates when the Sun enters and leaves each sign may change from year to year. Some people born near the cusp, or edge, of a sign have difficulty determining which is their Sun sign. But in this book a Table of Cusps is provided for the years 1900 to 2015 (page 5) so you can find out what your true Sun sign is.

Here are the twelve signs of the Zodiac, their ancient zodiacal symbol, and the dates when the Sun enters and leaves each sign for the year 2013. Remember, these dates may change from year to year.

ARIES	Ram	March 20–April 19
TAURUS	Bull	April 19–May 20
GEMINI	Twins	May 20–June 21
CANCER	Crab	June 21–July 22
LEO	Lion	July 22–August 22
VIRGO	Virgin	August 22–September 22
LIBRA	Scales	September 22–October 23
SCORPIO	Scorpion	October 23–November 22
SAGITTARIUS	Archer	November 22–December 21
CAPRICORN	Sea Goat	December 21–January 19
AQUARIUS	Water Bearer	January 19–February 18
PISCES	Fish	February 18–March 20

It is possible to draw significant conclusions and make meaningful predictions based simply on the Sun sign of a person. There are many people who have been amazed at the accuracy of the description of their own character based only on the Sun sign. But an astrologer needs more information than just your Sun sign to interpret the photograph that is your horoscope.

The Rising Sign and the Zodiacal Houses

An astrologer needs the exact time and place of your birth in order to construct and interpret your horoscope. The illustration on the next page shows the flat chart, or natural wheel, an astrologer uses. Note the inner circle of the wheel labeled 1 through 12. These 12 divisions are known as the houses of the Zodiac.

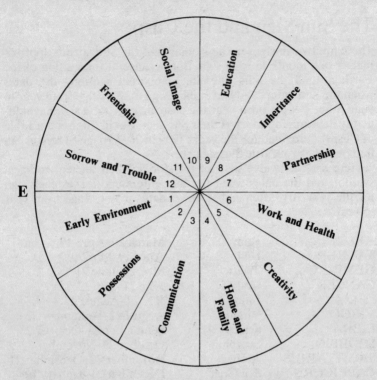

The 1st house always starts from the position marked E, which corresponds to the eastern horizon. The rest of the houses 2 through 12 follow around in a "counterclockwise" direction. The point where each house starts is known as a cusp, or edge.

The cusp, or edge, of the 1st house (point E) is where an astrologer would place your Rising sign, the Ascendant. And, as already noted, the exact time of your birth determines your Rising sign. Let's see how this works.

As the Earth rotates on its axis once every 24 hours, each one of the twelve signs of the Zodiac appears to be "rising" on the horizon, with a new one appearing about every 2 hours. Actually it is the turning of the Earth that exposes each sign to view, but in our astrological work we are discussing apparent motion. This Rising sign marks the Ascendant, and it colors the whole orientation of a horoscope. It indicates the sign governing the 1st house of the chart, and will thus determine which signs will govern all the other houses.

To visualize this idea, imagine two color wheels with twelve divisions superimposed upon each other. For just as the Zodiac is divided into twelve constellations that we identify as the signs, another twelvefold division is used to denote the houses. Now imagine one wheel (the signs) moving slowly while the other wheel (the houses) remains still. This analogy may help you see how the signs keep shifting the "color" of the houses as the Rising sign continues to change every two hours. To simplify things, a Table of Rising Signs has been provided (pages 8–9) for your specific Sun sign.

Once your Rising sign has been placed on the cusp of the 1st house, the signs that govern the rest of the 11 houses can be placed on the chart. In any individual's horoscope the signs do not necessarily correspond with the houses. For example, it could be that a sign covers part of two adjacent houses. It is the interpretation of such variations in an individual's horoscope that marks the professional astrologer.

But to gain a workable understanding of astrology, it is not necessary to go into great detail. In fact, we just need a description of the houses and their meanings, as is shown in the illustration above and in the table below.

THE 12 HOUSES OF THE ZODIAC

1st	Individuality, body appearance, general outlook on life	Personality house
2nd	Finance, possessions, ethical principles, gain or loss	Money house
3rd	Relatives, communication, short journeys, writing, education	Relatives house
4th	Family and home, parental ties, land and property, security	Home house
5th	Pleasure, children, creativity, entertainment, risk	Pleasure house
6th	Health, harvest, hygiene, work and service, employees	Health house
7th	Marriage and divorce, the law, partnerships and alliances	Marriage house
8th	Inheritance, secret deals, sex, death, regeneration	Inheritance house
9th	Travel, sports, study, philosophy, religion	Travel house
10th	Career, social standing, success and honor	Business house
11th	Friendship, social life, hopes and wishes	Friends house
12th	Troubles, illness, secret enemies, hidden agendas	Trouble house

The Planets in the Houses

An astrologer, knowing the exact time and place of your birth, will use tables of planetary motion in order to locate the planets in your horoscope chart. He or she will determine which planet or planets are in which sign and in which house. It is not uncommon, in an individual's horoscope, for there to be two or more planets in the same sign and in the same house.

The characteristics of the planets modify the influence of the Sun according to their natures and strengths.

Sun: Source of life. Basic temperament according to the Sun sign. The conscious will. Human potential.

Moon: Emotions. Moods. Customs. Habits. Changeable. Adaptive. Nurturing.

Mercury: Communication. Intellect. Reasoning power. Curiosity. Short travels.

Venus: Love. Delight. Charm. Harmony. Balance. Art. Beautiful possessions.

Mars: Energy. Initiative. War. Anger. Adventure. Courage. Daring. Impulse.

Jupiter: Luck. Optimism. Generous. Expansive. Opportunities. Protection.

Saturn: Pessimism. Privation. Obstacles. Delay. Hard work. Research. Lasting rewards after long struggle.

Uranus: Fashion. Electricity. Revolution. Independence. Freedom. Sudden changes. Modern science.

Neptune: Sensationalism. Theater. Dreams. Inspiration. Illusion. Deception.

Pluto: Creation and destruction. Total transformation. Lust for power. Strong obsessions.

Superimpose the characteristics of the planets on the functions of the house in which they appear. Express the result through the character of the Sun sign, and you will get the basic idea.

Of course, many other considerations have been taken into account in producing the carefully worked out predictions in this book: the aspects of the planets to each other; their strength according to position and sign; whether they are in a house of exaltation or decline; whether they are natural enemies or not; whether a planet occupies its own sign; the position of a planet in relation to its own house or sign; whether the sign is male or female; whether the sign is a fire, earth, water, or air sign. These are only a few of the colors on the astrologer's pallet which he or she must mix with the inspiration of the artist and the accuracy of the mathematician.

How To Use These Predictions

A person reading the predictions in this book should understand that they are produced from the daily position of the planets for a group of people and are not, of course, individually specialized. To get the full benefit of them our readers should relate the predictions to their own character and circumstances, coordinate them, and draw their own conclusions from them.

If you are a serious observer of your own life, you should find a definite pattern emerging that will be a helpful and reliable guide.

The point is that we always retain our free will. The stars indicate certain directional tendencies but we are not compelled to follow. We can do or not do, and wisdom must make the choice.

We all have our good and bad days. Sometimes they extend into cycles of weeks. It is therefore advisable to study daily predictions in a span ranging from the day before to several days ahead.

Daily predictions should be taken very generally. The word "difficult" does not necessarily indicate a whole day of obstruction or inconvenience. It is a warning to you to be cautious. Your caution will often see you around the difficulty before you are involved. This is the correct use of astrology.

In another section (pages 78–84), detailed information is given about the influence of the Moon as it passes through each of the twelve signs of the Zodiac. There are instructions on how to use the Moon Tables (pages 85–92), which provide Moon Sign Dates throughout the year as well as the Moon's role in health and daily affairs. This information should be used in conjunction with the daily forecasts to give a fuller picture of the astrological trends.

HISTORY OF ASTROLOGY

The origins of astrology have been lost far back in history, but we do know that reference is made to it as far back as the first written records of the human race. It is not hard to see why. Even in primitive times, people must have looked for an explanation for the various happenings in their lives. They must have wanted to know why people were different from one another. And in their search they turned to the regular movements of the Sun, Moon, and stars to see if they could provide an answer.

It is interesting to note that as soon as man learned to use his tools in any type of design, or his mind in any kind of calculation, he turned his attention to the heavens. Ancient cave dwellings reveal dim crescents and circles representative of the Sun and Moon, rulers of day and night. Mesopotamia and the civilization of Chaldea, in itself the foundation of those of Babylonia and Assyria, show a complete picture of astronomical observation and well-developed astrological interpretation.

Humanity has a natural instinct for order. The study of anthropology reveals that primitive people—even as far back as prehistoric times—were striving to achieve a certain order in their lives. They tried to organize the apparent chaos of the universe. They had the desire to attach meaning to things. This demand for order has persisted throughout the history of man. So that observing the regularity of the heavenly bodies made it logical that primitive peoples should turn heavenward in their search for an understanding of the world in which they found themselves so random and alone.

And they did find a significance in the movements of the stars. Shepherds tending their flocks, for instance, observed that when the cluster of stars now known as the constellation Aries was in sight, it was the time of fertility and they associated it with the Ram. And they noticed that the growth of plants and plant life corresponded with different phases of the Moon, so that certain times were favorable for the planting of crops, and other times were not. In this way, there grew up a tradition of seasons and causes connected with the passage of the Sun through the twelve signs of the Zodiac.

Astrology was valued so highly that the king was kept informed of the daily and monthly changes in the heavenly bodies, and the results of astrological studies regarding events of the future. Head astrologers were clearly men of great rank and position, and the office was said to be a hereditary one.

Omens were taken, not only from eclipses and conjunctions of the Moon or Sun with one of the planets, but also from storms and earthquakes. In the eastern civilizations, particularly, the reverence inspired by astrology appears to have remained unbroken since the very earliest days. In ancient China, astrology, astronomy, and religion went hand in hand. The astrologer, who was also an astronomer, was part of the official government service and had his own corner in the Imperial Palace. The duties of the Imperial astrologer, whose office was one of the most important in the land, were clearly defined, as this extract from early records shows:

This exalted gentleman must concern himself with the stars in the heavens, keeping a record of the changes and movements of the Planets, the Sun and the Moon, in order to examine the movements of the terrestrial world with the object of prognosticating good and bad fortune. He divides the territories of the nine regions of the empire in accordance with their dependence on particular celestial bodies. All the fiefs and principalities are connected with the stars and from this their prosperity or misfortune should be ascertained. He makes prognostications according to the twelve years of the Jupiter cycle of good and evil of the terrestrial world. From the colors of the five kinds of clouds, he determines the coming of floods or droughts, abundance or famine. From the twelve winds, he draws conclusions about the state of harmony of heaven and earth, and takes note of good and bad signs that result from their accord or disaccord. In general, he concerns himself with five kinds of phenomena so as to warn the Emperor to come to the aid of the government and to allow for variations in the ceremonies according to their circumstances.

The Chinese were also keen observers of the fixed stars, giving them such unusual names as Ghost Vehicle, Sun of Imperial Concubine, Imperial Prince, Pivot of Heaven, Twinkling Brilliance, Weaving Girl. But, great astrologers though they may have been, the Chinese lacked one aspect of mathematics that the Greeks applied to astrology—deductive geometry. Deductive geometry was the basis of much classical astrology in and after the time of the Greeks, and this explains the different methods of prognostication used in the East and West.

Down through the ages the astrologer's art has depended, not so much on the uncovering of new facts, though this is important, as on the interpretation of the facts already known. This is the essence of the astrologer's skill.

But why should the signs of the Zodiac have any effect at all on the formation of human character? It is easy to see why people thought they did, and even now we constantly use astrological expressions in our everyday speech. The thoughts of "lucky star," "ill-fated," "star-crossed," "mooning around," are interwoven into the very structure of our language.

Wherever the concept of the Zodiac is understood and used, it could well appear to have an influence on the human character. Does this mean, then, that the human race, in whose civilization the idea of the twelve signs of the Zodiac has long been embedded, is divided into only twelve types? Can we honestly believe that it is really as simple as that? If so, there must be pretty wide ranges of variation within each type. And if, to explain the variation, we call in heredity and environment, experiences in early childhood, the thyroid and other glands, and also the four functions of the mind together with extroversion and introversion, then one begins to wonder if the original classification was worth making at all. No sensible person believes that his favorite system explains everything. But even so, he will not find the system much use at all if it does not even save him the trouble of bothering with the others.

In the same way, if we were to put every person under only one sign of the Zodiac, the system becomes too rigid and unlike life. Besides, it was never intended to be used like that. It may be convenient to have only twelve types, but we know that in practice there is every possible gradation between aggressiveness and timidity, or between conscientiousness and laziness. How, then, do we account for this?

A person born under any given Sun sign can be mainly influenced by one or two of the other signs that appear in their individual horoscope. For instance, famous persons born under the sign of Gemini include Henry VIII, whom nothing and no one could have induced to abdicate, and Edward VIII, who did just that. Obviously, then, the sign Gemini does not fully explain the complete character of either of them.

Again, under the opposite sign, Sagittarius, were both Stalin, who was totally consumed with the notion of power, and Charles V, who freely gave up an empire because he preferred to go into a monastery. And we find under Scorpio many uncompromising characters such as Luther, de Gaulle, Indira Gandhi, and Montgomery, but also Petain, a successful commander whose name later became synonymous with collaboration.

A single sign is therefore obviously inadequate to explain the differences between people; it can only explain resemblances, such as the combativeness of the Scorpio group, or the far-reaching devotion of Charles V and Stalin to their respective ideals — the Christian heaven and the Communist utopia.

But very few people have only one sign in their horoscope chart. In addition to the month of birth, the day and, even more, the hour to the nearest minute if possible, ought to be considered. Without this, it is impossible to have an actual horoscope, for the word horoscope literally means "a consideration of the hour."

The month of birth tells you only which sign of the Zodiac was occupied by the Sun. The day and hour tell you what sign was occupied by the Moon. And the minute tells you which sign was rising on the eastern horizon. This is called the Ascendant, and, as some astrologers believe, it is supposed to be the most important thing in the whole horoscope.

The Sun is said to signify one's heart, that is to say, one's deepest desires and inmost nature. This is quite different from the Moon, which signifies one's superficial way of behaving. When the ancient Romans referred to the Emperor Augustus as a Capricorn, they meant that he had the Moon in Capricorn. Or, to take another example, a modern astrologer would call Disraeli a Scorpion because he had Scorpio Rising, but most people would call him Sagittarius because he had the Sun there. The Romans would have called him Leo because his Moon was in Leo.

So if one does not seem to fit one's birth month, it is always worthwhile reading the other signs, for one may have been born at a time when any of them were rising or occupied by the Moon. It also seems to be the case that the influence of the Sun develops as life goes on, so that the month of birth is easier to guess in people over the age of forty. The young are supposed to be influenced mainly by their Ascendant, the Rising sign, which characterizes the body and physical personality as a whole.

It is nonsense to assume that all people born at a certain time will exhibit the same characteristics, or that they will even behave in the same manner. It is quite obvious that, from the very moment of its birth, a child is subject to the effects of its environment, and that this in turn will influence its character and heritage to a decisive extent. Also to be taken into account are education and economic conditions, which play a very important part in the formation of one's character as well.

People have, in general, certain character traits and qualities which, according to their environment, develop in either a positive or a negative manner. Therefore, selfishness (inherent selfishness, that is) might emerge as unselfishness; kindness and consideration as cruelty and lack of consideration toward others. In the same way, a naturally constructive person may, through frustration, become destructive, and so on. The latent characteristics with which people are born can, therefore, through environment and good or bad training, become something that would appear to be its opposite, and so give the lie to the astrologer's description of their character. But this is not the case. The true character is still there, but it is buried deep beneath these external superficialities.

Careful study of the character traits of various signs of the Zodiac are of immeasurable help, and can render beneficial service to the intelligent person. Undoubtedly, the reader will already have discovered that, while he is able to get on very well with some people, he just "cannot stand" others. The causes sometimes seem inexplicable. At times there is intense dislike, at other times immediate sympathy. And there is, too, the phenomenon of love at first sight, which is also apparently inexplicable. People appear to be either sympathetic or unsympathetic toward each other for no apparent reason.

Now if we look at this in the light of the Zodiac, we find that people born under different signs are either compatible or incompatible with each other. In other words, there are good and bad interrelating factors among the various signs. This does not, of course, mean that humanity can be divided into groups of hostile camps. It would be quite wrong to be hostile or indifferent toward people who happen to be born under an incompatible sign. There is no reason why everybody should not, or cannot, learn to control and adjust their feelings and actions, especially after they are aware of the positive qualities of other people by studying their character analyses, among other things.

Every person born under a certain sign has both positive and negative qualities, which are developed more or less according to our free will. Nobody is entirely good or entirely bad, and it is up to each of us to learn to control ourselves on the one hand and at the same time to endeavor to learn about ourselves and others.

It cannot be emphasized often enough that it is free will that determines whether we will make really good use of our talents and abilities. Using our free will, we can either overcome our failings or allow them to rule us. Our free will enables us to exert sufficient willpower to control our failings so that they do not harm ourselves or others.

Astrology can reveal our inclinations and tendencies. Astrology can tell us about ourselves so that we are able to use our free will to overcome our shortcomings. In this way astrology helps us do our best to become needed and valuable members of society as well as helpmates to our family and our friends. Astrology also can save us a great deal of unhappiness and remorse.

Yet it may seem absurd that an ancient philosophy could be a prop to modern men and women. But below the materialistic surface of modern life, there are hidden streams of feeling and thought. Symbology is reappearing as a study worthy of the scholar; the psychosomatic factor in illness has passed from the writings of the crank to those of the specialist; spiritual healing in all its forms is no longer a pious hope but an accepted phenomenon. And it is into this context that we consider astrology, in the sense that it is an analysis of human types.

Astrology and medicine had a long journey together, and only parted company a couple of centuries ago. There still remain in medical language such astrological terms as "saturnine," "choleric," and "mercurial," used in the diagnosis of physical tendencies. The herbalist, for long the handyman of the medical profession, has been dominated by astrology since the days of the Greeks. Certain herbs traditionally respond to certain planetary influences, and diseases must therefore be treated to ensure harmony between the medicine and the disease.

But the stars are expected to foretell and not only to diagnose.

Astrological forecasting has been remarkably accurate, but often it is wide of the mark. The brave person who cares to predict world events takes dangerous chances. Individual forecasting is less clear cut; it can be a help or a disillusionment. Then we come to the nagging question: if it is possible to foreknow, is it right to foretell? This is a point of ethics on which it is hard to pronounce judgment. The doctor faces the same dilemma if he finds that symptoms of a mortal disease are present in his patient and that he can only prognosticate a steady decline. How much to tell an individual in a crisis is a problem that has perplexed many distinguished scholars. Honest and conscientious astrologers in this modern world, where so many people are seeking guidance, face the same problem.

Five hundred years ago it was customary to call in a learned man who was an astrologer who was probably also a doctor and a philosopher. By his knowledge of astrology, his study of planetary influences, he felt himself qualified to guide those in distress. The world has moved forward at a fantastic rate since then, and yet people are still uncertain of themselves. At first sight it seems fantastic in the light of modern thinking that they turn to the most ancient of all studies, and get someone to calculate a horoscope for them. But is it really so fantastic if you take a second look? For astrology is concerned with tomorrow, with survival. And in a world such as ours, tomorrow and survival are the keywords for the twenty-first century.

SPECIAL OVERVIEW 2011–2020

The second decade of the twenty-first century opens on major planetary shifts that set the stage for challenge, opportunity, and change. The personal planets—notably Jupiter and Saturn—and the generational planets—Uranus, Neptune, and Pluto—have all moved forward into new signs of the zodiac. These fresh planetary influences act to shape unfolding events and illuminate pathways to the future.

Jupiter, the big planet that attracts luck, spends about one year in each zodiacal sign. It takes approximately twelve years for Jupiter to travel through all twelve signs of the zodiac in order to complete a cycle. In 2011 a new Jupiter cycle is initiated with Jupiter transiting Aries, the first sign of the zodiac. As each year progresses over the course of the decade, Jupiter moves forward into the next sign, following the natural progression of the zodiac. Jupiter visits Taurus in 2012, Gemini in 2013, Cancer in 2014, Leo in 2015, Virgo in 2016, Libra in 2017, Scorpio in 2018, Sagittarius in 2019, Capricorn in 2020. Then in late December 2020 Jupiter enters Aquarius just two weeks before the decade closes. Jupiter's vibrations are helpful and fruitful, a source of good luck and a protection against bad luck. Opportunity swells under Jupiter's powerful rays. Learning takes leaps of faith.

Saturn, the beautiful planet of reason and responsibility, spends about two and a half years in each zodiacal sign. A complete Saturn cycle through all twelve signs of the zodiac takes about twenty-nine to thirty years. Saturn is known as the lawgiver: setting boundaries and codes of conduct, urging self-discipline and structure within a creative framework. The rule of law, the role of government, the responsibility of the individual are all sourced from Saturn. Saturn gives as it takes. Once a lesson is learned, Saturn's reward is just and full.

Saturn transits Libra throughout 2011 until early autumn of 2012. Here Saturn seeks to harmonize, to balance, to bring order out of chaos. Saturn in Libra ennobles the artist, the judge, the high-minded, the honest. Saturn next visits Scorpio from autumn 2012 until late December 2014. With Saturn in Scorpio, tactic and strategy combine to get workable solutions and desired results. Saturn's problem-solving tools here can harness dynamic energy for the common good. Saturn in Sagittarius, an idealistic and humanistic transit that stretches from December 2014 into the last day of autumn 2017, promotes activism over mere dogma and debate. Saturn in Sagittarius can be a driving force for good. Saturn tours Capricorn, the sign that Saturn rules, from the first day of winter 2017 into early spring 2020. Saturn in Capricorn is a consolidating transit, bringing things forth and into fruition. Here a plan can be made right, made whole, then launched for success. Saturn starts to visit Aquarius, a sign that Saturn corules and a very good sign for Saturn to visit, in the very last year of the decade. Saturn in Aquarius fosters team spirit, the unity of effort amid diversity. The transit of Saturn in Aquarius until early 2023 represents a period of enlightened activism and unprecedented growth.

Uranus, Neptune, and Pluto spend more than several years in each sign. They produce the differences in attitude, belief, behavior, and taste that distinguish one generation from another—and so are called the generational planets.

Uranus, planet of innovation and surprise, is known as the awakener. Uranus spends seven to eight years in each sign. Uranus started a new cycle when it entered Aries, the first sign of the zodiac, in May 2010. Uranus tours Aries until May 2018. Uranus in Aries accents originality, freedom, independence, unpredictability. There can be a start-stop quality to undertakings given this transit. Despite contradiction and confrontation, significant invention and productivity mark this transit. Uranus next visits Taurus through the end of the decade into 2026. Strategic thinking and timely action characterize the transit of Uranus in Taurus. Here intuition is backed up by common sense, leading to fresh discoveries upon which new industries can be built.

Neptune spends about fourteen years in each sign. Neptune, the visionary planet, enters Pisces, the sign Neptune rules and the final sign of the zodiac, in early April 2011. Neptune journeys through Pisces until 2026 to complete the Neptune cycle of visiting all twelve zodiacal signs. Neptune's tour of Pisces ushers in a long period of great potentiality: universal understanding, universal good, universal love, universal generosity, universal forgiveness—the universal spirit affects all. Neptune in Pisces can oversee the fruition of such noble aims as human rights for all and liberation from all forms of tyranny. Neptune in Pisces is a pervasive influence that changes concepts, consciences, attitudes, actions. The impact of Neptune in Pisces is to illuminate and to inspire.

Pluto, dwarf planet of beginnings and endings, entered the earthy sign of Capricorn in 2008 and journeys there for sixteen years into late 2024. Pluto in Capricorn over the course of this extensive visit has the capacity to change the landscape as well as the humanscape. The transforming energy of Pluto combines with the persevering power of Capricorn to give depth and character to potential change. Pluto in Capricorn brings focus and cohesion to disparate, diverse creativities. As new forms arise and take root, Pluto in Capricorn organizes the rebuilding process. Freedom versus limitation, freedom versus authority is in the framework during this transit. Reasonableness struggles with recklessness to solve divisive issues. Pluto in Capricorn teaches important lessons about adversity, and the lessons will be learned.

THE SIGNS OF THE ZODIAC

Dominant Characteristics

Aries: March 21–April 20

The Positive Side of Aries

The Aries has many positive points to his character. People born under this first sign of the Zodiac are often quite strong and enthusiastic. On the whole, they are forward-looking people who are not easily discouraged by temporary setbacks. They know what they want out of life and they go out after it. Their personalities are strong. Others are usually quite impressed by the Ram's way of doing things. Quite often they are sources of inspiration for others traveling the same route. Aries men and women have a special zest for life that can be contagious; for others, they are a fine example of how life should be lived.

The Aries person usually has a quick and active mind. He is imaginative and inventive. He enjoys keeping busy and active. He generally gets along well with all kinds of people. He is interested in mankind, as a whole. He likes to be challenged. Some would say he thrives on opposition, for it is when he is set against that he often does his best. Getting over or around obstacles is a challenge he generally enjoys. All in all, Aries is quite positive and young-thinking. He likes to keep abreast of new things that are happening in the world. Aries are often fond of speed. They like things to be done quickly, and this sometimes aggravates their slower colleagues and associates.

The Aries man or woman always seems to remain young. Their whole approach to life is youthful and optimistic. They never say

31

die, no matter what the odds. They may have an occasional setback, but it is not long before they are back on their feet again.

The Negative Side of Aries

Everybody has his less positive qualities—and Aries is no exception. Sometimes the Aries man or woman is not very tactful in communicating with others; in his hurry to get things done he is apt to be a little callous or inconsiderate. Sensitive people are likely to find him somewhat sharp-tongued in some situations. Often in his eagerness to get the show on the road, he misses the mark altogether and cannot achieve his aims.

At times Aries can be too impulsive. He can occasionally be stubborn and refuse to listen to reason. If things do not move quickly enough to suit the Aries man or woman, he or she is apt to become rather nervous or irritable. The uncultivated Aries is not unfamiliar with moments of doubt and fear. He is capable of being destructive if he does not get his way. He can overcome some of his emotional problems by steadily trying to express himself as he really is, but this requires effort.

Taurus: April 21–May 20

The Positive Side of Taurus

The Taurus person is known for his ability to concentrate and for his tenacity. These are perhaps his strongest qualities. The Taurus man or woman generally has very little trouble in getting along with others; it's his nature to be helpful toward people in need. He can always be depended on by his friends, especially those in trouble.

Taurus generally achieves what he wants through his ability to persevere. He never leaves anything unfinished but works on something until it has been completed. People can usually take him at his word; he is honest and forthright in most of his dealings. The Taurus person has a good chance to make a success of his life because of his many positive qualities. The Taurus who aims high seldom falls short of his mark. He learns well by experience. He is thorough and does not believe in shortcuts of any kind. The Bull's thoroughness pays off in the end, for through his deliberateness he learns how to rely on himself and what he has learned. The Taurus person tries to get along with others, as a rule.

He is not overly critical and likes people to be themselves. He is a tolerant person and enjoys peace and harmony—especially in his home life.

Taurus is usually cautious in all that he does. He is not a person who believes in taking unnecessary risks. Before adopting any one line of action, he will weigh all of the pros and cons. The Taurus person is steadfast. Once his mind is made up it seldom changes. The person born under this sign usually is a good family person—reliable and loving.

The Negative Side of Taurus

Sometimes the Taurus man or woman is a bit too stubborn. He won't listen to other points of view if his mind is set on something. To others, this can be quite annoying. Taurus also does not like to be told what to do. He becomes rather angry if others think him not too bright. He does not like to be told he is wrong, even when he is. He dislikes being contradicted.

Some people who are born under this sign are very suspicious of others—even of those persons close to them. They find it difficult to trust people fully. They are often afraid of being deceived or taken advantage of. The Bull often finds it difficult to forget or forgive. His love of material things sometimes makes him rather avaricious and petty.

Gemini: May 21–June 20

The Positive Side of Gemini

The person born under this sign of the Heavenly Twins is usually quite bright and quick-witted. Some of them are capable of doing many different things. The Gemini person very often has many different interests. He keeps an open mind and is always anxious to learn new things.

Gemini is often an analytical person. He is a person who enjoys making use of his intellect. He is governed more by his mind than by his emotions. He is a person who is not confined to one view; he can often understand both sides to a problem or question. He knows how to reason, how to make rapid decisions if need be.

He is an adaptable person and can make himself at home almost anywhere. There are all kinds of situations he can adapt to. He is a person who seldom doubts himself; he is sure of his talents and his ability to think and reason. Gemini is generally most satisfied when he is in a situation where he can make use of his intellect. Never short of imagination, he often has strong talents for invention. He is rather a modern person when it comes to life; Gemini almost always moves along with the times—perhaps that is why he remains so youthful throughout most of his life.

Literature and art appeal to the person born under this sign. Creativity in almost any form will interest and intrigue the Gemini man or woman.

The Gemini is often quite charming. A good talker, he often is the center of attraction at any gathering. People find it easy to like a person born under this sign because he can appear easygoing and usually has a good sense of humor.

The Negative Side of Gemini

Sometimes the Gemini person tries to do too many things at one time—and as a result, winds up finishing nothing. Some Twins are easily distracted and find it rather difficult to concentrate on one thing for too long a time. Sometimes they give in to trifling fancies and find it rather boring to become too serious about any one thing. Some of them are never dependable, no matter what they promise.

Although the Gemini man or woman often appears to be well-versed on many subjects, this is sometimes just a veneer. His knowledge may be only superficial, but because he speaks so well he gives people the impression of erudition. Some Geminis are sharp-tongued and inconsiderate; they think only of themselves and their own pleasure.

Cancer: June 21–July 20

The Positive Side of Cancer

The Moon Child's most positive point is his understanding nature. On the whole, he is a loving and sympathetic person. He would never go out of his way to hurt anyone. The Cancer man or woman is often very kind and tender; they give what they can to others. They hate to see others suffering and will do what they can to help someone in less fortunate circumstances than themselves. They are often very concerned about the world. Their interest in people generally goes beyond that of just their own families and close friends; they have a deep sense of community and respect humanitarian values. The Moon Child means what he says, as a rule; he is honest about his feelings.

The Cancer man or woman is a person who knows the art of patience. When something seems difficult, he is willing to wait until the situation becomes manageable again. He is a person who knows how to bide his time. Cancer knows how to concentrate on one thing at a time. When he has made his mind up he generally sticks with what he does, seeing it through to the end.

Cancer is a person who loves his home. He enjoys being surrounded by familiar things and the people he loves. Of all the signs, Cancer is the most maternal. Even the men born under this sign often have a motherly or protective quality about them. They like to take care of people in their family—to see that they are well loved and well provided for. They are usually loyal and faithful. Family ties mean a lot to the Cancer man or woman. Parents and in-laws are respected and loved. Young Cancer responds very well to adults who show faith in him. The Moon Child has a strong sense of tradition. He is very sensitive to the moods of others.

The Negative Side of Cancer

Sometimes Cancer finds it rather hard to face life. It becomes too much for him. He can be a little timid and retiring, when things don't go too well. When unfortunate things happen, he is apt to just shrug and say, "Whatever will be will be." He can be fatalistic to a fault. The uncultivated Cancer is a bit lazy. He doesn't have very much ambition. Anything that seems a bit difficult he'll gladly leave to others. He may be lacking in initiative. Too sensitive, when he feels he's been injured, he'll crawl back into his shell and nurse his imaginary wounds. The immature Moon Child often is given to crying when the smallest thing goes wrong.

Some Cancers find it difficult to enjoy themselves in environments outside their homes. They make heavy demands on others, and need to be constantly reassured that they are loved. Lacking such reassurance, they may resort to sulking in silence.

Leo: July 21–August 21

The Positive Side of Leo

Often Leos make good leaders. They seem to be good organizers and administrators. Usually they are quite popular with others. Whatever group it is that they belong to, the Leo man or woman is almost sure to be or become the leader. Loyalty, one of the Lion's noblest traits, enables him or her to maintain this leadership position.

Leo is generous most of the time. It is his best characteristic. He or she likes to give gifts and presents. In making others happy, the Leo person becomes happy himself. He likes to splurge when spending money on others. In some instances it may seem that the Lion's generosity knows no boundaries. A hospitable person, the Leo man or woman is very fond of welcoming people to his house and entertaining them. He is never short of company.

Leo has plenty of energy and drive. He enjoys working toward some specific goal. When he applies himself correctly, he gets what he wants most often. The Leo person is almost never unsure of himself. He has plenty of confidence and aplomb. He is a person who is direct in almost everything he does. He has a quick mind and can make a decision in a very short time.

He usually sets a good example for others because of his ambitious manner and positive ways. He knows how to stick to something once he's started. Although Leo may be good at making a joke, he is not superficial or glib. He is a loving person, kind and thoughtful.

There is generally nothing small or petty about the Leo man or woman. He does what he can for those who are deserving. He is a person others can rely upon at all times. He means what he says. An honest person, generally speaking, he is a friend who is valued and sought out.

The Negative Side of Leo

Leo, however, does have his faults. At times, he can be just a bit too arrogant. He thinks that no one deserves a leadership position except him. Only he is capable of doing things well. His opinion of himself is often much too high. Because of his conceit, he is sometimes rather unpopular with a good many people. Some Leos are too materialistic; they can only think in terms of money and profit.

Some Leos enjoy lording it over others—at home or at their place of business. What is more, they feel they have the right to. Egocentric to an impossible degree, this sort of Leo cares little about how others think or feel. He can be rude and cutting.

Virgo: August 22–September 22

The Positive Side of Virgo

The person born under the sign of Virgo is generally a busy person. He knows how to arrange and organize things. He is a good planner. Above all, he is practical and is not afraid of hard work.

Often called the sign of the Harvester, Virgo knows how to attain what he desires. He sticks with something until it is finished. He never shirks his duties, and can always be depended upon. The Virgo person can be thoroughly trusted at all times.

The man or woman born under this sign tries to do everything to perfection. He doesn't believe in doing anything halfway. He always aims for the top. He is the sort of a person who is always learning and constantly striving to better himself—not because he wants more money or glory, but because it gives him a feeling of accomplishment.

The Virgo man or woman is a very observant person. He is sensitive to how others feel, and can see things below the surface of a situation. He usually puts this talent to constructive use.

It is not difficult for the Virgo to be open and earnest. He believes in putting his cards on the table. He is never secretive or underhanded. He's as good as his word. The Virgo person is generally plainspoken and down to earth. He has no trouble in expressing himself.

The Virgo person likes to keep up to date on new developments in his particular field. Well-informed, generally, he sometimes has a keen interest in the arts or literature. What he knows, he knows well. His ability to use his critical faculties is well-developed and sometimes startles others because of its accuracy.

Virgos adhere to a moderate way of life; they avoid excesses. Virgo is a responsible person and enjoys being of service.

The Negative Side of Virgo

Sometimes a Virgo person is too critical. He thinks that only he can do something the way it should be done. Whatever anyone else does is inferior. He can be rather annoying in the way he quibbles over insignificant details. In telling others how things should be done, he can be rather tactless and mean.

Some Virgos seem rather emotionless and cool. They feel emotional involvement is beneath them. They are sometimes too tidy, too neat. With money they can be rather miserly. Some Virgos try to force their opinions and ideas on others.

Libra: September 23–October 22

The Positive Side of Libra

Libras love harmony. It is one of their most outstanding character traits. They are interested in achieving balance; they admire beauty and grace in things as well as in people. Generally speaking, they are kind and considerate people. Libras are usually very sympathetic. They go out of their way not to hurt another person's feelings. They are outgoing and do what they can to help those in need.

People born under the sign of Libra almost always make good friends. They are loyal and amiable. They enjoy the company of others. Many of them are rather moderate in their views; they believe in keeping an open mind, however, and weighing both sides of an issue fairly before making a decision.

Alert and intelligent, Libra, often known as the Lawgiver, is always fair-minded and tries to put himself in the position of the other person. They are against injustice; quite often they take up for the underdog. In most of their social dealings, they try to be tactful and kind. They dislike discord and bickering, and most Libras strive for peace and harmony in all their relationships.

The Libra man or woman has a keen sense of beauty. They appreciate handsome furnishings and clothes. Many of them are artistically inclined. Their taste is usually impeccable. They know how to use color. Their homes are almost always attractively arranged and inviting. They enjoy entertaining people and see to it that their guests always feel at home and welcome.

Libra gets along with almost everyone. He is well-liked and socially much in demand.

The Negative Side of Libra

Some people born under this sign tend to be rather insincere. So eager are they to achieve harmony in all relationships that they will even go so far as to lie. Many of them are escapists. They find facing the truth an ordeal and prefer living in a world of make-believe.

In a serious argument, some Libras give in rather easily even when they know they are right. Arguing, even about something they believe in, is too unsettling for some of them.

Libras sometimes care too much for material things. They enjoy possessions and luxuries. Some are vain and tend to be jealous.

Scorpio: October 23–November 22

The Positive Side of Scorpio

The Scorpio man or woman generally knows what he or she wants out of life. He is a determined person. He sees something through to the end. Scorpio is quite sincere, and seldom says anything he doesn't mean. When he sets a goal for himself he tries to go about achieving it in a very direct way.

The Scorpion is brave and courageous. They are not afraid of hard work. Obstacles do not frighten them. They forge ahead until they achieve what they set out for. The Scorpio man or woman has a strong will.

Although Scorpio may seem rather fixed and determined, inside he is often quite tender and loving. He can care very much for others. He believes in sincerity in all relationships. His feelings about someone tend to last; they are profound and not superficial.

The Scorpio person is someone who adheres to his principles no matter what happens. He will not be deterred from a path he believes to be right.

Because of his many positive strengths, the Scorpion can often achieve happiness for himself and for those that he loves.

He is a constructive person by nature. He often has a deep understanding of people and of life, in general. He is perceptive and unafraid. Obstacles often seem to spur him on. He is a positive person who enjoys winning. He has many strengths and resources; challenge of any sort often brings out the best in him.

The Negative Side of Scorpio

The Scorpio person is sometimes hypersensitive. Often he imagines injury when there is none. He feels that others do not bother to recognize him for his true worth. Sometimes he is given to excessive boasting in order to compensate for what he feels is neglect.

Scorpio can be proud, arrogant, and competitive. They can be sly when they put their minds to it and they enjoy outwitting persons or institutions noted for their cleverness.

Their tactics for getting what they want are sometimes devious and ruthless. They don't care too much about what others may think. If they feel others have done them an injustice, they will do their best to seek revenge. The Scorpion often has a sudden, violent temper; and this person's interest in sex is sometimes quite unbalanced or excessive.

Sagittarius: November 23–December 20

The Positive Side of Sagittarius

People born under this sign are honest and forthright. Their approach to life is earnest and open. Sagittarius is often quite adult in his way of seeing things. They are broad-minded and tolerant people. When dealing with others the person born under the sign of the Archer is almost always open and forthright. He doesn't believe in deceit or pretension. His standards are high. People who associate with Sagittarius generally admire and respect his tolerant viewpoint.

The Archer trusts others easily and expects them to trust him. He is never suspicious or envious and almost always thinks well of others. People always enjoy his company because he is so friendly and easygoing. The Sagittarius man or woman is often good-humored. He can always be depended upon by his friends, family, and co-workers.

The person born under this sign of the Zodiac likes a good joke every now and then. Sagittarius is eager for fun and laughs, which makes him very popular with others.

A lively person, he enjoys sports and outdoor life. The Archer is fond of animals. Intelligent and interesting, he can begin an ani-

mated conversation with ease. He likes exchanging ideas and discussing various views.

He is not selfish or proud. If someone proposes an idea or plan that is better than his, he will immediately adopt it. Imaginative yet practical, he knows how to put ideas into practice.

The Archer enjoys sport and games, and it doesn't matter if he wins or loses. He is a forgiving person, and never sulks over something that has not worked out in his favor.

He is seldom critical, and is almost always generous.

The Negative Side of Sagittarius

Some Sagittarius are restless. They take foolish risks and seldom learn from the mistakes they make. They don't have heads for money and are often mismanaging their finances. Some of them devote much of their time to gambling.

Some are too outspoken and tactless, always putting their feet in their mouths. They hurt others carelessly by being honest at the wrong time. Sometimes they make promises which they don't keep. They don't stick close enough to their plans and go from one failure to another. They are undisciplined and waste a lot of energy.

Capricorn: December 21–January 19

The Positive Side of Capricorn

The person born under the sign of Capricorn, known variously as the Mountain Goat or Sea Goat, is usually very stable and patient. He sticks to whatever tasks he has and sees them through. He can always be relied upon and he is not averse to work.

An honest person, Capricorn is generally serious about whatever he does. He does not take his duties lightly. He is a practical person and believes in keeping his feet on the ground.

Quite often the person born under this sign is ambitious and knows how to get what he wants out of life. The Goat forges ahead and never gives up his goal. When he is determined about something, he almost always wins. He is a good worker—a hard worker. Although things may not come easy to him, he will not complain, but continue working until his chores are finished.

He is usually good at business matters and knows the value of money. He is not a spendthrift and knows how to put something away for a rainy day; he dislikes waste and unnecessary loss.

Capricorn knows how to make use of his self-control. He can apply himself to almost anything once he puts his mind to it. His ability to concentrate sometimes astounds others. He is diligent and does well when involved in detail work.

The Capricorn man or woman is charitable, generally speaking, and will do what is possible to help others less fortunate. As a friend, he is loyal and trustworthy. He never shirks his duties or responsibilities. He is self-reliant and never expects too much of the other fellow. He does what he can on his own. If someone does him a good turn, then he will do his best to return the favor.

The Negative Side of Capricorn

Like everyone, Capricorn, too, has faults. At times, the Goat can be overcritical of others. He expects others to live up to his own high standards. He thinks highly of himself and tends to look down on others.

His interest in material things may be exaggerated. The Capricorn man or woman thinks too much about getting on in the world and having something to show for it. He may even be a little greedy.

He sometimes thinks he knows what's best for everyone. He is too bossy. He is always trying to organize and correct others. He may be a little narrow in his thinking.

Aquarius: January 20–February 18

The Positive Side of Aquarius

The Aquarius man or woman is usually very honest and forthright. These are his two greatest qualities. His standards for himself are generally very high. He can always be relied upon by others. His word is his bond.

Aquarius is perhaps the most tolerant of all the Zodiac personalities. He respects other people's beliefs and feels that everyone is entitled to his own approach to life.

He would never do anything to injure another's feelings. He is never unkind or cruel. Always considerate of others, the Water

Bearer is always willing to help a person in need. He feels a very strong tie between himself and all the other members of mankind.

The person born under this sign, called the Water Bearer, is almost always an individualist. He does not believe in teaming up with the masses, but prefers going his own way. His ideas about life and mankind are often quite advanced. There is a saying to the effect that the average Aquarius is fifty years ahead of his time.

Aquarius is community-minded. The problems of the world concern him greatly. He is interested in helping others no matter what part of the globe they live in. He is truly a humanitarian sort. He likes to be of service to others.

Giving, considerate, and without prejudice, Aquarius have no trouble getting along with others.

The Negative Side of Aquarius

Aquarius may be too much of a dreamer. He makes plans but seldom carries them out. He is rather unrealistic. His imagination has a tendency to run away with him. Because many of his plans are impractical, he is always in some sort of a dither.

Others may not approve of him at all times because of his unconventional behavior. He may be a bit eccentric. Sometimes he is so busy with his own thoughts that he loses touch with the realities of existence.

Some Aquarius feel they are more clever and intelligent than others. They seldom admit to their own faults, even when they are quite apparent. Some become rather fanatic in their views. Their criticism of others is sometimes destructive and negative.

Pisces: February 19–March 20

The Positive Side of Pisces

Known as the sign of the Fishes, Pisces has a sympathetic nature. Kindly, he is often dedicated in the way he goes about helping others. The sick and the troubled often turn to him for advice and assistance. Possessing keen intuition, Pisces can easily understand people's deepest problems.

He is very broad-minded and does not criticize others for their faults. He knows how to accept people for what they are. On the whole, he is a trustworthy and earnest person. He is loyal to his friends and will do what he can to help them in time of need. Generous and good-natured, he is a lover of peace; he is often willing to help others solve their differences. People who have taken a wrong turn in life often interest him and he will do what he can to persuade them to rehabilitate themselves.

He has a strong intuitive sense and most of the time he knows how to make it work for him. Pisces is unusually perceptive and often knows what is bothering someone before that person, himself, is aware of it. The Pisces man or woman is an idealistic person, basically, and is interested in making the world a better place in which to live. Pisces believes that everyone should help each other. He is willing to do more than his share in order to achieve cooperation with others.

The person born under this sign often is talented in music or art. He is a receptive person; he is able to take the ups and downs of life with philosophic calm.

The Negative Side of Pisces

Some Pisces are often depressed; their outlook on life is rather glum. They may feel that they have been given a bad deal in life and that others are always taking unfair advantage of them. Pisces sometimes feel that the world is a cold and cruel place. The Fishes can be easily discouraged. The Pisces man or woman may even withdraw from the harshness of reality into a secret shell of his own where he dreams and idles away a good deal of his time.

Pisces can be lazy. He lets things happen without giving the least bit of resistance. He drifts along, whether on the high road or on the low. He can be lacking in willpower.

Some Pisces people seek escape through drugs or alcohol. When temptation comes along they find it hard to resist. In matters of sex, they can be rather permissive.

Sun Sign Personalities

ARIES: Hans Christian Andersen, Pearl Bailey, Marlon Brando, Wernher Von Braun, Charlie Chaplin, Joan Crawford, Da Vinci, Bette Davis, Doris Day, W.C. Fields, Alec Guinness, Adolf Hitler, William Holden, Thomas Jefferson, Nikita Khrushchev, Elton John, Arturo Toscanini, J.P. Morgan, Paul Robeson, Gloria Steinem, Sarah Vaughn, Vincent van Gogh, Tennessee Williams

TAURUS: Fred Astaire, Charlotte Brontë, Carol Burnett, Irving Berlin, Bing Crosby, Salvador Dali, Tchaikovsky, Queen Elizabeth II, Duke Ellington, Ella Fitzgerald, Henry Fonda, Sigmund Freud, Orson Welles, Joe Louis, Lenin, Karl Marx, Golda Meir, Eva Peron, Bertrand Russell, Shakespeare, Kate Smith, Benjamin Spock, Barbra Streisand, Shirley Temple, Harry Truman

GEMINI: Ruth Benedict, Josephine Baker, Rachel Carson, Carlos Chavez, Walt Whitman, Bob Dylan, Ralph Waldo Emerson, Judy Garland, Paul Gauguin, Allen Ginsberg, Benny Goodman, Bob Hope, Burl Ives, John F. Kennedy, Peggy Lee, Marilyn Monroe, Joe Namath, Cole Porter, Laurence Olivier, Harriet Beecher Stowe, Queen Victoria, John Wayne, Frank Lloyd Wright

CANCER: "Dear Abby," Lizzie Borden, David Brinkley, Yul Brynner, Pearl Buck, Marc Chagall, Princess Diana, Babe Didrikson, Mary Baker Eddy, Henry VIII, John Glenn, Ernest Hemingway, Lena Horne, Oscar Hammerstein, Helen Keller, Ann Landers, George Orwell, Nancy Reagan, Rembrandt, Richard Rodgers, Ginger Rogers, Rubens, Jean-Paul Sartre, O.J. Simpson

LEO: Neil Armstrong, James Baldwin, Lucille Ball, Emily Brontë, Wilt Chamberlain, Julia Child, William J. Clinton, Cecil B. De Mille, Ogden Nash, Amelia Earhart, Edna Ferber, Arthur Goldberg, Alfred Hitchcock, Mick Jagger, George Meany, Annie Oakley, George Bernard Shaw, Napoleon, Jacqueline Onassis, Henry Ford, Francis Scott Key, Andy Warhol, Mae West, Orville Wright

VIRGO: Ingrid Bergman, Warren Burger, Maurice Chevalier, Agatha Christie, Sean Connery, Lafayette, Peter Falk, Greta Garbo, Althea Gibson, Arthur Godfrey, Goethe, Buddy Hackett, Michael Jackson, Lyndon Johnson, D.H. Lawrence, Sophia Loren, Grandma Moses, Arnold Palmer, Queen Elizabeth I, Walter Reuther, Peter Sellers, Lily Tomlin, George Wallace

LIBRA: Brigitte Bardot, Art Buchwald, Truman Capote, Dwight D. Eisenhower, William Faulkner, F. Scott Fitzgerald, Gandhi, George Gershwin, Micky Mantle, Helen Hayes, Vladimir Horowitz, Doris Lessing, Martina Navratalova, Eugene O'Neill, Luciano Pavarotti, Emily Post, Eleanor Roosevelt, Bruce Springsteen, Margaret Thatcher, Gore Vidal, Barbara Walters, Oscar Wilde

SCORPIO: Vivien Leigh, Richard Burton, Art Carney, Johnny Carson, Billy Graham, Grace Kelly, Walter Cronkite, Marie Curie, Charles de Gaulle, Linda Evans, Indira Gandhi, Theodore Roosevelt, Rock Hudson, Katherine Hepburn, Robert F. Kennedy, Billie Jean King, Martin Luther, Georgia O'Keeffe, Pablo Picasso, Jonas Salk, Alan Shepard, Robert Louis Stevenson

SAGITTARIUS: Jane Austen, Louisa May Alcott, Woody Allen, Beethoven, Willy Brandt, Mary Martin, William F. Buckley, Maria Callas, Winston Churchill, Noel Coward, Emily Dickinson, Walt Disney, Benjamin Disraeli, James Doolittle, Kirk Douglas, Chet Huntley, Jane Fonda, Chris Evert Lloyd, Margaret Mead, Charles Schulz, John Milton, Frank Sinatra, Steven Spielberg

CAPRICORN: Muhammad Ali, Isaac Asimov, Pablo Casals, Dizzy Dean, Marlene Dietrich, James Farmer, Ava Gardner, Barry Goldwater, Cary Grant, J. Edgar Hoover, Howard Hughes, Joan of Arc, Gypsy Rose Lee, Martin Luther King, Jr., Rudyard Kipling, Mao Tse-tung, Richard Nixon, Gamal Nasser, Louis Pasteur, Albert Schweitzer, Stalin, Benjamin Franklin, Elvis Presley

AQUARIUS: Marian Anderson, Susan B. Anthony, Jack Benny, John Barrymore, Mikhail Baryshnikov, Charles Darwin, Charles Dickens, Thomas Edison, Clark Gable, Jascha Heifetz, Abraham Lincoln, Yehudi Menuhin, Mozart, Jack Nicklaus, Ronald Reagan, Jackie Robinson, Norman Rockwell, Franklin D. Roosevelt, Gertrude Stein, Charles Lindbergh, Margaret Truman

PISCES: Edward Albee, Harry Belafonte, Alexander Graham Bell, Chopin, Adelle Davis, Albert Einstein, Golda Meir, Jackie Gleason, Winslow Homer, Edward M. Kennedy, Victor Hugo, Mike Mansfield, Michelangelo, Edna St. Vincent Millay, Liza Minelli, John Steinbeck, Linus Pauling, Ravel, Renoir, Diana Ross, William Shirer, Elizabeth Taylor, George Washington

The Signs and Their Key Words

		POSITIVE	NEGATIVE
ARIES	self	courage, initiative, pioneer instinct	brash rudeness, selfish impetuosity
TAURUS	money	endurance, loyalty, wealth	obstinacy, gluttony
GEMINI	mind	versatility	capriciousness, unreliability
CANCER	family	sympathy, homing instinct	clannishness, childishness
LEO	children	love, authority, integrity	egotism, force
VIRGO	work	purity, industry, analysis	faultfinding, cynicism
LIBRA	marriage	harmony, justice	vacillation, superficiality
SCORPIO	sex	survival, regeneration	vengeance, discord
SAGITTARIUS	travel	optimism, higher learning	lawlessness
CAPRICORN	career	depth	narrowness, gloom
AQUARIUS	friends	human fellowship, genius	perverse unpredictability
PISCES	confine-ment	spiritual love, universality	diffusion, escapism

The Elements and Qualities of The Signs

Every sign has both an *element* and a *quality* associated with it. The element indicates the basic makeup of the sign, and the quality describes the kind of activity associated with each.

Element	Sign	Quality	Sign
FIRE...........	ARIES	CARDINAL......	ARIES
	LEO		LIBRA
	SAGITTARIUS		CANCER
			CAPRICORN
EARTH	TAURUS		
	VIRGO		
	CAPRICORN	FIXED	TAURUS
			LEO
			SCORPIO
AIR.............	GEMINI		AQUARIUS
	LIBRA		
	AQUARIUS		
		MUTABLE........	GEMINI
WATER	CANCER		VIRGO
	SCORPIO		SAGITTARIUS
	PISCES		PISCES

Signs can be grouped together according to their element and quality. Signs of the same element share many basic traits in common. They tend to form stable configurations and ultimately harmonious relationships. Signs of the same quality are often less harmonious, but they share many dynamic potentials for growth as well as profound fulfillment.

Further discussion of each of these sign groupings is provided on the following pages.

The Fire Signs

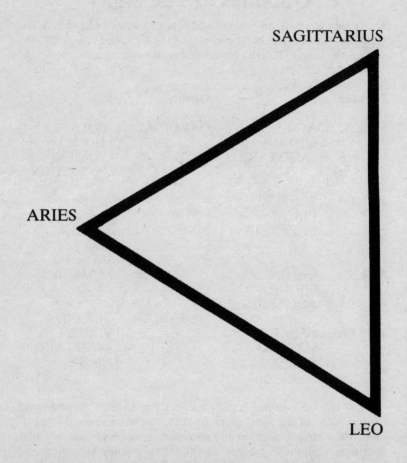

This is the fire group. On the whole these are emotional, volatile types, quick to anger, quick to forgive. They are adventurous, powerful people and act as a source of inspiration for everyone. They spark into action with immediate exuberant impulses. They are intelligent, self-involved, creative, and idealistic. They all share a certain vibrancy and glow that outwardly reflects an inner flame and passion for living.

The Earth Signs

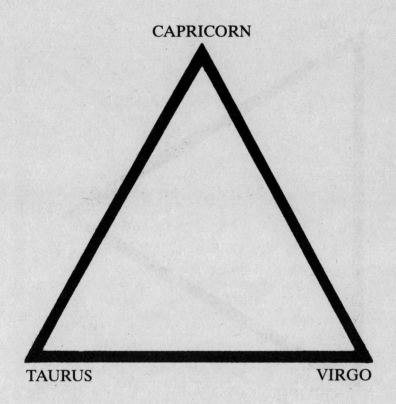

CAPRICORN

TAURUS   VIRGO

This is the earth group. They are in constant touch with the material world and tend to be conservative. Although they are all capable of spartan self-discipline, they are earthy, sensual people who are stimulated by the tangible, elegant, and luxurious. The thread of their lives is always practical, but they do fantasize and are often attracted to dark, mysterious, emotional people. They are like great cliffs overhanging the sea, forever married to the ocean but always resisting erosion from the dark, emotional forces that thunder at their feet.

The Air Signs

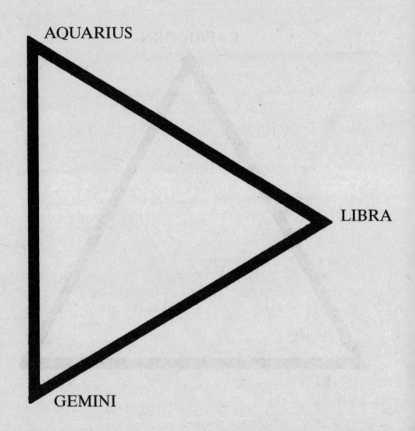

This is the air group. They are light, mental creatures desirous of contact, communication, and relationship. They are involved with people and the forming of ties on many levels. Original thinkers, they are the bearers of human news. Their language is their sense of word, color, style, and beauty. They provide an atmosphere suitable and pleasant for living. They add change and versatility to the scene, and it is through them that we can explore new territory of human intelligence and experience.

The Water Signs

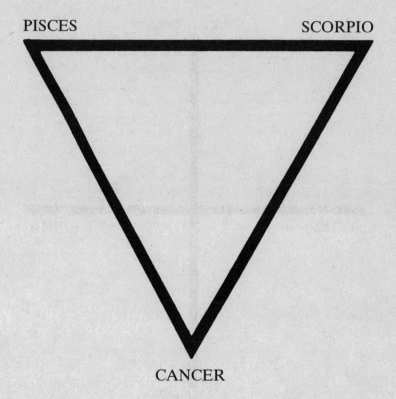

PISCES   SCORPIO

CANCER

This is the water group. Through the water people, we are all joined together on emotional, nonverbal levels. They are silent, mysterious types whose magic hypnotizes even the most determined realist. They have uncanny perceptions about people and are as rich as the oceans when it comes to feeling, emotion, or imagination. They are sensitive, mystical creatures with memories that go back beyond time. Through water, life is sustained. These people have the potential for the depths of darkness or the heights of mysticism and art.

The Cardinal Signs

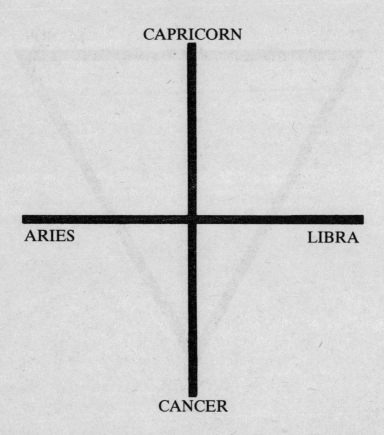

CAPRICORN

ARIES

LIBRA

CANCER

Put together, this is a clear-cut picture of dynamism, activity, tremendous stress, and remarkable achievement. These people know the meaning of great change since their lives are often characterized by significant crises and major successes. This combination is like a simultaneous storm of summer, fall, winter, and spring. The danger is chaotic diffusion of energy; the potential is irrepressible growth and victory.

The Fixed Signs

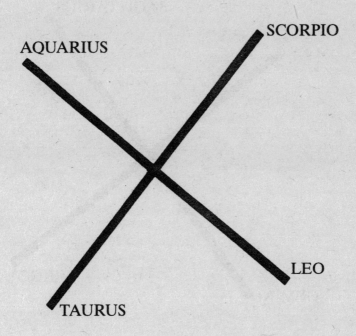

Fixed signs are always establishing themselves in a given place or area of experience. Like explorers who arrive and plant a flag, these people claim a position from which they do not enjoy being deposed. They are staunch, stalwart, upright, trusty, honorable people, although their obstinacy is well-known. Their contribution is fixity, and they are the angels who support our visible world.

The Mutable Signs

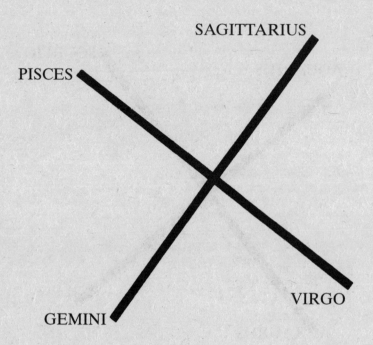

Mutable people are versatile, sensitive, intelligent, nervous, and deeply curious about life. They are the translators of all energy. They often carry out or complete tasks initiated by others. Combinations of these signs have highly developed minds; they are imaginative and jumpy and think and talk a lot. At worst their lives are a Tower of Babel. At best they are adaptable and ready creatures who can assimilate one kind of experience and enjoy it while anticipating coming changes.

THE PLANETS
OF THE SOLAR SYSTEM

This section describes the planets of the solar system. In astrology, both the Sun and the Moon are considered to be planets. Because of the Moon's influence in our day-to-day lives, the Moon is described in a separate section following this one.

The Planets and the Signs
They Rule

The signs of the Zodiac are linked to the planets in the following way. Each sign is governed or ruled by one or more planets. No matter where the planets are located in the sky at any given moment, they still rule their respective signs, and when they travel through the signs they rule, they have special dignity and their effects are stronger.

Following is a list of the planets and the signs they rule. After looking at the list, read the definitions of the planets and see if you can determine how the planet ruling *your* Sun sign has affected your life.

SIGNS	RULING PLANETS
Aries	Mars, Pluto
Taurus	Venus
Gemini	Mercury
Cancer	Moon
Leo	Sun
Virgo	Mercury
Libra	Venus
Scorpio	Mars, Pluto
Sagittarius	Jupiter
Capricorn	Saturn
Aquarius	Saturn, Uranus
Pisces	Jupiter, Neptune

Characteristics of the Planets

The following pages give the meaning and characteristics of the planets of the solar system. They all travel around the Sun at different speeds and different distances. Taken with the Sun, they all distribute individual intelligence and ability throughout the entire chart.

The planets modify the influence of the Sun in a chart according to their own particular natures, strengths, and positions. Their positions must be calculated for each year and day, and their function and expression in a horoscope will change as they move from one area of the Zodiac to another.

We start with a description of the sun.

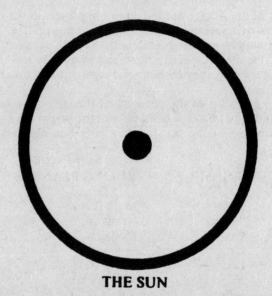

THE SUN

SUN

This is the center of existence. Around this flaming sphere all the planets revolve in endless orbits. Our star is constantly sending out its beams of light and energy without which no life on Earth would be possible. In astrology it symbolizes everything we are trying to become, the center around which all of our activity in life will always revolve. It is the symbol of our basic nature and describes the natural and constant thread that runs through everything that we do from birth to death on this planet.

To early astrologers, the Sun seemed to be another planet because it crossed the heavens every day, just like the rest of the bodies in the sky.

It is the only star near enough to be seen well—it is, in fact, a dwarf star. Approximately 860,000 miles in diameter, it is about ten times as wide as the giant planet Jupiter. The next nearest star is nearly 300,000 times as far away, and if the Sun were located as far away as most of the bright stars, it would be too faint to be seen without a telescope.

Everything in the horoscope ultimately revolves around this singular body. Although other forces may be prominent in the charts of some individuals, still the Sun is the total nucleus of being and symbolizes the complete potential of every human being alive. It is vitality and the life force. Your whole essence comes from the position of the Sun.

You are always trying to express the Sun according to its position by house and sign. Possibility for all development is found in the Sun, and it marks the fundamental character of your personal radiations all around you.

It is the symbol of strength, vigor, wisdom, dignity, ardor, and generosity, and the ability for a person to function as a mature individual. It is also a creative force in society. It is consciousness of the gift of life.

The underdeveloped solar nature is arrogant, pushy, undependable, and proud, and is constantly using force.

MERCURY

Mercury is the planet closest to the Sun. It races around our star, gathering information and translating it to the rest of the system. Mercury represents your capacity to understand the desires of your own will and to translate those desires into action.

In other words it is the planet of mind and the power of communication. Through Mercury we develop an ability to think, write, speak, and observe—to become aware of the world around us. It colors our attitudes and vision of the world, as well as our capacity to communicate our inner responses to the outside world. Some people who have serious disabilities in their power of verbal communication have often wrongly been described as people lacking intelligence.

Although this planet (and its position in the horoscope) indicates your power to communicate your thoughts and perceptions to the world, intelligence is something deeper. Intelligence is distributed throughout all the planets. It is the relationship of the planets to each other that truly describes what we call intelligence. Mercury rules speaking, language, mathematics, draft and design, students, messengers, young people, offices, teachers, and any pursuits where the mind of man has wings.

VENUS

Venus is beauty. It symbolizes the harmony and radiance of a rare and elusive quality: beauty itself. It is refinement and delicacy, softness and charm. In astrology it indicates grace, balance, and the aesthetic sense. Where Venus is we see beauty, a gentle drawing in of energy and the need for satisfaction and completion. It is a special touch that finishes off rough edges. It is sensitivity, and affection, and it is always the place for that other elusive phenomenon: love. Venus describes our sense of what is beautiful and loving. Poorly developed, it is vulgar, tasteless, and self-indulgent. But its ideal is the flame of spiritual love — Aphrodite, goddess of love, and the sweetness and power of personal beauty.

MARS

Mars is raw, crude energy. The planet next to Earth but outward from the Sun is a fiery red sphere that charges through the horoscope with force and fury. It represents the way you reach out for new adventure and new experience. It is energy and drive, initiative, courage, and daring. It is the power to start something and see it through. It can be thoughtless, cruel and wild, angry and hostile, causing cuts, burns, scalds, and wounds. It can stab its way through a chart, or it can be the symbol of healthy spirited adventure, well-channeled constructive power to begin and keep up the drive. If you have trouble starting things, if you lack the get-up-and-go to start the ball rolling, if you lack aggressiveness and self-confidence, chances are there's another planet influencing your Mars. Mars rules soldiers, butchers, surgeons, salesmen—any field that requires daring, bold skill, operational technique, or self-promotion.

JUPITER

This is the largest planet of the solar system. Scientists have recently learned that Jupiter reflects more light than it receives from the Sun. In a sense it is like a star itself. In astrology it rules good luck and good cheer, health, wealth, optimism, happiness, success, and joy. It is the symbol of opportunity and always opens the way for new possibilities in your life. It rules exuberance, enthusiasm, wisdom, knowledge, generosity, and all forms of expansion in general. It rules actors, statesmen, clerics, professional people, religion, publishing, and the distribution of many people over large areas.

Sometimes Jupiter makes you think you deserve everything, and you become sloppy, wasteful, careless and rude, prodigal and law-less, in the illusion that nothing can ever go wrong. Then there is the danger of overconfidence, exaggeration, undependability, and overindulgence.

Jupiter is the minimization of limitation and the emphasis on spirituality and potential. It is the thirst for knowledge and higher learning.

SATURN

Saturn circles our system in dark splendor with its mysterious rings, forcing us to be awakened to what ever we have neglected in the past. It will present real puzzles and problems to be solved, causing delays, obstacles, and hindrances. By doing so, Saturn stirs our own sensitivity to those areas where we are laziest.

Here we must patiently develop *method*, and only through painstaking effort can our ends be achieved. It brings order to a horoscope and imposes reason just where we are feeling least reasonable. By creating limitations and boundary, Saturn shows the consequences of being human and demands that we accept the changing cycles inevitable in human life. Saturn rules time, old age, and sobriety. It can bring depression, gloom, jealousy, and greed, or serious ac cep tance of responsibilities out of which success will develop. With Saturn there is nothing to do but face facts. It rules laborers, stones, granite, rocks, and crystals of all kinds.

THE OUTER PLANETS:
URANUS, NEPTUNE, PLUTO

Uranus, Neptune, Pluto are the outer planets. They liberate human beings from cultural conditioning, and in that sense are the lawbreakers. In early times it was thought that Saturn was the last planet of the system—the outer limit beyond which we could never go. The discovery of the next three planets ushered in new phases of human history, revolution, and technology.

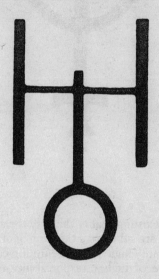

URANUS

Uranus rules unexpected change, upheaval, revolution. It is the symbol of total independence and asserts the freedom of an individual from all restriction and restraint. It is a breakthrough planet and indicates talent, originality, and genius in a horoscope. It usually causes last-minute reversals and changes of plan, unwanted separations, accidents, catastrophes, and eccentric behavior. It can add irrational rebelliousness and perverse bohemianism to a personality or a streak of unaffected brilliance in science and art. It rules technology, aviation, and all forms of electrical and electronic advancement. It governs great leaps forward and topsy-turvy situations, and *always* turns things around at the last minute. Its effects are difficult to predict, since it rules sudden last-minute decisions and events that come like lightning out of the blue.

NEPTUNE

Neptune dissolves existing reality the way the sea erodes the cliffs beside it. Its effects are subtle like the ringing of a buoy's bell in the fog. It suggests a reality higher than definition can usually describe. It awakens a sense of higher responsibility often causing guilt, worry, anxieties, or delusions. Neptune is associated with all forms of escape and can make things seem a certain way so convincingly that you are absolutely sure of something that eventually turns out to be quite different.

It is the planet of illusion and therefore governs the invisible realms that lie beyond our ordinary minds, beyond our simple factual ability to prove what is "real." Treachery, deceit, disillusionment, and disappointment are linked to Neptune. It describes a vague reality that promises eternity and the divine, yet in a manner so complex that we cannot really fathom it at all. At its worst Neptune is a cheap intoxicant; at its best it is the poetry, music, and inspiration of the higher planes of spiritual love. It has dominion over movies, photographs, and much of the arts.

PLUTO

Pluto lies at the outpost of our system and therefore rules finality in a horoscope—the final closing of chapters in your life, the passing of major milestones and points of development from which there is no return. It is a final wipeout, a closeout, an evacuation. It is a distant, subtle but powerful catalyst in all transformations that occur. It creates, destroys, then re creates. Sometimes Pluto starts its influence with a minor event or insignificant incident that might even go unnoticed. Slowly but surely, little by little, everything changes, until at last there has been a total transformation in the area of your life where Pluto has been operating. It rules mass thinking and the trends that society first rejects, then adopts, and finally outgrows.

Pluto rules the dead and the underworld—all the powerful forces of creation and destruction that go on all the time beneath, around, and above us. It can bring a lust for power with strong obsessions.

It is the planet that rules the metamorphosis of the caterpillar into a butterfly, for it symbolizes the capacity to change totally and forever a person's lifestyle, way of thought, and behavior.

THE MOON IN EACH SIGN

The Moon is the nearest planet to the Earth. It exerts more observable influence on us from day to day than any other planet. The effect is very personal, very intimate, and if we are not aware of how it works it can make us quite unstable in our ideas. And the annoying thing is that at these times we often see our own instability but can do nothing about it. A knowledge of what can be expected may help considerably. We can then be prepared to stand strong against the Moon's negative influences and use its positive ones to help us to get ahead. Who has not heard of going with the tide?

The Moon reflects, has no light of its own. It reflects the Sun—the life giver—in the form of vital movement. The Moon controls the tides, the blood rhythm, the movement of sap in trees and plants. Its nature is inconstancy and change so it signifies our moods, our superficial behavior—walking, talking, and especially thinking. Being a true reflector of other forces, the Moon is cold, watery like the surface of a still lake, brilliant and scintillating at times, but easily ruffled and disturbed by the winds of change.

The Moon takes about 27⅓ days to make a complete transit of the Zodiac. It spends just over 2¼ days in each sign. During that time it reflects the qualities, energies, and characteristics of the sign and, to a degree, the planet which rules the sign. When the Moon in its transit occupies a sign incompatible with our own birth sign, we can expect to feel a vague uneasiness, perhaps a touch of irritableness. We should not be discouraged nor let the feeling get us down, or, worse still, allow ourselves to take the discomfort out on others. Try to remember that the Moon has to change signs within 55 hours and, provided you are not physically ill, your mood will probably change with it. It is amazing how frequently depression lifts with the shift in the Moon's position. And, of course, when the Moon is transiting a sign compatible or sympathetic to yours, you will probably feel some sort of stimulation or just be plain happy to be alive.

In the horoscope, the Moon is such a powerful indicator that competent astrologers often use the sign it occupied at birth as the birth sign of the person. This is done particularly when the Sun is on the cusp, or edge, of two signs. Most experienced astrologers, however, coordinate both Sun and Moon signs by reading and confirming from one to the other and secure a far more accurate and personalized analysis.

For these reasons, the Moon tables which follow this section (see pages 86–92) are of great importance to the individual. They show the days and the exact times the Moon will enter each sign of the Zodiac for the year. Remember, you have to adjust the indicated times to local time. The corrections, already calculated for most of the main cities, are at the beginning of the tables. What follows now is a guide to the influences that will be reflected to the Earth by the Moon while it transits each of the twelve signs. The influence is at its peak about 26 hours after the Moon enters a sign. As you read the daily forecast, check the Moon sign for any given day and glance back at this guide.

MOON IN ARIES
This is a time for action, for reaching out beyond the usual self-imposed limitations and faint-hearted cautions. If you have plans in your head or on your desk, put them into practice. New ventures, applications, new jobs, new starts of any kind—all have a good chance of success. This is the period when original and dynamic impulses are being reflected onto Earth. Such energies are extremely vital and favor the pursuit of pleasure and adventure in practically every form. Sick people should feel an improvement. Those who are well will probably find themselves exuding confidence and optimism. People fond of physical exercise should find their bodies growing with tone and well-being. Boldness, strength, determination should characterize most of your activities with a readiness to face up to old challenges. Yesterday's problems may seem petty and exaggerated—so deal with them. Strike out alone. Self-reliance will attract others to you. This is a good time for making friends. Business and marriage partners are more likely to be impressed with the man and woman of action. Opposition will be overcome or thrown aside with much less effort than usual. CAUTION: Be dominant but not domineering.

MOON IN TAURUS
The spontaneous, action-packed person of yesterday gives way to the cautious, diligent, hardworking "thinker." In this period ideas will probably be concentrated on ways of improving finances. A great deal of time may be spent figuring out and going over schemes and plans. It is the right time to be careful with detail.

People will find themselves working longer than usual at their desks. Or devoting more time to serious thought about the future. A strong desire to put order into business and financial arrangements may cause extra work. Loved ones may complain of being neglected and may fail to appreciate that your efforts are for their ultimate benefit. Your desire for system may extend to criticism of arrangements in the home and lead to minor upsets. Health may be affected through overwork. Try to secure a reasonable amount of rest and relaxation, although the tendency will be to "keep going" despite good advice. Work done conscientiously in this period should result in a solid contribution to your future security. CAUTION: Try not to be as serious with people as the work you are engaged in.

MOON IN GEMINI
The humdrum of routine and too much work should suddenly end. You are likely to find yourself in an expansive, quicksilver world of change and self-expression. Urges to write, to paint, to experience the freedom of some sort of artistic outpouring, may be very strong. Take full advantage of them. You may find yourself finishing something you began and put aside long ago. Or embarking on something new which could easily be prompted by a chance meeting, a new acquaintance, or even an advertisement. There may be a yearning for a change of scenery, the feeling to visit another country (not too far away), or at least to get away for a few days. This may result in short, quick journeys. Or, if you are planning a single visit, there may be some unexpected changes or detours on the way. Familiar activities will seem to give little satisfaction unless they contain a fresh element of excitement or expectation. The inclination will be toward untried pursuits, particularly those that allow you to express your inner nature. The accent is on new faces, new places. CAUTION: Do not be too quick to commit yourself emotionally.

MOON IN CANCER
Feelings of uncertainty and vague insecurity are likely to cause problems while the Moon is in Cancer. Thoughts may turn frequently to the warmth of the home and the comfort of loved ones. Nostalgic impulses could cause you to bring out old photographs and letters and reflect on the days when your life seemed to be much more rewarding and less demanding. The love and understanding of parents and family may be important, and, if it is not forthcoming, you may have to fight against bouts of self-pity. The cordiality of friends and the thought of good times with them that are sure to be repeated will help to restore you to a happier frame

of mind. The desire to be alone may follow minor setbacks or re-buffs at this time, but solitude is unlikely to help. Better to get on the telephone or visit someone. This period often causes peculiar dreams and upsurges of imaginative thinking which can be help-ful to authors of occult and mystical works. Preoccupation with the personal world of simple human needs can overshadow any mate-rial strivings. CAUTION: Do not spend too much time thinking—seek the company of loved ones or close friends.

MOON IN LEO

New horizons of exciting and rather extravagant activity open up. This is the time for exhilarating entertainment, glamorous and lav-ish parties, and expensive shopping sprees. Any merrymaking that relies upon your generosity as a host has every chance of being a spectacular success. You should find yourself right in the center of the fun, either as the life of the party or simply as a person whom happy people like to be with. Romance thrives in this heady atmo-sphere and friendships are likely to explode unexpectedly into seri-ous attachments. Children and younger people should be attracted to you and you may find yourself organizing a picnic or a visit to a fun-fair, the movies, or the beach. The sunny company and vitality of youthful companions should help you to find some unsuspected energy. In career, you could find an opening for promotion or ad-vancement. This should be the time to make a direct approach. The period favors those engaged in original research. CAUTION: Bask in popularity, not in flattery.

MOON IN VIRGO

Off comes the party cap and out steps the busy, practical worker. He wants to get his personal affairs straight, to rearrange them, if necessary, for more efficiency, so he will have more time for more work. He clears up his correspondence, pays outstanding bills, makes numerous phone calls. He is likely to make inquiries, or sign up for some new insurance and put money into gilt-edged investment. Thoughts probably revolve around the need for future security—to tie up loose ends and clear the decks. There may be a tendency to be "finicky," to interfere in the routine of others, particularly friends and family members. The motive may be a genuine desire to help with suggestions for updating or streamlining their affairs, but these will probably not be welcomed. Sympathy may be felt for less fortunate sections of the community and a flurry of some sort of voluntary ser-vice is likely. This may be accompanied by strong feelings of respon-sibility on several fronts and health may suffer from extra efforts made. CAUTION: Everyone may not want your help or advice.

MOON IN LIBRA
These are days of harmony and agreement and you should find yourself at peace with most others. Relationships tend to be smooth and sweet-flowing. Friends may become closer and bonds deepen in mutual understanding. Hopes will be shared. Progress by cooperation could be the secret of success in every sphere. In business, established partnerships may flourish and new ones get off to a good start. Acquaintances could discover similar interests that lead to congenial discussions and rewarding exchanges of some sort. Love, as a unifying force, reaches its optimum. Marriage partners should find accord. Those who wed at this time face the prospect of a happy union. Cooperation and tolerance are felt to be stronger than dissension and impatience. The argumentative are not quite so loud in their bellowings, nor as inflexible in their attitudes. In the home, there should be a greater recognition of the other point of view and a readiness to put the wishes of the group before selfish insistence. This is a favorable time to join an art group. CAUTION: Do not be too independent—let others help you if they want to.

MOON IN SCORPIO
Driving impulses to make money and to economize are likely to cause upsets all around. No area of expenditure is likely to be spared the ax, including the household budget. This is a time when the desire to cut down on extravagance can become near fanatical. Care must be exercised to try to keep the aim in reasonable perspective. Others may not feel the same urgent need to save and may retaliate. There is a danger that possessions of sentimental value will be sold to realize cash for investment. Buying and selling of stock for quick profit is also likely. The attention turns to organizing, reorganizing, tidying up at home and at work. Neglected jobs could suddenly be done with great bursts of energy. The desire for solitude may intervene. Self-searching thoughts could disturb. The sense of invisible and mysterious energies in play could cause some excitability. The reassurance of loves ones may help. CAUTION: Be kind to the people you love.

MOON IN SAGITTARIUS
These are days when you are likely to be stirred and elevated by discussions and reflections of a religious and philosophical nature. Ideas of faraway places may cause unusual response and excitement. A decision may be made to visit someone overseas, perhaps a person whose influence was important to your earlier character development. There could be a strong resolution to get away from

present intellectual patterns, to learn new subjects, and to meet more interesting people. The superficial may be rejected in all its forms. An impatience with old ideas and unimaginative contacts could lead to a change of companions and interests. There may be an upsurge of religious feeling and metaphysical inquiry. Even a new insight into the significance of astrology and other occult studies is likely under the curious stimulus of the Moon in Sagittarius. Physically, you may express this need for fundamental change by spending more time outdoors: sports, gardening, long walks appeal. CAUTION: Try to channel any restlessness into worthwhile study.

MOON IN CAPRICORN

Life in these hours may seem to pivot around the importance of gaining prestige and honor in the career, as well as maintaining a spotless reputation. Ambitious urges may be excessive and could be accompanied by quite acquisitive drives for money. Effort should be directed along strictly ethical lines where there is no possibility of reproach or scandal. All endeavors are likely to be characterized by great earnestness, and an air of authority and purpose which should impress those who are looking for leadership or reliability. The desire to conform to accepted standards may extend to sharp criticism of family members. Frivolity and unconventional actions are unlikely to amuse while the Moon is in Capricorn. Moderation and seriousness are the orders of the day. Achievement and recognition in this period could come through community work or organizing for the benefit of some amateur group. CAUTION: Dignity and esteem are not always self-awarded.

MOON IN AQUARIUS

Moon in Aquarius is in the second last sign of the Zodiac where ideas can become disturbingly fine and subtle. The result is often a mental "no-man's land" where imagination cannot be trusted with the same certitude as other times. The dangers for the individual are the extremes of optimism and pessimism. Unless the imagination is held in check, situations are likely to be misread, and rosy conclusions drawn where they do not exist. Consequences for the unwary can be costly in career and business. Best to think twice and not speak or act until you think again. Pessimism can be a cruel self-inflicted penalty for delusion at this time. Between the two extremes are strange areas of self-deception which, for example, can make the selfish person think he is actually being generous. Eerie dreams which resemble the reality and even seem to continue into the waking state are also possible. CAUTION: Look for the fact and not just for the image in your mind.

MOON IN PISCES

Everything seems to come to the surface now. Memory may be crystal clear, throwing up long-forgotten information which could be valuable in the career or business. Flashes of clairvoyance and intuition are possible along with sudden realizations of one's own nature, which may be used for self-improvement. A talent, never before suspected, may be discovered. Qualities not evident before in friends and marriage partners are likely to be noticed. As this is a period in which the truth seems to emerge, the discovery of false characteristics is likely to lead to disenchantment or a shift in attachments. However, when qualities are accepted, it should lead to happiness and deeper feeling. Surprise solutions could bob up for old problems. There may be a public announcement of the solving of a crime or mystery. People with secrets may find someone has "guessed" correctly. The secrets of the soul or the inner self also tend to reveal themselves. Religious and philosophical groups may make some interesting discoveries. CAUTION: Not a time for activities that depend on secrecy.

NOTE: When you read your daily forecasts, use the Moon Sign Dates that are provided in the following section of Moon Tables. Then you may want to glance back here for the Moon's influence in a given sign.

MOON TABLES

Atlanta, Boston, Detroit, Miami, Washington, Montreal,
Ottawa, Quebec, Bogota, Havana, Lima, Santiago...... Same time
Chicago, New Orleans, Houston, Winnipeg, Churchill,
Mexico City .... Deduct 1 hour
Albuquerque, Denver, Phoenix, El Paso, Edmonton,
Helena.. Deduct 2 hours
Los Angeles, San Francisco, Reno, Portland,
Seattle, Vancouver.. Deduct 3 hours
Honolulu, Anchorage, Fairbanks, Kodiak .... Deduct 5 hours
Nome, Samoa, Tonga, Midway .... Deduct 6 hours
Halifax, Bermuda, San Juan, Caracas, La Paz,
Barbados.. Add 1 hour
St. John's, Brasilia, Rio de Janeiro, Sao Paulo,
Buenos Aires, Montevideo .... Add 2 hours
Azores, Cape Verde Islands.. Add 3 hours
Canary Islands, Madeira, Reykjavik .... Add 4 hours
London, Paris, Amsterdam, Madrid, Lisbon,
Gibraltar, Belfast, Raba .... Add 5 hours
Frankfurt, Rome, Oslo, Stockholm, Prague,
Belgrade... Add 6 hours
Bucharest, Beirut, Tel Aviv, Athens, Istanbul, Cairo,
Alexandria, Cape Town, Johannesburg...................... Add 7 hours
Moscow, Leningrad, Baghdad, Dhahran,
Addis Ababa, Nairobi, Teheran, Zanzibar .... Add 8 hours
Bombay, Calcutta, Sri Lanka .... Add 10½
Hong Kong, Shanghai, Manila, Peking, Perth............. Add 13 hours
Tokyo, Okinawa, Darwin, Pusan .... Add 14 hours
Sydney, Melbourne, Port Moresby, Guam.................... Add 15 hours
Auckland, Wellington, Suva, Wake .... Add 17 hours

2013 MOON SIGN DATES — NEW YORK TIME

JANUARY		FEBRUARY		MARCH	
Day Moon Enters		**Day Moon Enters**		**Day Moon Enters**	
1. Virgo	12.36 pm	1. Libra		1. Scorp.	12.35 pm
2. Virgo		2. Scorp.	7:03 am	2. Scorp	
3. Libra	8:12 pm	3. Scorp.		3. Sagitt.	4:12 pm
4. Libra		4. Sagitt.	10:46 am	4. Sagitt.	
5. Libra		5. Sagitt.		5. Capric.	7:15 pm
6. Scorp.	1:10 am	6. Capric.	12:56 pm	6. Capric.	
7. Scorp.		7. Capric.		7. Aquar.	10:03 pm
8. Sagitt.	3:29 am	8. Aquar.	1:18 pm	8. Aquar.	
9. Sagitt.		9. Aquar.		9. Aquar.	
10. Capric.	3:55 am	10. Pisces	4:21 pm	10. Pisces	1:20 am
11. Capric.		11. Pisces		11. Pisces	
12. Aquar.	4:02 am	12. Aries	8:52 pm	12. Aries	6:18 am
13. Aquar.		13. Aries		13. Aries	
14. Pisces	5:50 am	14. Aries		14. Taurus	2:09 pm
15. Pisces		15. Taurus	5:09 am	15. Taurus	
16. Aries	11:08 am	16. Taurus		16. Taurus	
17. Aries		17. Gemini	4:51 pm	17. Gemini	1:10 am
18. Taurus	8:37 pm	18. Gemini		18. Gemini	
19. Taurus		19. Gemini		19. Cancer	1:56 pm
20. Taurus		20. Cancer	5:46 am	20. Cancer	
21. Gemini	9:05 am	21. Cancer		21. Cancer	
22. Gemini		22. Leo	5:13 pm	22. Leo	1:51 am
23. Cancer	10:01 pm	23. Leo		23. Leo	
24. Cancer		24. Leo		24. Virgo	10:50 am
25. Cancer		25. Virgo	1:54 am	25. Virgo	
26. Leo	9:21 am	26. Virgo		26. Libra	4:33 pm
27. Leo		27. Libra	8:03 am	27. Libra	
28. Virgo	6:28 pm	28. Libra		28. Scorp.	7:55 pm
29. Virgo				29. Scorp.	
30. Virgo				30. Sagitt.	10:14 pm
31. Libra	1:37 am			31. Sagitt.	

Daylight saving time to be considered where applicable.

2013 MOON SIGN DATES —
NEW YORK TIME

APRIL		MAY		JUNE	
Day Moon Enters		Day Moon Enters		Day Moon Enters	
1. Sagitt.		1. Aquar.	9:21 am	1. Pisces	
2. Capric.	12:36 am	2. Aquar.		2. Aries	1:34 am
3. Capric.		3. Pisces	1:26 pm	3. Aries	
4. Aquar.	3:43 am	4. Pisces		4. Taurus	10:55 am
5. Aquar.		5. Aries	8:04 pm	5. Taurus	
6. Pisces	8:01 am	6. Aries		6. Gemini	10:33 pm
7. Pisces		7. Aries		7. Gemini	
8. Aries	2:03 pm	8. Taurus	5:10 am	8. Gemini	
9. Aries		9. Taurus		9. Cancer	11:17 am
10. Taurus	10:23 pm	10. Gemini	4:22 pm	10. Cancer	
11. Taurus		11. Gemini		11. Leo	11:59 pm
12. Taurus		12. Gemini		12. Leo	
13. Gemini	9:14 am	13. Cancer	4:58 am	13. Leo	
14. Gemini		14. Cancer		14. Virgo	11:27 am
15. Cancer	9:50 pm	15. Leo	5:39 pm	15. Virgo	
16. Cancer		16. Leo		16. Libra	8:20 pm
17. Cancer		17. Leo		17. Libra	
18. Leo	10:15 am	18. Virgo	4:34 am	18. Libra	
19. Leo		19. Virgo		19. Scorp.	1:40 am
20. Virgo	8:10 pm	20. Libra	12:08 pm	20. Scorp.	
21. Virgo		21. Libra		21. Sagitt.	3:32 am
22. Virgo		22. Scorp.	3:56 pm	22. Sagitt.	
23. Libra	2:26 am	23. Scorp.		23. Capric.	3:09 am
24. Libra		24. Sagitt.	4:50 pm	24. Capric.	
25. Scorp.	5:26 am	25. Sagitt.		25. Aquar.	2:28 am
26. Scorp.		26. Capric.	4:30 pm	26. Aquar.	
27. Sagitt.	6:33 am	27. Capric.		27. Pisces	3:33 am
28. Sagitt.		28. Aquar.	4:49 pm	28. Pisces	
29. Capric.	7:22 am	29. Aquar.		29. Aries	8:08 am
30. Capric.		30. Pisces	7:31 pm	30. Aries	
		31. Pisces			

Daylight saving time to be considered where applicable.

2013 MOON SIGN DATES — NEW YORK TIME

JULY		AUGUST		SEPTEMBER	
Day Moon Enters		**Day Moon Enters**		**Day Moon Enters**	
1. Taurus	4:44 pm	1. Gemini		1. Leo	7:02 pm
2. Taurus		2. Cancer	11:31 pm	2. Leo	
3. Taurus		3. Cancer		3. Leo	
4. Gemini	4:23 am	4. Cancer		4. Virgo	5:45 am
5. Gemini		5. Leo	11:59 am	5. Virgo	
6. Cancer	5:15 pm	6. Leo		6. Libra	2:14pm
7. Cancer		7. Virgo	10:58 pm	7. Libra	
8. Cancer		8. Virgo		8. Scorp.	8:45 pm
9. Leo	5:49 am	9. Virgo		9. Scorp.	
10. Leo		10. Libra	8:09 am	10. Scorp.	
11. Virgo	5:13 pm	11. Libra		11. Sagitt.	1:37 am
12. Virgo		12. Scorp.	3:19 pm	12. Sagitt.	
13. Virgo		13. Scorp.		13. Capric.	4:57 am
14. Libra	2:42 am	14. Sagitt.	8:05 pm	14. Capric.	
15. Libra		15. Sagitt.		15. Aquar.	7:06 am
16. Scorp.	9:25 am	16. Capric.	10:26 pm	16. Aquar.	
17. Scorp.		17. Capric.		17. Pisces	8:59 am
18. Sagitt.	12:55 pm	18. Aquar.	11:08 pm	18. Pisces	
19. Sagitt.		19. Aquar.		19. Aries	11:59 am
20. Capric.	1:40 pm	20. Pisces	11:44 pm	20. Aries	
21. Capric.		21. Pisces		21. Taurus	5:34 pm
22. Aquar.	1:06 pm	22. Pisces		22. Taurus	
23. Aquar.		23. Aries	2:14 am	23. Taurus	
24. Pisces	1:23 pm	24. Aries		24. Gemini	2:35 am
25. Pisces		25. Taurus	8:14 am	25. Gemini	
26. Aries	4:30 pm	26. Taurus		26. Cancer	2:26 pm
27. Aries		27. Gemini	6:09 pm	27. Cancer	
28. Taurus	11:44 pm	28. Gemini		28. Cancer	
29. Taurus		29. Gemini		29. Leo	2:58 am
30. Taurus		30. Cancer	6:34 am	30. Leo	
31. Gemini	10:43 am	31. Cancer			

Daylight saving time to be considered where applicable.

2013 MOON SIGN DATES —
NEW YORK TIME

OCTOBER Day Moon Enters		NOVEMBER Day Moon Enters		DECEMBER Day Moon Enters	
1. Virgo	1:53 pm	1. Libra		1. Scorp.	
2. Virgo		2. Scorp.	12:36 pm	2. Sagitt.	1:32 am
3. Libra	10:01 pm	3. Scorp.		3. Sagitt.	
4. Libra		4. Sagitt.	3:15 pm	4. Capric.	1:50 am
5. Libra		5. Sagitt.		5. Capric.	
6. Scorp.	3:34 am	6. Capric.	4:45 pm	6. Aquar.	1:54 am
7. Scorp.		7. Capric.		7. Aquar.	
8. Sagitt.	7:23 am	8. Aquar.	6:31 pm	8. Pisces	3:35 am
9. Sagitt.		9. Aquar.		9. Pisces	
10. Capric.	10:18 am	10. Pisces	9:37 pm	10. Aries	8:07 am
11. Capric.		11. Pisces		11. Aries	
12. Aquar.	1:01 pm	12. Pisces		12. Taurus	3:41 pm
13. Aquar.		13. Aries	2:40 am	13. Taurus	
14. Pisces	4:07 pm	14. Aries		14. Taurus	
15. Pisces		15. Taurus	9:50 am	15. Gemini	1:42 am
16. Aries	8:19 pm	16. Taurus		16. Gemini	
17. Aries		17. Gemini	7:08 pm	17. Cancer	1:18 pm
18. Aries		18. Gemini		18. Cancer	
19. Taurus	2:28 am	19. Gemini		19. Cancer	
20. Taurus		20. Cancer	6:24 am	20. Leo	1:49 am
21. Gemini	11:15 am	21. Cancer		21. Leo	
22. Gemini		22. Leo	6:58 pm	22. Virgo	2:20 pm
23. Cancer	10:39 am	23. Leo		23. Virgo	
24. Cancer		24. Leo		24. Virgo	
25. Cancer		25. Virgo	7:12 am	25. Libra	1:18 am
26. Leo	11:13 am	26. Virgo		26. Libra	
27. Leo		27. Libra	5:01 pm	27. Scorp.	8:59 am
28. Virgo	10:46 pm	28. Libra		28. Scorp.	
29. Virgo		29. Scorp.	11:04 pm	29. Sagitt.	12:38 pm
30. Virgo		30. Scorp.		30. Sagitt.	
31. Libra	7:23 am			31. Capric.	1:02 pm

Daylight saving time to be considered where applicable.

2013 PHASES OF THE MOON—
NEW YORK TIME

New Moon	First Quarter	Full Moon	Last Quarter
Dec. 13 ('12)	Dec. 20	Dec. 28	Jan. 4
Jan. 11	Jan. 18	Jan. 27	Feb. 4
Feb. 10	Feb. 17	Feb. 25	March 4
March 11	March 19	March 27	April 3
April 10	April 18	April 25	May 2
May 9	May 17	May 25	May 31
June 8	June 16	June 23	June 30
July 8	July 15	July 22	July 29
August 6	August 14	August 20	August 28
Sept. 5	Sept. 12	Sept. 19	Sept. 27
Oct. 4	Oct. 11	Oct. 18	Oct. 26
Nov. 3	Nov. 10	Nov. 17	Nov. 25
Dec. 2	Dec. 9	Dec. 17	Dec. 25

Each phase of the Moon lasts approximately seven to eight days, during which the Moon's shape gradually changes as it comes out of one phase and goes into the next.

There will be a solar eclipse during the New Moon phase on May 9 and November 3.

There will be a lunar eclipse during the Full Moon phase on April 25, May 25, and October 18.

2013 FISHING GUIDE

	Good	Best
January	4-5-9-13-29-23	6-15-25
February	2-11-16-17-21-22	3-12-19-28
March	2-3-11-12-21-22	4-13-19-20-27
April	5-7-8-9-17-23	4-15-24-28
May	4-9-14-15-21-23-24	2-5-12-21
June	1-10-19-21-26-27-28	3-11-17-20-22
July	8-8-16-23-25-26	7-15-17-21
August	5-10-11-14-22-23	4-13-19-27
September	1-8-9-10-19-28-29	7-9-16-18-20
October	8-16-18-20-22-27	6-15-19-24-26
November	2-3-13-18-23-30	4-12-15-18-21
December	3-12-13-14-18-30	5-9-19-28

2013 PLANTING GUIDE

	Aboveground Crops	Root Crops
January	2-6-15-25-29	4-11-20-25
February	3-12-14-21-26	7-19-24-28
March	4-6-21-25-29	2-6-18-29
April	7-17-22-26	2-12-24
May	4-14-19-23-31	9-10-21-27
June	1-11-15-20-28	6-17-20-24
July	8-12-17-25	3-15-21-30
August	4-9-13-22	11-17-27
September	1-5-9-18-28	7-14-23
October	3-7-15-25-30	4-5-11-20
November	3-12-21-26	1-7-16-29
December	1-9-19-24-28	5-14-26

	Pruning	Weeds and Pests
January	9-18-20	13-18-23-27
February	5-14-15	9-14-19-24
March	4-13-14	8-18-23
April	9-10-28	5-15-20
May	6-7-25	2-12-17-29
June	3-4-21-22	8-13-26
July	1-19-27-28	5-10-23
August	15-16-24-25	2-19-30
September	11-12-20-21	3-16-25-30
October	9-18-19	1-13-23-28
November	5-14-15	9-19-24
December	3-11-12-30	7-16-21

MOON'S INFLUENCE OVER PLANTS

Centuries ago it was established that seeds planted when the Moon is in signs and phases called Fruitful will produce more growth than seeds planed when the Moon is in a Barren sign.

Fruitful Signs: Taurus, Cancer, Libra, Scorpio, Capricorn, Pisces
Barren Signs: Aries, Gemini, Leo, Virgo, Sagittarius, Aquarius
Dry Signs: Aries, Gemini, Sagittarius, Aquarius

Activity	Moon In
Mow lawn; trim plants	**Fruitful sign:** 1st & 2nd quarter
Plant flowers	**Fruitful sign:** 2nd quarter; best in Cancer and Libra
Prune	**Fruitful sign:** 3rd & 4th quarter
Destroy pests; spray	**Barren sign:** 4th quarter
Harvest potatoes, root crops	**Dry sign:** 3rd & 4th quarter; Taurus, Leo, and Aquarius

MOON'S INFLUENCE OVER YOUR HEALTH

ARIES	Head, brain, face, upper jaw
TAURUS	Throat, neck, lower jaw
GEMINI	Hands, arms, lungs, shoulders, ner vous system
CANCER	Esophagus, stomach, breasts, womb, liver
LEO	Heart, spine
VIRGO	Intestines, liver
LIBRA	Kidneys, lower back
SCORPIO	Sex and eliminative organs
SAGITTARIUS	Hips, thighs, liver
CAPRICORN	Skin, bones, teeth, knees
AQUARIUS	Circulatory system, lower legs
PISCES	Feet, tone of being

Try to avoid work being done on that part of the body when the Moon is in the sign governing that part.

MOON'S INFLUENCE OVER DAILY AFFAIRS

The Moon makes a complete transit of the Zodiac every 27 days 7 hours and 43 minutes. In making this transit the Moon forms different aspects with the planets and consequently has favorable or unfavorable bearings on affairs and events for persons according to the sign of the Zodiac under which they were born.

When the Moon is in conjunction with the Sun it is called a New Moon; when the Moon and Sun are in opposition it is called a Full Moon. From New Moon to Full Moon, first and second quarter—which takes about two weeks—the Moon is increasing or waxing. From Full Moon to New Moon, third and fourth quarter, the Moon is decreasing or waning.

Activity	Moon In
Business: buying and selling new, requiring public support	Sagittarius, Aries, Gemini, Virgo 1st and 2nd quarter
meant to be kept quiet	3rd and 4th quarter
Investigation	3rd and 4th quarter
Signing documents	1st & 2nd quarter, Cancer, Scorpio, Pisces
Advertising	2nd quarter, Sagittarius
Journeys and trips	1st & 2nd quarter, Gemini, Virgo
Renting offices, etc.	Taurus, Leo, Scorpio, Aquarius
Painting of house/apartment	3rd & 4th quarter, Taurus, Scorpio, Aquarius
Decorating	Gemini, Libra, Aquarius
Buying clothes and accessories	Taurus, Virgo
Beauty salon or barber shop visit	1st & 2nd quarter, Taurus, Leo, Libra, Scorpio, Aquarius
Weddings	1st & 2nd quarter

Leo

LEO

Character Analysis

The person born under the sign of Leo usually knows how to handle a position of authority well. Others have a deep respect for the decisions he makes. The Leo man or woman generally has something aristocratic about him that commands respect. The person born under this fifth sign of the Zodiac generally knows how to stand on his own two feet. He is independent in many things that he does. He knows how to direct his energies so that he will be able to achieve his ends. He seldom wastes time; he is to the point. In love matters, the Leo is quite passionate. He doesn't stint when it comes to romance and is capable of deep emotions. The Leo is a stable person; he has the ability to see things through to the end without wavering on his standpoint.

Leo people are quite generous in all that they do. They give themselves fully to every situation. To others they often appear quite lordly; they are often at the helm of organizations, running things.

The Leo person does not believe in being petty or small. Quite often he goes out of his way to make others happy. He would never stoop to doing anything which he felt was beneath his dignity. He has a deep feeling of self-respect. He would never treat others badly. He is kindhearted, sometimes to a fault. Although he does his best not to hurt others, he is apt to have his moments of irritation when he feels that it is better to speak outright than to give a false impression of his attitudes.

Leo people generally learn to shoulder certain responsibilities at an early age. They have an understanding of life that others sometimes never attain. They do not shy away from conflict or troubles. They believe in dealing with opposition directly. They are quite active in their approach to problems. Life, to them, should be attacked with zest and vigor. There is nothing lazy or retiring about a person born under this sign. He is outgoing, often fond of strenuous sports, keenly interested in having a good time. Everything about his attitudes is likely to be king-sized.

When the Leo man or woman knows what he wants in life, he goes out after it. He is not a person who gives up easily. He perseveres until he wins. He is not interested in occupying a position where he has to be told what to do. He is too independent for that sort of thing. He wants to be the person who runs things and he seems almost naturally suited for an authoritative position. His bearing is that of someone who expects others to listen to him when he speaks. He is a forceful person; he knows how to command respect. He is seldom unsure of himself, but when he is, he sees to it that others do not notice. He is quite clever at organizing things. He is a person who likes order. He knows how to channel his creative talents in such a way that the results of whatever he does are always constructive and original. Leadership positions bring out the best in a person born under this sign.

The Leo person is generally quite tolerant and open-minded. He believes in live-and-let-live as long as the other person does not infringe on what he believes to be his natural rights. In most things, he is fair. He believes in being frank and open. On the whole, the Leo person is active and high-strung. If something irritates him or runs against his grain, he will let it be known. He can be short-tempered if the occasion calls for it.

He is a person who believes in sticking to his principles. He is not interested in making compromises—especially if he feels that his standpoint is the correct one. He can become angry if opposed. But, all in all, his bad temper does not last for a long time. He is the kind of person who does not hold grudges.

The Leo person often has a flair for acting. Some of the best actors in the world have been people born under the sign of the Lion. Their dramatic talents are often considerable. Even as children Leo people have a strong understanding of drama. There is also something poetic about them. They can be quite romantic at times. They have a deep love and appreciation of beauty. They are fond of display and have a love of luxury that often startles modest people.

On the whole, Lion or Lioness is a proud person. His head is easily turned by a compliment. The cultivated Leo, however, knows how to take flattery in his stride. Others may try to get around him by flattering him. They generally succeed with the weaker Leos, for they are quite caught up with themselves and feel that no compliment is too great. This should not be interpreted as pure vanity. The Leo person has a clear understanding of his own superiority and worth.

In spite of the fact that he is generous in most things, the person born under Leo may not appreciate others making demands of him. He may not mind offering favors, but he does not like them to be asked of him.

Leo men and women feel that it is important to be your own boss. He does not like others to tell him what to do. He is quite capable, he feels, of handling his own affairs—and quite well. If he has to work with others, he may become impatient, especially if they are somewhat slow or unsure. He does not like to be kept waiting. Teamwork for the Lion is sometimes a very frustrating experience. He likes to be on his own.

Health

The Leo person is generally well built. He is a sturdy person, capable of taking a lot of stress and strain if necessary. Still, he may take on more than he can manage from time to time, and this is likely to exhaust him physically. He enjoys challenge, however, and finds it difficult to turn down a proposition which gives him a chance to demonstrate his worth—even if it is beyond his real capabilities.

Although he is basically an active person, he does have his limits. If he refuses to recognize them, he may become the victim of a nervous disorder. Some people born under this sign are fond of keeping late hours, especially in pursuit of pleasure or of fame. They can keep this up for some time, but in the end it does have a telling effect on their health. People born under this sign often wear themselves out by going from one extreme to the other.

The weak parts of the Leo are his spine and heart. He should see to it that he does nothing that might affect these areas of his body. In many instances, the Leo has to restrain himself in order to protect his health. Heart disease or rheumatic fever sometimes strikes people born under this sign. In spite of this, the Leo generally has a strong resistance to disease. His constitution is good. Whenever he does fall ill, he generally recovers rather quickly. The Leo man or woman cannot stand being sick. He has to be up and around; lying in bed is quite bothersome for him.

On the whole, Leo is a brave person. However, he may have to learn the art of being physically courageous. This is generally not one of his natural attributes. When physical dangers threaten, he may be somewhat paralyzed by fear. But intellectually Leo is fearless. If ideas or principles are at stake he is not afraid to stand up and let others know his opinion.

The Leo man or woman has a deep love of life. He can be quite pleasure-oriented. He likes the good things that life has to offer. Sometimes he is overenthusiastic in his approach to things, and as a result accidents occur. Under certain conditions he may take chances that others wouldn't. It is important that the person born as a Lion or Lioness learn how to curb impulsiveness, as often it works against him.

Even when they become older, Leo people remain energetic. Their zest for life never dies. They can prolong their lives by avoiding excesses in drinking or by adopting a balanced and moderate lifestyle.

Occupation

Leo seems to gravitate to jobs where he will have a chance to exercise his ability to manage. He is best suited to positions of authority; people respect the decisions he makes. He seems to be a natural-born leader. He knows how to take command of any situation in which he finds himself. The decisions he makes are usually just. He is direct in the way he handles his business affairs. When dealing with others he is open. He says what he means—even if he runs the danger of being blunt or offensive. He is the kind of person who believes that honesty is the best policy. Lies don't go down well with him. The truth—even if it is painful—is better than a kind lie.

In spite of the fact that the Leo man or woman is sometimes critical to a fault, the people who work under him generally respect him and try to understand him. They seldom have reason to question his authority.

In work situations, Leo always tries to do his best. His interest in being the top person has considerable motivational force. He is not interested in second place; only the top position is good enough for him. He will strive until he gets the position he feels is his due. The Leo individual generally has a good understanding of the way things work and how to improve work situations so that better results can be obtained. He knows how to handle people—how they think and how they behave. His understanding of human nature is considerable. He is not the kind of person to rest on his laurels. He is always in search of ways to better an existing situation. He knows how to move along with the times and always tries to keep abreast of new developments in his field.

Leo is proud. In every struggle—be it physical or intellectual—he fights to win. Failure is something he finds difficult to accept. He seldom considers the possibility; success is the only thing he keeps in mind as he works. He coordinates all of his energies and efforts so that success is almost guaranteed. Dull, routine work he is glad to leave to others. His interest lies in the decision-making area of business. He wants to discuss important issues and have a hand in making policies.

Leo leads things well; there can be no question of that. He or she is deeply interested in people's welfare. Leo would never abuse his position as supervisor or manager, but would use it to help those working under him.

On the whole, Leo is a responsible person. He handles his duties capably. He does not, however, enjoy being told what to do. When others try to lord it over him, he is likely to resent it—sometimes quite violently. He feels that no one is in a position to lead him. He often finds fault with the way others try to run things; sometimes he is quite just in his criticism.

The person born under this fifth sign of the Zodiac usually does well in a position where he has to deal with the public. He knows how to be persuasive in his argument. Others seldom have reason to doubt his word, for he is usually sure of what he has to say. A Leo person is likely to do well in any kind of business where he is given an opportunity to make use of his managerial skills. Politics is another area where the man or woman born under the sign of the Lion is apt to do quite well.

As was mentioned before, many Leos seem to be natural-born actors. They have convincing ease when on the stage. They know how to immerse themselves completely in a dramatic role. They do well in almost any kind of creative work. They have the soul of an artist or poet. In whatever field he enters—theater, art, politics, advertising, or industrial management—the Lion or Lioness will do what they can to occupy the top position. If they do not have it in the beginning, you can be sure they are working toward it.

The Leo person is far from being stingy. He loves entertaining his friends and relatives in a royal manner. Generous, sometimes to a fault, he is far from being careless with his money. He has a deep-hidden fear of being poor. He'll do what he can to protect his interests. The Leo man or woman is generally fortunate enough to occupy a position that pays well. If he earns a lot, he is apt to spend a lot. He does not like to have to count pennies. Luxurious surroundings give him the feeling of success. Money is seldom a problem to the wise Leo man or woman. Some of them wind up considerably well-off early in life. They usually don't mind taking chances with their finances. Quite often they are lucky in speculation or gambling.

If Leo feels that someone is in serious financial trouble, he does not mind helping out. He is generous and good-hearted when it comes to lending money. But he doesn't like to be taken advantage of. If someone makes unnecessary demands of him financially, he is apt to become disagreeable.

Leo likes to treat the people he cares for and to give them presents. The gifts he gives are usually expensive and in good taste. He likes to please others—to make them grateful for the gifts he has given them. He likes others to think well of him and that is perhaps why he is eager to give presents. He likes to be the one others turn to when in trouble or lean on for support.

A show of wealth makes Leo men or women feel important. The cultivated Leo sees to it that their extravagance never becomes unreasonable or unbearable.

Home and Family

The Leo man or woman needs a place where he can relax in peace and quiet. His home is his castle. He likes to live in a place that radiates comfort and harmony. Home life is important to the Leo person. He likes to feel that his family needs him—financially as well as emotionally. He likes to be the one who runs things at home. He expects his standards to be upheld by the other members of his family. He is generally a good provider.

The Leo individual makes an excellent host. He knows how to make his guests feel at home. He likes to entertain his close friends quite often. The Leo woman does everything she can to make her guests feel they are liked and cared for. She is usually a very attentive hostess.

When the Leo person spends money, it is often to show that he is capable of spending it. For him it is a display of power or success. It lets others know what he is worth. He sees to it that his home has all of the latest appliances and luxuries. He enjoys impressing others by his clothes and furnishings, even though this may encourage them to envy him.

The woman born under this sign usually enjoys dressing well. Her wardrobe is apt to be large. If she is able, she may not wear the same thing more than once or twice. She is very conscious of being in style. If her husband is not a big earner, she may be quite a burden, for her extravagance is sometimes boundless. If she is married to a man who is not in a top earning position, she will do what she can to help him achieve it.

The Leo person is fond of children. Leos enjoy taking care of them and seeing them grow up. Sometimes, however, they are too forceful as parents and don't give their children a chance to develop their own potential. They like to be proud of their children and appreciate it when others pay them compliments about their children's behavior.

Some Leo parents love their children so much that they are blind to their faults. They become angry if others should accuse them of spoiling their children. They are anxious to see their children succeed and sometimes expect too much of them too soon. When the children reach adulthood and assert their own will, the Leo parent is apt to feel that his children are not appreciative of all that he has done for them. He may resent the youngsters' show of independence.

Social Relationships

Leo people have no trouble making friends. People seem to gravitate to them. It is unusual for someone born under this sign not to be popular. They are warm, friendly, and considerate. People like them because of their sure, authoritative ways. Leo people know how to keep the friends they make. They are outgoing, open, and helpful. They never refuse someone in real need.

They usually have what is popularly known as "personality".They are never dull or retiring people. They are always out front where they can easily be seen. They like having a rich and active social life. Sometimes they make considerable gains in their business affairs through social activities. For them, business and pleasure can mix. They are never short of important contacts.

Those who love Leos accept their leadership without having any qualms. They trust Leos' good judgment and their ability to regulate things.

Leo is tremendously loyal to true friends, so firm friendships may last a lifetime. But a problem can arise in finding true friends. Because Leos believe everyone is as noble as they are, a naive belief at best, they often immediately claim an associate or casual acquaintance as a friend. The trouble begins when the person does not live up to Leo's expectations of what a friend should be.

Such disappointing experiences prove to be useful lessons for the young Lion. As they mature, and as a defense against hurt or betrayal, Leos will maintain a measure of aloofness in many of their personal relationships. For that reason, many Leo men and women have few really intimate friends or close confidantes. Leo likes to mix with people, but he or she may feel it necessary to keep some distance.

The Lion's desire to win in any situation makes for a very competitive personality. This basic competitive nature sometimes interferes with an ability to get along with teammates. Also, many people who are peers and might become good friends may be regarded as rivals on any playing field. Of course, Leos are just as likely to compliment a worthy rival as to criticize a weak and undeserving one.

But Leo is all heart. Leo is deeply sympathetic with anyone who is perceived to lack the advantages. Leos go out of their way to nurture, aid, and lead this person to a richer, fuller life. Some of Leo's friends are those unfortunates who need a helping hand. Family members or associates may pick on Leo for such unconventional choices. But a generosity of spirit rises above what Leos consider to be petty considerations of wealth, class, and rank.

Love and Marriage

Leo is the sign of life and love of life. Leo is also the sign of pleasure and of children. Love together with love of life linked in the union of two loving individuals is the basis for pleasure and children. The supreme force of love motivates the Lion or Lioness in every aspect of living. But Leo's love is not strictly sexual nor earthily sensual nor purely mental. Leo's love embraces each kind yet extends to the romantic, idealistic, unrestrained, universal love that sustains all of humankind.

Because of love's impelling force, it can hardly be said that Leo men and women are cool, easygoing lovers. Quite the contrary! Most Lions are incredibly impulsive, even unpredictable, in affairs of the heart—and as a result Leos are very vulnerable.

With their intense emotionality, Leos are apt to get carried away in love. They throw caution to the winds. They take all kinds of risks in order to win someone they are chasing. When amorous and ardent, Leos may lose all sense of what is wrong and what is right.

Leos are sentimental and easily moved. Every love affair is serious to them. They may flirt from time to time, but when earnest in love they do what they can to make it permanent.

A Leo is very affectionate by nature and he displays this in private. He or she is not fond of being demonstrative in public places. Somehow Leo feels this is undignified. Love and affection should be kept between two people in private.

When in love, Leos are faithful. They do not believe in cheating. Constancy is important to the Lion and Lioness. But if a lover cheats, Leo cannot endure such unhappiness even long enough to resolve what might be only a testing situation. Leo quickly switches interest to another potential mate and wholeheartedly resumes the chase. The same is true of unrequited love. If the adored one is not responding, Leo doesn't hang around acting like a pest. He or she eagerly looks for another beloved on whom to lavish attention and affection.

Generally, Leo individuals are attractive and are never at a loss for company. The opposite sex falls under the charm of a Leo person quite easily.

When looking for a permanent mate, the wise and cultivated Leo chooses someone who is not jealous or possessive—someone who won't suspect him of infidelity if he finds someone else attractive and is quite frank about it.

Romance and the Leo Woman

The Leo woman is often charming and beautiful. She seldom has any trouble in finding a mate. Men are drawn to her almost automatically because of her grace and poise. Lady Lions are known for their attractive eyes and regal bearing. Their features are often fine and delicate. There is seldom anything gross about a woman born under the sign of Leo, even when they tend to be heavy-set or large. There is always something fine that is easy to recognize in their build and carriage.

The Leo woman is passionate by nature. She is very warm and giving when in love. Men find her a very desirable creature and are apt to lose their heads over her when in love. She has an undeniable charm for the opposite sex. Other women are not apt to care for her when men are in the vicinity, for she has no trouble in outshining them all. She is serious when it comes to love. She may have many love affairs before she settles down, but all of them will be serious. She almost never flirts. She doesn't like a jealous or possessive man. She wants the person she loves to trust her implicitly. She doesn't like her love to be doubted.

She likes to be active socially. She enjoys being catered to by the man who loves her. She is fond of parties and entertainment. The man who courts her may have to spend quite a bit of money in order to please her. Sometimes, she is dreamy and idealistic when in love, and so chooses the wrong man for a partner.

She is the kind of woman who stands behind her man in all that she does. She does what she can to help him ascend the ladder of success. She is an intelligent conversationalist and can often entertain her husband's business associates in such a way that her husband can make important gains. She is a charming hostess.

The Leo mother is affectionate and understanding. She will do all she can to see to it that her children are brought up properly.

Romance and the Leo Man

The Leo man is considered a real Casanova by many. He is passionate when in love and will stop at nothing to please the object of his affection. Women love his fiery, sure nature. They feel safe and secure when they are with him. He is a difficult person for many a woman to resist. When romancing someone, Leo does what he can to keep the affair exciting and happy. He lavishes gifts on the person he loves. Dining and dancing at the best places in town are something that Leo is fond of when dating.

If Leo loves someone, he is likely to be blind to her faults. He may be more in love with his idea of a person than with the person herself. So caught up is he in his passion that he is likely to forget all practical matters. Sometimes Leo marries unluckily because of this. He idolizes his love to such an extent that he feels she is incapable of human faults and weaknesses.

The Leo man is a passionate lover. He woos the woman of his choice until he wins her. It is important for him to love, and to have that love returned. Women are easily attracted to him because of his charming ways. He knows how to make a woman feel important and wanted.

He is serious about love. He doesn't believe in meaningless flings.

He is very concerned with appearance and is easily attracted to a good-looking woman. He is apt to build a certain fantasy world around the woman he loves and set her on a high pedestal. He will do everything he can to make her happy. He is an attentive lover and is fond of presenting his loved one with presents. He does not like possessive or jealous women. He wants his sweetheart or wife to give him the freedom he feels he is entitled to. Although he may be attracted to other women after marriage, it is unlikely that he will ever be unfaithful.

As a parent and husband Leo is an excellent provider. He likes to be admired by his family. He may become quite irritable if he feels his family is not as loving and as affectionate as he is. He wants his family to be one he can be proud of.

Woman—Man

LEO WOMAN
ARIES MAN
The man born under the sign of Aries is often attracted to the Leo woman. After all, you are both fire signs. In you he can find that mixture of intellect and charm that is often difficult to find in a woman.

In some ways, the lamb and the lion are an idealized union. Your lively Ram lover may even lead the way. Aries has an insatiable thirst for knowledge. He is ambitious and is apt to have his finger in many pies. He can do with a woman like you—someone attractive, quick-witted, and smart.

He is not interested in a clinging vine for a wife. He wants someone who is there when he needs her; someone who listens and understands what he says; someone who can give advice if he should ever have to ask for it—which is not likely to be often. The Aries man wants a woman who is a good companion and a good sport.

He is looking for a woman who will look good on his arm without hanging on it too heavily. He is looking for a woman who has both feet on the ground and yet is mysterious and enticing—a kind of domestic Helen of Troy whose face or fine dinner can launch a thousand business deals if need be. That woman he is in search of sounds a little like you, doesn't it? If the shoe fits, wear it. It will make you feel like Cinderella.

The Aries man makes a good husband. He is faithful and attentive. He is an affectionate kind of man. He'll make you feel needed and loved. Love is a serious matter for the Aries man. He does not believe in flirting or playing the field—especially after he's found the woman of his dreams. He'll expect you to be as constant in your affection as he is in his. He'll expect you to be one hundred percent his; he won't put up with any nonsense while romancing you.

The Aries man may be pretty progressive and modern about many things. However, when it comes to wearing the pants he's downright conventional; it's strictly male attire. The best role you can take in the relationship is a supporting one. He's the boss and that's that. Once you have learned to accept that, you'll find the going easy.

The Aries man, with his endless energy and drive, likes to relax in the comfort of his home at the end of the day. The good home-maker can be sure of holding his love. He's keen on watching news programs and special reports from a comfortable armchair. If you see to it that everything in the house is where he expects to find it, you'll have no difficulty keeping the relationship on an even keel.

Life and love with an Aries man may be just the medicine you need. He'll be a good provider. He'll spoil you if he's financially able.

The Aries father is young at heart and can get along easily with children. His ability to jump from one activity to another will suit and delight a young child's attention span.

LEO WOMAN
TAURUS MAN

If you've got your heart set on a man born under the sign of Taurus, you'll have to learn the art of being patient. Taurus take their time about everything—even love.

The steady and deliberate Taurus man is a little slow on the draw. It may take him quite a while before he gets around to popping that question. For the Leo woman who doesn't mind twiddling her thumbs, the waiting and anticipating almost always pay off in the end. Taurus men want to make sure that every step they take is a good one, particularly if they feel that the path they're on could lead to the altar.

If you are in the mood for a whirlwind romance, you had better cast your net in shallower waters. Moreover, most Taurus prefer to do the angling themselves. They are not happy when a woman takes the lead. Once she does, he's likely to drop her like a dead fish. If you let yourself get caught on his terms, you'll find that he's fallen for you—hook, line, and sinker.

The Taurus man is fond of a comfortable home life. It is very important to him. If you keep those home fires burning, you will have no trouble keeping that flame in your Taurus lover's heart aglow. You have a talent for homemaking; use it. Your taste in furnishings is excellent. You know how to make a house come alive with inviting colors and decorations.

Taurus, the strong, steady, and protective Bull, could be the answer to your prayers. Perhaps he could be the anchor for your dreams and plans. He could help you acquire a more balanced outlook and approach to your life. If you're given to impulsiveness, he could help you to curb it. He's the man who is always there when you need him.

When you tie the knot with a man born under Taurus, you can put away fears about creditors pounding on the front door. Taurus are practical about everything including bill paying. When he carries you over that threshold, you can be certain that the entire house is paid for, not only the doorsill.

As a homemaker, you won't have to worry about putting aside your many interests for the sake of back-breaking house chores. Your Taurus husband will see to it that you have all the latest time-saving appliances and comforts.

You can forget about acquiring premature gray hairs due to unruly, ruckus-raising children under your feet. Papa Taurus is a master at keeping the youngsters in line. He's crazy about kids, but he also knows what's good for them.

LEO WOMAN
GEMINI MAN

The Gemini man is quite a catch. Many a woman has set her cap for him and failed to bag him. Generally, Gemini men are intelligent, witty, and outgoing. Many of them tend to be versatile and multi-faceted. The Gemini man could easily wind up being your better half.

One thing that causes a Twin's mind and affection to wander is a bore, and it is unlikely that an active Leo woman would ever allow herself to be accused of that. The Gemini man who has caught your heart will admire you for your ideas and intellect—perhaps even more than for your homemaking talents and good looks.

The Leo woman needn't feel that once she's made her marriage vows that she'll have to store her interests and ambition in the attic somewhere. The Gemini man will admire you for your zeal and liveliness. He's the kind of guy who won't scowl if you let him shift for himself in the kitchen once in a while. In fact, he'll enjoy the challenge of wrestling with pots and pans himself for a change. Chances are, too, that he might turn out to be a better cook than you—that is, if he isn't already.

The man born under the sign of the Twins is a very active person. There aren't many women who have enough pep to keep up with him. But pep is no problem for the spry Leo woman. You are both dreamers, planners, and idealists. The strong Leo woman can easily fill the role of rudder for her Gemini's ship-without-a-sail. If you are a cultivated, purposeful Leo, he won't mind it at all.

The intelligent Twin is often aware of his shortcomings and doesn't resent it if someone with better bearings gives him a shove in the right direction—when it's needed. The average Gemini does not have serious ego hang-ups and will even accept a well-deserved chewing out from his mate quite gracefully.

When you and your Gemini man team up, you'll probably always have a houseful of people to entertain—interesting people, too. Geminis find it hard to tolerate sluggish minds and impassive dispositions.

People born under Gemini generally have two sides to their natures, as different as night and day. It's very easy for them to be happy-go-lucky one minute, then down in the dumps the next. They hate to be bored and will generally do anything to make their lives interesting, vivid, and action-packed.

Gemini men are always attractive to the opposite sex. You'll perhaps have to allow him an occasional harmless flirt—it will seldom amount to more than that if you're his proper mate.

The Gemini father is a pushover for the kids. He loves them so much, he generally lets them do what they want. Gemini's sense of humor is infectious, so the children will naturally come to see the fun and funny sides of life.

LEO WOMAN
CANCER MAN

Chances are you won't hit it off too well with the man born under Cancer if love is your object, but then Cupid has been known to do some pretty unlikely things. The Cancer man is very sensitive. He is thin-skinned and occasionally moody. You've got to keep on your toes—and not step on his—if you're determined to make a go of the relationship.

The Cancer man may be lacking in many of the qualities you seek in a man, but when it comes to being faithful and being a good provider, he's hard to beat.

It is the perceptive Leo woman who will not mistake the Crab's quietness for sullenness or his thriftiness for penny-pinching. In some respects, he is like that wise old owl out on a limb; he may look like he's dozing but actually he hasn't missed a thing. Cancers often possess a well of knowledge about human behavior. They can come across with some pretty helpful advice to those in trouble. He can certainly guide you in making investments both in time and in money. He may not say much, but he's always got his wits about him.

The Crab may not be the match or the catch for many a

Leo woman. In fact, he is likely to seem downright dull to the on-the-move Leo girl. True to his sign, he can be fairly cranky and crabby when handled the wrong way. He is perhaps more sensitive than he should be.

Leo people are usually as smart as a whip. If you're clever, you will never in any way convey the idea that you consider your Cancer a little slow on the uptake. Browbeating is a surefire way of sending the Crab angrily scurrying back to his shell. And it's quite possible that all of that lost ground will never be recovered.

The Crab is most himself at home. Once settled down for the night or the weekend, wild horses couldn't drag him any farther than the gatepost—that is, unless those wild horses were dispatched by his mother. The Crab is sometimes a Momma's boy. If his mate doesn't put her foot down, he will see to it that his mother always comes first. No self-respecting Leo would ever allow herself to play second fiddle, even if it's to an elderly mother-in-law. If the Lioness is tactful, she'll discover that slipping into the number-one position is as easy as pie (that legendary pie his mother used to bake).

If you pamper your Cancer man, you'll find that "mother" turns up less and less both at the front door as well as in conversations.

Cancers make protective, proud, and patient fathers. But they can be a little too protective. Sheltering may interfere with a youngster's burgeoning independence. Still, the Cancer father doesn't want to see his youngster learning about life the hard way.

LEO WOMAN
LEO MAN

You probably won't have any trouble understanding the Leo man as you were born under the same sign. Still, some conflict is possible due to the fact that you both are very much alike. Be tactful and tolerant in a Leo-Leo relationship.

For many women, Leo is the sign of love. When the Lion puts his mind to romance, he doesn't stint. If he has it his way, he will be wining, dining, and dancing with his Lioness till the wee hours of the morning.

The Leo man is all heart and knows how to make his woman feel like a woman. More often than not, he is a man a woman can look up to. He's a man who manages to have full control of just about any situation he finds himself in. He's a winner.

The Leo man may not look like Tarzan, but he knows how to roar and beat his chest if he has to. He's the kind of man you can lean upon. He'll also give you support in your plans and projects. He's often capable of giving advice that pays off. Leo men are direct. They don't pussyfoot around.

Leo men often rise to the top of their profession, and through their examples prove to be great sources of inspiration to others.

Although he's a ladies' man, Leo is very particular about his ladies. His standards are high when it comes to love interests. He believes that romance should be played on a fair give-and-take basis. He won't put up with any monkey business in a love relationship. It's all or nothing.

You'll find him a frank, honest person. He generally says what is on his mind.

If you decide that a Leo man is the one for you, be prepared to stand behind him full force. He expects it—and usually deserves it. He's the head of the house and can handle that position without a hitch. He knows how to go about breadwinning and, if he has his way (and most Leos do have their own way), he'll see to it that you'll have all the luxuries you crave and the comforts you need.

It's unlikely that the romance in your marriage will ever die out. Lions need love like flowers need sunshine. They're ever amorous and generally expect equal attention and affection from their mate. Lions are fond of going out on the town. They love to give parties as well as go to them. You should encounter no difficulties in sharing his interests in this direction.

Leo fathers can be strict when they think that the rules of the royal kingdom are being broken. You'll have to do your best to smooth over the children's roughed-up feelings.

LEO WOMAN
VIRGO MAN

The Virgo man is all business—or he may seem so to you. He is usually very cool, calm, and collected. He's perhaps too much of a fussbudget to wake up deep romantic interests in a Leo woman. Torrid romancing to the Virgo man is just so much sentimental mush. He can do without it and can make that quite evident.

The Virgo man regards chastity as a virtue. If necessary, he can lead a sedentary, sexless life without caring too much about the fun others think he's missing. In short, you are apt to find him a first-class dud. He doesn't have much of an imagination; flights of fancy don't interest him. He is always correct and likes to be handled correctly. Almost everything about him is orderly. There's a place for everything and everything in its place is likely to be an adage he'll fall upon quite regularly.

He does have an honest-to-goodness heart, believe it or not. The Leo woman who finds herself strangely attracted to his cool, feet-flat-on-the-ground ways will discover that his is a constant heart, not one that goes in for flings or sordid affairs. Virgos take an awfully long time to warm up to someone. A practical man, even in matters of the heart, he wants to know just what kind of a person you are before he takes a chance on you.

The impulsive Leo girl had better not make the mistake of kissing her Virgo friend on the street—even if it's only a peck on the cheek. He's not at all demonstrative and hates public displays of affection. Love, according to him, should be kept within the confines of one's home—with the curtains drawn. Once he believes that you are on the level with him as far as your love is concerned, you'll see how fast he can lose his cool. Virgos are considerate, gentle lovers. He'll spend a long time, though, getting to know you. He'll like you before he loves you.

A Leo-Virgo romance can be a sometime—or, rather, a one-time thing. If the bottom ever falls out, don't bother reaching for the adhesive tape. Nine times out of ten he won't care about patching up. He's a once-burnt-twice-shy guy. When he crosses your telephone number out of his address book, he's crossing you out of his life for good.

Neat as a pin, he's thumbs-down on what he considers sloppy housekeeping. An ashtray with just one stubbed-out cigarette in it can annoy him even if it's just two seconds old. Glassware should always sparkle and shine.

If you marry a Virgo man, instill a sense of order in the kids, or at least have them behaving by the time he gets home. The Virgo father wants his children to be kind and courteous and always helpful to the neighbors.

LEO WOMAN
LIBRA MAN

If there's a Libra in your life, you are most likely a very happy woman. Men born under this sign have a way with women. You'll always feel at ease in a Libra's company. You can be yourself when you're with him.

Like you, he can be moody at times. His moodiness, though, is more puzzling. One moment he comes on hard and strong with declarations of his love, the next moment you find that he's left you like yesterday's mashed potatoes. He'll come back, though; don't worry. Libras are like that. Deep down inside he really knows what he wants even though he may not appear to.

You'll appreciate his admiration of beauty and harmony. If you're dressed to the teeth and never looked lovelier, you'll get a ready compliment—and one that's really deserved. Libras don't indulge in idle flattery. If they don't like something, they are tactful enough to remain silent.

Libras will go to great lengths to preserve peace and harmony— even tell a fat lie if necessary. They don't like showdowns or disagreeable confrontations. The frank Leo woman is all for getting whatever is bothering her off her chest and out into the open, even if it comes out all wrong. To the Libra, making a clean breast of everything seems like sheer folly sometimes.

You may lose your patience while waiting for your Libra friend to make up his mind. It takes him ages sometimes to make a decision. He weighs both sides carefully before committing himself to anything. You seldom dillydally—at least about small things—and so it's likely that you will find it difficult to see eye-to-eye with a hesitating Libra when it comes to decision-making methods.

All in all, though, he is kind, gentle, and fair. He is interested in the "real" truth. He'll try to balance everything out until he has all the correct answers. It is not difficult for him to see both sides of a story.

He's a peace-loving man. The mere prospect of an explosive scene will turn him off.

Libras are not show-offs. Generally, they are well-balanced people. Honest, wholesome, and affectionate, they are serious about every love encounter they have. If he should find that the woman he's dating is not really suited to him, he will end the relationship in such a tactful manner that no hard feelings will come about.

The Libra father is gentle and patient. He can be firm without exercising undue strictness. Although he can be a harsh judge at times, with youngsters growing up he will radiate sweetness and light.

LEO WOMAN
SCORPIO MAN

Many people have a hard time understanding a man born under the sign of Scorpio. Few, however, are able to resist his magnetic charm.

When angered, he can act like an overturned wasps' nest; his sting is capable of leaving an almost permanent mark. If you find yourself interested in a man born under this sign, you'd better learn how to keep on the good side of him. If he's in love with you, you'll know about it. Scorpio men let no one get in their way when they are out to win a certain heart. When it comes to romance, they never take no for an answer.

The Scorpio man can be quite blunt when he chooses. At times, he'll strike you as being a brute. His touchiness may get on your nerves after a while. If it does, you'd better tiptoe away from the scene rather than chance an explosive confrontation. He's capable of a firestorm of emotion that drives even fiery Leo away.

You're the kind of woman who can put up with almost anything once you put your mind and heart to it. A stormy Scorpio relationship may be worth its ups and downs. Scorpio men are all quite perceptive and intelligent. In some respects, they know how to use their brains more effectively than others. They believe in winning in whatever they do. And in business, they usually achieve the position they want through drive and intellect.

He doesn't give a hoot for home life, generally. He doesn't like being tied down. He would rather be out on the battlefield of life, belting away at what he feels is a just and worthy cause.

Many women are easily attracted to him. You are perhaps no exception. Know what you're getting into before you go making any promises to him. Women who allow themselves to be swept off their feet by a Scorpio man soon find that they're dealing with a pepper pot of seething excitement. He's passion with a capital P, make no mistake about that.

Scorpios are straight to the point. They can be as sharp as a razor blade and just as cutting. Don't give him cause to find fault with you, and you'll do just fine.

If you decide to marry him and take the bitter with the sweet, prepare yourself for a challenging relationship. Chances are you won't have as much time for your own interests as you'd like. Your Scorpio man may keep you at his beck and call.

In spite of the extremes in his personality, the Scorpio man is able to transform conflicting characteristics when he becomes a father. He is adept with difficult youngsters because he knows how to tap the best in a child.

LEO WOMAN
SAGITTARIUS MAN

If you've set your cap for a man born under the sign of Sagittarius, you may have to apply an awful lot of strategy before you can persuade him to get down on bended knee. Although some Sagittarius may be marriage-shy, they're not ones to skitter away from romance. You'll find a love relationship with a Sagittarius—whether it is a fling or the real thing—a very enjoyable experience.

As a rule, Sagittarius are bright, happy, and healthy people. They have a strong sense of fair play. Often they are a source of inspiration to others. They are full of drive and ideas.

You'll be taken by the Archer's infectious grin and his light-hearted friendly nature. If you do wind up being the woman in his life, you'll find that he's apt to treat you more like a buddy than the love of his life. It's just his way. Sagittarius are often more chummy than romantic.

You'll admire his broad-mindedness in most matters—including those of the heart. If, while dating you, he claims that he still wants to play the field, he'll expect you to enjoy the same liberty. Once he's promised to love, honor, and obey, however, he does just that. Marriage for him, once he's taken that big step, is very serious business.

The Sagittarius man is quick-witted. He has a genuine interest in equality. He hates prejudice and injustice. Generally, Sagittarius are good at sports. They love the great out-of-doors and respect wildlife in all its forms.

He's not much of a homebody. Quite often he's occupied with faraway places either in his daydreams or in reality. He enjoys being on the move. He's got ants in his pants and refuses to sit still for long stretches at a time. Humdrum routine—especially at home—bores him. At the drop of a hat, he may ask you to put on your party clothes and dine out for a change. He likes surprising people. He'll take great pride in showing you off to his friends. He'll always be a considerate mate. He will never embarrass or disappoint you intentionally.

His friendly, sunny nature is capable of attracting many people. Like you, he's very tolerant when it comes to friends. You will probably spend a great deal of time entertaining.

The Sagittarius father will dote on any son or daughter, but he may be bewildered by the newborn baby. As soon as the children are old enough to walk and talk, the Sagittarius dad encourages each and every visible sign of talent or skill.

LEO WOMAN
CAPRICORN MAN

A with-it Leo woman is likely to find the average Capricorn man a bit of a drag. The man born under the sign of the Goat is often a closed person and difficult to get to know. Even if you do get to know him, you may not find him very interesting.

In romance, Capricorn men are a little on the rusty side. You'll probably have to make all the passes.

You may find his plodding manner irritating, and his conservative, traditional ways downright maddening. He's not one to take chances on anything. He believes in the motto: If it was good enough for my father, it's good enough for me. He follows a way that is tried and true.

Whenever adventure rears its tantalizing head, the Goat may turn the other way. He's more interested in succeeding at what he's already doing.

He may be just as ambitious as you are—perhaps even more so—but his ways of accomplishing his aims are more subterranean or, at least, seem so. He operates from the background a good deal of the time. At a gathering you may never even notice him. But he's there, taking in everything and sizing up everyone—planning his next careful move.

Although Capricorns may be intellectual to a degree, it is generally not the kind of intelligence you appreciate. He may not be as quick or as bright as you; it may take ages for him to understand a simple joke.

If you decide to take up with a man born under this sign, you ought to be pretty good in the cheering-up department. The Capricorn man often acts as though he's constantly being followed by a cloud of gloom.

The Capricorn man is most himself when in the comfort and privacy of his own home. The security possible within four walls can make him a happy man. He'll spend as much time as he can at home. If he is loaded down with extra work, he'll bring it home instead of working overtime at the office.

You'll most likely find yourself frequently confronted by his relatives. Family is very important to the Capricorn—his family, that is. They had better take a pretty important place in your life, too, if you want to keep your home a happy one.

Although his caution in most matters may all but drive you up the wall, you'll find his concerned way with money justified most of the time. He'll plan everything right down to the last penny.

The Capricorn father's empire is rather like the Leo mother's royal realm. There are goals to be achieved, and there is the right way to achieve them. He can be quite a scold when it comes to disciplining the youngsters. You'll have to step in and bend the rules sometimes.

LEO WOMAN
AQUARIUS MAN

Aquarius individuals love everybody—even their worst enemies, sometimes. Through your relationship with an Aquarius man, you'll find yourself running into all sorts of people, ranging from near-genius to downright insane—and they're all friends of his.

As a rule, Aquarius are extremely friendly and open. Of all the signs of the Zodiac, they are perhaps the most tolerant. In the thinking department, they are often miles ahead of others.

You'll most likely find your relationship with this man a challenging one. Your high respect for intelligence and imagination may be reason enough for you to settle your heart on a Water Bearer. You'll find that you can learn a lot from him.

In the holding-hands phase of your romance, you may find that your Water Bearer friend has cold feet. Aquarius take quite a bit of warming up before they are ready to come across with that first goodnight kiss. More than likely, he'll just want to be your pal in the beginning. For him, that's an important first step in any relationship—love, included.

The poetry and flowers stage—if it ever comes—will be later. The Aquarius is all heart. Still, when it comes to tying himself down to one person and for keeps, he is apt to hesitate. He may even try to get out of it if you breathe down his neck too heavily.

The Aquarius man is no Valentino and wouldn't want to be. The kind of love life he's looking for is one that's made up mainly for companionship. Although he may not be very romantic, the memory of his first romance will always hold an important position in his heart. Sometimes Aquarius wind up marrying their childhood sweethearts.

You won't find it difficult to look up to a man born under the sign of the Water Bearer. But you may find the challenge of trying to keep up with him dizzying. He can pierce through the most complicated problem as if it were a simple math puzzle. You may find him a little too lofty and high-minded—but don't judge him too harshly if that's the case; he's way ahead of his time—your time, too, most likely.

If you marry this man, he'll stay true to you. Don't think that once the honeymoon is over, you'll be chained to the kitchen sink forever. Your Aquarius husband will encourage you to keep active in your own interests and affairs. You'll most likely have a minor tiff now and again but never anything serious.

The Aquarius father can be a shining example for the children because he sees them as individuals in their own right, not as extensions of himself. Kids love him and vice versa. He'll be as tolerant with them as he is with adults.

LEO WOMAN
PISCES MAN

The man born under Pisces is quite a dreamer. Sometimes he's so wrapped up in his dreams that he's difficult to reach. To the average ambitious woman, he may seem a little passive.

He's easygoing most of the time. He seems to take things in his stride. He'll entertain all kinds of views and opinions from just about anyone, nodding or smiling vaguely, giving the impression that he's with them one hundred percent while that may not be the case at all. His attitude may be why bother when he is confronted with someone wrong who thinks he's right. The Pisces man will seldom speak his mind if he thinks he'll be rigidly opposed.

The Pisces man is oversensitive at times. He's afraid of getting his feelings hurt. He'll sometimes imagine a personal injury when none's been made at all. Chances are you'll find this complex of his maddening; at times you may feel like giving him a swift kick where it hurts the most. It wouldn't do any good, though. It would just add fuel to the fire of his persecution complex.

One thing you will admire about Pisces is his concern for people who are sickly or troubled. He'll make his shoulder available to anyone in the mood for a good cry. He can listen to one hard-luck story after another without seeming to tire. When his advice is asked, he is capable of coming across with some pretty important words of wisdom. He often knows what is bothering someone before that person is aware of it himself. It's almost intuitive with Pisces, it seems.

Still, at the end of the day, the Pisces man looks forward to some peace and quiet. If you've got a problem on your mind when he comes home, don't unload it in his lap. If you do, you're likely to find him short-tempered. He's a good listener, but he can only take so much.

Pisces men are not aimless although they may seem so at times. The positive sort of Pisces man is quite often successful in his profession and is likely to wind up rich and influential. Material gain, however, is not a direct goal for a Pisces who devotes his life's work to helping people in need.

The weaker Pisces is usually content to stay put on the level where he finds himself. He won't complain too much if the roof leaks and the fence is in need of repair. He'll just shrug it off as a minor inconvenience.

Because of their seemingly laissez-faire manner, Pisces individuals are immensely popular with children. For tots the Pisces father plays the double role of confidant and playmate. It will never enter his mind to discipline a child, no matter how spoiled or incorrigible that child becomes.

Man—Woman

LEO MAN
ARIES WOMAN

The Aries woman is quite a charmer. When she tugs at the strings of your heart, you'll know it. She's a woman who's in search of a knight in shining armor. She is a very particular person with very high ideals. She won't accept anyone but the man of her dreams.

The Aries woman never plays around with passion; she means business when it comes to love.

Don't get the idea that she's a dewy-eyed damsel. She isn't. In fact, she can be pretty practical and to the point when she wants. She's a woman with plenty of drive and ambition. With an Aries woman behind you, you can go far in life. She knows how to help her man get ahead. She's full of wise advice; you only have to ask. In some cases, the Aries woman has a keen business sense; many of them become successful career women. There is nothing hesitant or retiring about her. She is equipped with a good brain and she knows how to use it.

Your union with her could be something strong, secure, and romantic. If both of you have your sights fixed in the same direction, there is almost nothing that you could not accomplish.

The Aries woman is proud and capable of being quite jealous. While you're with her, never cast your eye in another woman's direction. It could spell disaster for your relationship. The Aries woman won't put up with romantic nonsense when her heart is at stake.

If the Aries woman backs you up in your business affairs, you can be sure of succeeding. However, if she only is interested in advancing her own career and puts her interests before yours, she will surely be rocking the boat. It will put a strain on the relationship. The overambitious Aries woman can be a pain in the neck and make you forget that you were in love with her once.

The cultivated Aries woman makes a wonderful wife and mother. She has a natural talent for homemaking. With a pot of paint and some wallpaper, she can transform the dreariest domicile into an abode of beauty and snug comfort. The perfect hostess—even when friends just happen by—she knows how to make guests feel at home.

You'll also admire your Aries because she knows how to stand on her own two feet. Hers is an independent nature. She won't break down and cry when things go wrong, but pick herself up and try to patch things up.

The Aries woman is skilled at juggling both career and motherhood, so her kids will never feel that she is an absentee parent. In fact, as the youngsters grow older, they might want a little more of the liberation that is so important to her.

LEO MAN
TAURUS WOMAN

The woman born under the sign of Taurus may lack a little of the sparkle and bubble you often like to find in a woman. The Taurus woman is generally down to earth and never flighty. It's important to her that she keep both feet flat on the ground. She is not fond of bounding all over the place, especially if she's under the impression that there's no profit in it.

On the other hand, if you hit it off with a Taurus woman, you won't be disappointed at all in the romance area. The Taurus woman is all woman and proud of it, too. She can be very devoted and loving once she decides that her relationship with you is no fly-by-night romance. Basically, she's a passionate person. In sex, she's direct and to the point. If she really loves you, she'll let you know she's yours—and without reservations. Better not flirt with other women once you've committed yourself to her. She is capable of being jealous and possessive.

She'll stick by you through thick and thin. It's almost certain that if the going ever gets rough, she'll not go running home to her mother. She can adjust to hard times just as graciously as she can to the good times.

Taurus are, on the whole, pretty even-tempered. They like to be treated with kindness. Pretty things and soft things make them purr like kittens.

You may find her a little slow and deliberate. She likes to be safe and sure about everything. Let her plod along if she likes; don't coax her but just let her take her own sweet time. Everything she does is done thoroughly and, generally, without mistakes. Don't deride her for being a kind of slowpoke. It could lead to flying pots and pans and a fireworks display that would light up the sky. The Taurus woman doesn't anger readily but when prodded often enough, she's capable of letting loose with a cyclone of ill will. If you treat her with kindness and consideration, you'll have no cause for complaint.

The Taurus woman loves doing things for her man. She's a whiz in the kitchen and can whip up feasts fit for a king if she thinks they'll be royally appreciated. She may not fully understand you, but she'll adore you and be faithful to you if she feels you're worthy of it.

The woman born under Taurus will make a wonderful mother. She knows how to keep her children well-loved, cuddled, and warm. She may find them difficult to manage, however, when they reach the teenage stage.

LEO MAN
GEMINI WOMAN

You may find a romance with a woman born under the sign of the Twins a many-splendored thing. In her you can find the intellectual companionship you often look for in a friend or mate. A Gemini partner can appreciate your aims and desires because she travels pretty much the same road as you do intellectually—that is, at least part of the way. She may share your interest but she will lack your tenacity.

She suffers from itchy feet. She can be here, there, all over the place and at the same time, or so it would seem. Her eagerness to be on the move may make you dizzy. Still, you'll enjoy and appreciate her liveliness and mental agility.

Geminis often have sparkling personalities. You'll be attracted by her warmth and grace. While she's on your arm you'll probably notice that many male eyes are drawn to her. She may even return a gaze or two, but don't let that worry you. All women born under this sign have nothing against a harmless flirt once in a while. They enjoy this sort of attention. If she feels she is already spoken for, however, she will never let it get out of hand.

Although she may not be as handy as you'd like in the kitchen, you'll never go hungry for a filling and tasty meal. She's as much in a hurry as you are, and won't feel like she's cheating by breaking out the instant mashed potatoes or the frozen peas. She may not be much of a cook but she is clever. With a dash of this and a suggestion of that, she can make an uninteresting TV dinner taste like a gourmet meal. Then, again, maybe you've struck it rich and have a Gemini lover who finds complicated recipes a challenge to her intellect. If so, you'll find every meal a tantalizing and mouth-watering surprise.

When you're beating your brains out over the Sunday crossword puzzle and find yourself stuck, just ask your Gemini mate. She'll give you all the right answers without batting an eyelash.

Like you, she loves all kinds of people. You may even find that you're a bit more particular than she. Often all that a Gemini requires is that her friends be interesting—and stay interesting. One thing she's not able to abide is a dullard.

Leave the party organizing to your Gemini sweetheart or mate, and you'll never have a chance to know what a dull moment is. She'll bring the swinger out in you if you give her half a chance.

A Gemini mother enjoys her children, which can be the truest form of love. Like them, she's often restless, adventurous, and easily bored. She will never complain about their fleeting interests because she understands the changes they will go through as they mature.

LEO MAN
CANCER WOMAN
If you fall in love with a Cancer woman, be prepared for anything. Cancers are sometimes difficult to understand when it comes to love. In one hour, she can unravel a whole gamut of emotions that will leave you in a tizzy. She'll keep you guessing, that's for sure.

You may find her a little too uncertain and sensitive for your liking. You'll most likely spend a good deal of time encouraging her, helping her to erase her foolish fears. Tell her she's a living doll a dozen times a day, and you'll be well loved in return.

Be careful of the jokes you make when in her company. Don't let any of them revolve around her, her personal interests, or her family. If you do, you'll most likely reduce her to tears. She can't stand being made fun of. It will take bushels of roses and tons of chocolates—not to mention the apologies—to get her to come back out of her shell.

In matters of money managing, she may not easily come around to your way of thinking. Money will never burn a hole in her pocket. You may get the notion that your Cancer sweetheart or mate is a direct descendent of Scrooge. If she has her way, she'll hang onto that first dollar you earned. She's not only that way with money, but with everything right on up from bakery string to jelly jars. She's a saver; she never throws anything away, no matter how trivial.

Once she returns your love, you'll have an affectionate, self-sacrificing, and devoted woman for life. Her love for you will never alter unless you want it to. She'll put you high upon a pedestal and will do everything—even if it's against your will—to keep you up there.

Cancer women love home life. For them, marriage is an easy step. They're domestic with a capital D. She'll do her best to make your home comfortable and cozy. She is more at ease at home than anywhere else. She makes an excellent hostess. The best in her comes out when she is in her own environment.

Cancer women make the best mothers of all the signs of the Zodiac. She'll consider every complaint of her child a major catastrophe. With her, children always come first. If you're lucky, you'll run a close second. You'll perhaps see her as too devoted to the children. You may have a hard time convincing her that her apron strings are a little too long.

LEO MAN
LEO WOMAN

If you can manage a woman who likes to kick up her heels every now and again, then Leo was made for you. You'll have to learn to put away jealous fears—or at least forget about them—when you take up with a woman born under this sign. She's often the kind that makes heads turn and tongues wag. You don't necessarily have to believe any of what you hear—it's most likely just jealous gossip. Take up with a Leo woman and you'll be taking off on a romance full of fire and ice. Be prepared to take the good things with the bad—the bitter with the sweet.

The Leo woman has more than a fair share of grace and glamour. She is aware of her charms and knows how to put them to good use. Needless to say, other women in her vicinity turn green with envy and will try anything short of shoving her into the nearest lake, in order to put her out of commission.

If she's captured your heart and fancy, woo her full force if your intention is to eventually win her. Shower her with expensive gifts and promise her the moon—if you're in a position to go that far—then you'll find her resistance beginning to weaken. It's not that she's such a difficult cookie—she'll probably adore you once she's decided you're the man for her—but she does enjoy a lot of attention. What's more, she feels she's entitled to it. Her mild arrogance, though, is becoming. The Leo woman knows how to transform the crime of excessive pride into a very charming misdemeanor. It sweeps most men right off their feet. Those who do not succumb to her leonine charm are few and far between.

If you've got an important business deal to clinch and you have doubts as to whether or not it will go over, bring your Leo lover along to that business luncheon and it's a cinch that that contract will be yours. She won't have to do or say anything—just be there at your side. The grouchiest oil magnate can be transformed into a gushing, obedient schoolboy if there's a Leo woman in the room.

If you're rich and want to stay that way, don't give your Leo mate a free hand with the charge accounts and credit cards. If you're poor, the luxury-loving Leo will most likely never enter your life.

The Leo mother is strict yet easygoing with the children. She wants her youngsters to follow the rules, and she is a patient teacher. She loves to pal around with the kids, proudly showing them off on every occasion.

LEO MAN
VIRGO WOMAN

The Virgo woman may be a little too difficult for you to understand at first. Her waters run deep. Even when you think you know her, don't take any bets on it. She's capable of keeping things hidden in the deep recesses of her womanly soul—things she'll only release when she's sure that you're the man she's been looking for. It may take her some time to come around to this decision. Virgos are finicky about almost everything; everything has to be letter-perfect before they're satisfied. Many of them have the idea that the only people who can do things correctly are Virgos.

Nothing offends a Virgo woman more than slovenly dress, sloppy character, or a careless display of affection. Make sure your tie is not crooked and your shoes sport a bright shine before you go calling on this lady. Keep your off-color jokes for the locker room; she'll have none of that. Take her arm when crossing the street. Don't rush the romance. Trying to corner her in the back of a cab may be one way of striking out. Never criticize the way she looks. In fact, the best policy would be to agree with her as much as possible.

Still, there's just so much a man can take. All those dos and don'ts you'll have to observe if you want to get to first base with a Virgo may be just a little too much to ask of you. After a few dates, you may come to the conclusion that she just isn't worth all that trouble. However, the Virgo woman is mysterious enough, generally speaking, to keep her men running back for more. Chances are you'll be intrigued by her airs and graces.

If lovemaking means a lot to you, you'll be disappointed at first in the cool ways of your Virgo lover. However, under her glacial facade there lies a hot cauldron of seething excitement. If you're patient and artful in your romantic approach, you'll find that all that caution was well worth the trouble. When Virgos love, they don't stint. It's all or nothing as far as they're concerned. Once they're convinced that they love you, they go all the way, right off the bat— tossing all cares to the wind.

One thing a Virgo woman can't stand in love is hypocrisy. They don't give a hoot about what the neighbors say, if their hearts tell them to go ahead. They're very concerned with human truths—so much so that if their hearts stumble upon another fancy, they're likely to be true to that new heartthrob and leave you standing in the rain.

She's honest to her heart and will be as true to you as you are with her, generally. Do her wrong once, however, and it's farewell.

The Virgo mother has high expectations for her children, and she will strive to bring out the very best in them. She is more tender than strict, though, and will nag rather than discipline. But youngsters sense her unconditional love for them, and usually turn out just as she hoped they would.

LEO MAN
LIBRA WOMAN

You'll probably find that the woman born under the sign of Libra is worth more than her weight in gold. She's a woman after your own heart.

With her, you'll always come first—make no mistake about that. She'll always be behind you 100 percent, no matter what you do. When you ask her advice about almost anything, you'll most likely get a very balanced and realistic opinion. She is good at thinking things out and never lets her emotions run away with her when clear logic is called for.

As a homemaker she is hard to beat. She is very concerned with harmony and balance. You can be sure she'll make your house a joy to live in; she'll see to it that the house is tastefully furnished and decorated. A Libra cannot stand filth or disarray. Anything that does not radiate harmony, in fact, runs against her orderly grain.

She is chock-full of charm and womanly ways. She can sweep just about any man off his feet with one winning smile. When it comes to using her brains, she can outthink almost anyone and, sometimes, with half the effort. She is diplomatic enough, though, never to let this become glaringly apparent. She may even turn the conversation around so that you think you were the one who did all the brainwork. She couldn't care less, really, just as long as you wind up doing what is right.

The Libra woman will put you up on a pretty high pedestal. You are her man and her idol. She'll leave all the decision making, large or small, up to you. She's not interested in running things and will only offer her assistance if she feels you really need it.

Some find her approach to reason masculine. However, in the areas of love and affection the Libra woman is all woman. She'll literally shower you with love and kisses during your romance with her. She doesn't believe in holding out. You shouldn't, either, if you want to hang onto her.

Libra is the kind of lover who likes to snuggle up to you in front of the fire on chilly autumn nights, the kind who will bring you breakfast in bed Sunday. She'll be very thoughtful about anything that concerns you. If anyone dares suggest you're not the grandest guy in the world, she'll give that person what-for. She'll defend you till her dying breath. The Libra woman will be everything you want her to be.

The Libra mother is sensitive and sensible, with an intuitive understanding of what a child needs. Her youngsters will never lack for anything that could make their lives easier and richer. Still, you will always come before the children.

LEO MAN
SCORPIO WOMAN

The Scorpio woman can be a whirlwind of passion—perhaps too much passion to really suit you. When her temper flies, you'd better lock up the family heirlooms and take cover. When she chooses to be sweet, you're apt to think that butter wouldn't melt in her mouth—but, of course, it would.

The Scorpio woman can be as hot as a tamale or as cool as a cucumber, but whatever mood she's in, she's in it for real. She does not believe in posing or putting on airs.

The Scorpio woman is often sultry and seductive. Her femme

fatale charm can pierce through the hardest of hearts like a laser beam. She may not look like Mata Hari (quite often Scorpios resemble the tomboy next door) but once she's fixed you with her tantalizing eyes, you're a goner.

Life with the Scorpio woman will not be all smiles and smooth sailing. When prompted, she can unleash a gale of venom. Generally, she'll have the good grace to keep family battles within the walls of your home. When company visits, she's apt to give the impression that married life with you is one great big joyride. It's just one of her ways of expressing her loyalty to you—at least in front of others. She may fight you tooth and nail in the confines of your living room, but at a ball or during an evening out, she'll hang onto your arm and have stars in her eyes.

Scorpio women are good at keeping secrets. She may even keep a few buried from you if she feels like it.

Never cross her up on even the smallest thing. When it comes to revenge, she's an eye-for-an-eye woman. She's not too keen on forgiveness—especially if she feels she's been wronged unfairly. You'd be well-advised not to give her any cause to be jealous, either. When the Scorpio woman sees green, your life will be made far from rosy. Once she's put you in the doghouse, you can be sure that you're going to stay there awhile.

You may find life with a Scorpio woman too draining. Although she may be full of the old paprika, it's quite likely that she's not the kind of woman you'd like to spend the rest of your natural life with. You'd prefer someone gentler and not so hot-tempered; someone who can take the highs with the lows and not bellyache; someone who is flexible and understanding. A woman born under Scorpio can be heavenly, but she can also be the very devil when she chooses.

The Scorpio mother is protective yet encouraging. The opposites within her nature mirror the very contradictions of life itself. Under her skillful guidance, the children learn how to cope with extremes and grow up to become many-faceted individuals.

LEO MAN
SAGITTARIUS WOMAN
You'll most likely never come across a more good-natured woman than the one born under the sign of Sagittarius. Generally, they're full of bounce and good cheer. Their sunny disposition seems almost permanent and can be relied upon even on the rainiest of days.

Women born under this sign are almost never malicious. If ever they seem to be it is only unintentional. Sagittarius are often a little short on tact and say literally anything that comes into their minds no matter what the occasion. Sometimes the words that tumble out of their mouths seem downright cutting and cruel. Still, no matter what she says, she means well. The Sagittarius woman is quite capable of losing some of her friends—and perhaps even some of yours—through a careless slip of the lip.

On the other hand, you will appreciate her honesty and good intentions. To you, qualities of this sort play an important part in life. With a little patience and practice, you can probably help cure your Sagittarius lover of her loose tongue. In most cases, she'll give in to your better judgment and try to follow your advice to the letter.

Chances are she'll be the outdoors type. Long hikes, fishing trips, and white-water canoeing will most likely appeal to her. She's a busy person; no one could ever call her a slouch. She sets great store in mobility. Her feet are itchy and she won't sit still for a minute if she doesn't have to.

She is great company most of the time and, generally, lots of fun. Even if your buddies drop by for poker and beer, she won't have any trouble fitting in.

On the whole, she is a very kind and sympathetic woman. If she feels she's made a mistake, she'll be the first to call your attention to it. She's not afraid to own up to her faults and shortcomings.

You might lose your patience with her once or twice. After she's seen how upset her shortsightedness or tendency to blab has made you, she'll do her best to straighten up.

The Sagittarius woman is not the kind who will pry into your business affairs. But she'll always be there, ready to offer advice if you need it. If you come home with red stains on your collar and you say it's paint and not lipstick, she'll believe you.

She'll seldom be suspicious. Your word will almost always be good enough for her.

The Sagittarius mother is a wonderful and loving friend to her children. She is not afraid if a youngster learns some street smarts along the way. She will broaden her children's knowledge and see that they get a well-rounded education.

LEO MAN
CAPRICORN WOMAN

If you are not a successful businessman, or at least on your way to success, it's quite possible that a Capricorn woman will have no interest in entering your life. Generally speaking, she is a very security-minded female; she'll see to it that she invests her time only in sure things. Men who whittle away their time with one unsuccessful scheme or another seldom attract a Capricorn. Men who are interested in getting somewhere in life and keep their noses close to the grindstone quite often have a Capricorn woman behind them, helping them to get ahead.

Although she is a kind of social climber she is not what you could call cruel or hard-hearted. Beneath that cool, seemingly calculating exterior there's a warm and desirable woman. She just happens to think that it is just as easy to fall in love with a rich or ambitious man as it is with a poor or lazy one. She's practical.

The Capricorn woman may be keenly interested in rising to the top, but she'll never be aggressive about it. She'll seldom step on someone's feet or nudge competitors away with her elbows. She's quiet about her desires. She sits, waits, and watches. When an opening or opportunity does appear, she'll latch onto it. For an on-the-move man, an ambitious Capricorn wife or lover can be quite an asset. She can probably give you some very good advice about business matters. When you invite the boss and his wife for dinner, she'll charm them both.

The Capricorn woman is thorough in whatever she does: cooking, cleaning, making a success out of life. Capricorns are excellent hostesses as well as guests. Generally, they are very well mannered and gracious, no matter what their backgrounds are. They seem to have a built-in sense of what is right. Crude behavior or a careless faux pas can offend them no end.

If you should marry a woman born under Capricorn, you need never worry about her going on a wild shopping spree. Capricorns are careful with every cent that comes into their hands. They understand the value of money better than most women and have no room in their lives for careless spending.

Capricorn women are usually very fond of family—their own, that is. With them, family ties run very deep. Don't make jokes about her relatives; she won't stand for it. You'd better check her family out before you get down on bended knee; after your marriage you'll undoubtedly be seeing lots of them.

The Capricorn mother is very ambitious for her children. She wants them to have every advantage and to benefit from things she perhaps lacked as a child. She will train her youngsters to be polite and kind and to honor traditional codes of conduct.

LEO MAN
AQUARIUS WOMAN

If you find that you've fallen head over heels for a woman born under the sign of the Water Bearer, you'd better fasten your safety belt. It may take you quite a while to actually discover what this woman is like. Even then, you may have nothing to go on but a string of vague hunches. Aquarius is like a rainbow, full of bright and shining hues; she's like no other women you've ever known. There is something elusive about her—something delightfully mysterious. You'll most likely never be able to put your finger on it. It's nothing calculated, either. Aquarius doesn't believe in phony charm.

There will never be a dull moment in your life with this Water Bearer woman; she seems to radiate adventure and magic. She'll most likely be the most open-minded and tolerant woman you've ever met. She has a strong dislike for injustice and prejudice. Narrow-mindedness runs against her grain.

She is very independent by nature and quite capable of shifting for herself if necessary. She may receive many proposals for marriage from all sorts of people without ever really taking them seriously. Marriage is a very big step for her; she wants to be sure she knows what she's getting into. If she thinks that it will seriously curb her independence and love of freedom, she's apt to shake her head and give the man his engagement ring back—if indeed she's let the romance get that far.

The line between friendship and romance is a pretty fuzzy one for an Aquarius. It's not difficult for her to remain buddy-buddy with an ex-lover. She's tolerant, remember? So if you should see her on the arm of an old love, don't jump to any hasty conclusions.

She's not a jealous person herself and doesn't expect you to be, either. You'll find her pretty much of a free spirit most of the time. Just when you think you know her inside out, you'll discover that you don't really know her at all.

She's a very sympathetic and warm person; she can be helpful to people in need of assistance and advice.

She'll seldom be suspicious even if she has every right to be. If the man she loves slips and allows himself a little fling, chances are she'll just ignore it—at least the first time. Her tolerance does have its limits, though, and her man should press never his luck fooling around.

The Aquarius mother is bighearted and seldom refuses her children anything. Her open-minded attitude is easily transmitted to her youngsters. They have every chance of growing up as respectful and tolerant individuals who feel at ease anywhere.

LEO MAN
PISCES WOMAN

Many a man dreams of an alluring Pisces woman. You're perhaps no exception. She's soft and cuddly and very domestic. She'll let you be the brains of the family; she's contented to play a behind-the-scenes role in order to help you achieve your goals. The illusion that you are the master of the household is the kind of magic that the Pisces woman is adept at creating.

She can be very ladylike and proper. Your business associates and friends will be dazzled by her warmth and femininity. Although she's a charmer, there is a lot more to her than just a pretty exterior. There is a brain ticking away behind that soft, womanly facade. You may never become aware of it—that is, until you're married to her. It's no cause for alarm, however; she'll most likely never use it against you, only to help you and possibly set you on a more successful path.

If she feels you're botching up your married life through careless behavior or if she feels you could be earning more money than you do, she'll tell you about it. But any wife would, really. She will never try to usurp your position as head and breadwinner of the family.

No one had better dare say one uncomplimentary word about you in her presence. It's likely to cause her to break into tears. Pisces women are usually very sensitive beings. Their reaction to adversity, frustration, or anger is just a plain, good, old-fashioned cry. They can weep buckets when inclined.

She can do wonders with a house. She is very fond of dramatic and beautiful things. There will always be plenty of fresh-cut flowers around the house. She will choose charming artwork and antiques, if they are affordable. She'll see to it that the house is decorated in a dazzling yet welcoming style.

She'll have an extra special dinner prepared for you when you come home from an important business meeting. Don't dwell on the boring details of the meeting, though. But if you need that grand vision, the big idea, to seal a contract or make a conquest, your Pisces woman is sure to confide a secret that will guarantee your success. She is canny and shrewd with money, and once you are on her wavelength you can manage the intricacies on your own.

Treat her with tenderness and generosity and your relationship will be an enjoyable one. She's most likely fond of chocolates. A bunch of beautiful flowers will never fail to make her eyes light up. See to it that you never forget her birthday or your anniversary. These things are very important to her. If you let them slip your mind, you'll send her into a crying fit that could last a considerable length of time. If you are patient and kind, you can keep a Pisces woman happy for a lifetime. She, however, is not without her faults. Her sensitivity may get on your nerves after a while. You may find her lacking in practicality and good old-fashioned stoicism. You may even feel that she uses her tears as a method of getting her own way.

The Pisces woman makes a strong, self-sacrificing mother. She will teach her children the value of service to the community while not letting them lose their individuality.

LEO
LUCKY NUMBERS 2013

Lucky numbers and astrology can be linked through the movements of the Moon. Each phase of the thirteen Moon cycles vibrates with a sequence of numbers for your Sign of the Zodiac over the course of the year. Using your lucky numbers is a fun system that connects you with tradition.

New Moon	First Quarter	Full Moon	Last Quarter
Dec. 13 ('12)	Dec. 20	Dec. 28	Jan. 4
8566	9731	9868	8374
Jan. 11	Jan. 18	Jan. 27	Feb. 3
4025	3065	0248	8396
Feb. 10	Feb. 17	Feb. 25	March 4
6708	6575	7726	6391
March 11	March 19	March 27	April 3
1042	9897	9485	5236
April 10	April 18	April 25	May 2
6421	0796	4528	8931
May 9	May 17	May 25	May 31
1876	6469	8078	8297
June 8	June 16	June 23	June 30
7653	3594	1745	8643
July 8	July 15	July 22	July 29
3292	2607	5447	5320
August 6	August 14	August 20	August 28
0805	5963	2479	7653
Sept. 5	Sept. 12	Sept. 19	Sept. 27
3594	4078	3298	7646
Oct. 4	Oct. 11	Oct. 18	Oct. 26
6052	2893	6087	0979
Nov. 3	Nov. 10	Nov. 17	Nov. 25
4852	2364	4219	7137
Dec. 2	Dec. 9	Dec. 17	Dec. 25
2856	6975	2431	1837

LEO
YEARLY FORECAST 2013

*Forecast for 2013 Concerning Business
and Financial Affairs, Job Prospects,
Travel, Health, Romance and Marriage
for Persons born with the Sun
in the Zodiacal Sign of Leo.
July 21–August 21*

For those born under the zodiacal sign of Leo, ruled by the Sun, life force of the solar system and the source of vitality and zest, 2013 will be a time of adventure, change, and inspiring challenges to align yourself and your actions with true meaning and purpose. This is also a time of new beginnings with a drive to advance your long-term goals successfully and productively. You can begin to move upward and forward to achieve your ambitions and build a safe and solid foundation on which you can feel personally secure. Many new opportunities to do so will appear on your horizon. But these opportunities will often be accompanied by challenges to transform those aspects of yourself that are no longer serving you. As such, this is a great time for Leo individuals to become involved in psychological counseling and any other forms of therapy that encourage self-awareness. In this way you can overcome the subconscious complexes that fuel the motivations and desires that inhibit growth and success.

Dependable associations and friendships will be an asset to you as you gain support for ideas as well as trustworthy feedback on what is viable and what isn't. Joint ventures are likely to be in the offing, but will need to be scrutinized for your protection and safety. Health will be on the agenda and you would be wise to resolve to live a healthy and moderate lifestyle to protect your greatest resources of all: your body and your mind. Travel also figures strongly in your desire to learn and explore new horizons. You may turn to study and broaden your thinking and your opportunities to advance in your chosen career. You can change the course of your life's direction as you discover your true calling in life. Relationships are going through a time of healing. New loves can heal old hurts and old ones can be renewed.

In business, there is the promise of success if you are willing to work hard at it. But dedication to your responsibilities and honesty in your dealings are necessary. July promises the ability to sense the subtle undercurrents in market forces that will enable you to move into an area of growth and productivity. For the best success, start your own business and maintain control. If you go into business with a partner or associates, you may expect disagreements and power struggles. Because of this, any partnership enterprises should be established on a legal basis to provide protection to all parties. You will be challenged to maintain your integrity and honesty, as there are likely to be many opportunities to cut corners for a quick return.

Be careful when choosing who you do business with. You are more susceptible to another person's influence this year and could be more gullible than you would like to think you are. This influence will be particularly strong in September, so keep your wits about you and you won't get led astray. You will need to get in touch with your hidden motivations if this occurs, because there is a reason why you are attracted to the other person, and that reason will show you more about your inner desires. Armed with awareness, you can stay true to your own course and fulfill your own desires without allowing another to take advantage of you.

Nebulous Neptune is touring the sign of Pisces, your solar eighth sector of joint resources and finances. Neptune here clouds some dealings with fogginess and confusion and allows for misunderstandings and underhanded dealings driven by unconscious motivations. Hidden forces could be at work behind the scenes that prevent you from knowing what is happening. Because of this it is not a good time to borrow money. It is also not recommended that you speculate on the stock market unless you are involved in it professionally, and even then you may find circumstances can suffer a setback that you, and everybody else, hadn't foreseen. It can be harder than usual to get financing, and that is a good thing. Ensure that your business and financial proposition is aboveboard and secure. This is not a good time to borrow money from friends, as the nature of private borrowings leaves the situation open for the worst type of misunderstandings. Inheritances and compensation payouts can be fraught with problems, causing a long and drawn-out process before it can be finalized. The message with finances is to be honest and maintain strong and fair boundaries, resorting to legal guidelines and protection when necessary. The period from February 23 until March 17 should be spent redeploying your debts and reallocating resources; you will not regret it.

As far as employment goes, don't be surprised if you leave your present employment and go in an unprecedented direction that offers better job satisfaction. Pluto, the planet of transformation, is moving through Capricorn, your solar sector of daily work, health, and employment conditions. Pluto here will bring about a fundamental change in your approach to work over the next few years. Some of you might experience retrenchment and find yourself out of work for the first time in your life. Others may have to change occupations due to ill health. Or you may just feel an underlying lack of satisfaction, purpose, or meaning in life that causes you to change how you live and your daily routine and working life. You might decide to go back to school and train in an art, skill, or philosophy that will give you the credentials to move into an area of work that you are drawn to. Leos can develop a need to be of service and desire to work in an area that is productive and beneficial to others. Any areas of work that deal with dismantling or wrecking, rebuilding, computer technology, the arts, detective or secretive work, volunteer work, the health industry, and even palliative care might offer the satisfaction and meaning you now crave.

Leo people may have to reorganize your domestic environment due to a reshuffling of personal relationships. Perhaps a relationship breaks down and the family home is no longer. Or you may take on the care of an elderly parent and need to redefine your living area to ensure everyone still has their privacy and space. Caring for a parent could be tied up with your inheritance. Your parent may offer you the family home or financial backing in return for your care and support. In this case you do need to do some honest reflection on your inner motivations for accepting or refusing this role. If you feel you are honestly happy to take on this responsibility, you also need to ensure the rest of the family members feel the same.

Clarity is needed here to avoid misunderstandings with siblings, especially in December. For some the home may become a burden as the repayments, bills, and repairs add up to more than you can afford, making changes necessary again. Perhaps you may sell the family home and downsize into a flat or unit and have to make all sorts of adjustments to your lifestyle and daily routine because of this. Regardless of the cause for the reorganization, this is a good time to build secure foundations. Be sure to stay true to yourself and don't sacrifice personal pleasures that may cause inner resentments.

Health matters are likely to affect your daily routine in one way or another this year. Watch out for an obsession with work, or workaholic tendencies. It's not good for you to have all work and no play. Factor in time for pleasure, friendship, and relaxation; otherwise health issues will force you to stop. Some of you might decide to change your diet and exercise routine to improve your health simply because you are aware of the need to look after your body and your mind, to ensure a healthy and active old age. Psychological issues can affect your health also. If you are holding on to resentments, anger, grief, or self-pity from the past it must invariably come out in a physical way. A health problem might force you to address these underlying psychological matters. Spiritual interests will be strong for many of you, and yoga and meditation will be invaluable aids for your health and your spiritual search for meaning. All Leos would be advised to work on developing self-awareness now as it will improve all areas of your life.

Travel is likely, as your desire for adventure and learning inspires you to explore other environments and cultures. A trip to another country can change your life forever and the urge for change will make other countries that much more inviting. Be prepared for travel plans to go awry and have an alternative route up your sleeve for safety, especially when traveling through countries experiencing unrest. Also, you could get caught up in airline problems and get stuck somewhere you don't want to be. Some of you might work in the armed forces and decide to take a post overseas, even finding dangerous missions attractive and exciting. There is a strong possibility that you will have a relationship with a foreigner and start learning the language and belief systems that go along with their culture. The more you learn, the more you may want to learn, and you certainly won't be happy to go back to the way you were. As your understanding of reality undergoes a transformation, so too will your view of your home and roots.

Relationships are also going through a strong period of change as you learn more about yourself and your motivations and desires, and you develop stronger boundaries and a sense of purpose regarding what is important to you personally. In these times of growth it can happen that we outgrow our partner and a relationship ends so that both parties can move forward. But there is a strong possibility that relationships based on true love will transform for the better. As both of you grow in understanding and awareness, the bonds of love and caring grow stronger. With Neptune in Pisces impacting your solar sector of commitment, you would be wise to enjoy a period of courtship before making long-term commitments such as marriage, as this will enable you to learn about all aspects of your partner, and they you. To discover if you are compatible for a long-term relationship, it is important to know that your goals and beliefs harmonize for a happy union.

Romance will not be lacking whether you are single or not, but singles could experience more than one sexual relationship this year. This is all part and parcel of learning about yourself and what you like in another. Be careful not to make commitments before you are ready and watch out for the company you keep. The likelihood that you will be attracted to someone because of other factors such as money, beauty or success, can cause you to confuse attraction with love. Work on knowing yourself and you will make healthy choices for future happiness in your loving relationships.

The end of the year is starred for romance and children, so ensure you use contraception if you don't want to start a family.

Be aware during the three periods of Mercury retrograde. These retrograde periods signal the times when it would be fruitful to re-hash, review, rejuvenate, refine, reflect, repair, recheck, reschedule, realign, rewrite, reformulate. Take inventory of what has occurred over the previous three months and reconsider and reexamine your experiences. These periods are February 23 to March 17 when the focus is on Leo finances, June 26 to July 20 when the focus in on your home and family, and October 21 to November 10 when your relationships and shared resources will come under scrutiny.

Overall, this year offers Leo the chance to revitalize your life and realign yourself with those things that give you the most satisfaction. Spiritual pursuits will help you to find peace of mind and give you the essential meaning to your existence that you crave. Focus on developing a personal daily routine that will order all areas of your life. But above all you are being asked to be honest and to pursue and live up to your own personal ideals. There is much for Leo to learn this year with regard to understanding the difference between what you expect and understand of an alliance and what the other person expects and understands. Of course you will be expected to support your friends and associations also and will gain a lot from selfless acts even though you might think you are time poor.

LEO
DAILY FORECAST

January–December 2013

JANUARY

1. TUESDAY. Expressive. Allow plenty of time to prepare for whatever is on your agenda later in the day. Your appearance could be very important and a little extra time spent on dressing to suit the occasion will add to your self-confidence. Issues around relationships might arise and you would be wise to take your own counsel before making any important decisions. Gaining advice from other people will only confuse the situation. Focus on the things you value, and if you are unsure of what they are, then take a moment to get in touch with your feelings. Sometimes our minds are too full of false ideas and expectations, but your feelings never lie. Watch your spending if you are on a budget.

2. WEDNESDAY. Creative. Don't hold back when it comes to the things you value. If you concentrate on what matters, your sense of satisfaction will be worth it. An issue with a teenage child could fill you with fear for their well-being, but if you focus on the love you have for them and be honest with them, you can reach a happy outcome. An important ingredient to success in any matter is to listen and try to be as broad-minded as possible. There may be something that doesn't fit with your belief system. Instead of denying it has any validity, consider that there could be some truth in it and you will broaden your understanding so much more. Romance is on the cards this evening.

3. THURSDAY. Valuable. Financial problems can arise early, especially if you allow your desires to take control. A girlfriend or female colleague may be troublesome, but this is probably because of a misunderstanding. Take the time to ensure you coordinate your energy with anyone you will be working with in tandem, and you'll both reap the benefits. Expensive tastes could reduce your bank balance and put you in the red. Take stock of your budget and avoid expensive places and you won't be tempted. A lovers' quarrel might highlight different values. Examine where your values vary and be honest with yourself about how far you are willing to make compromises.

4. FRIDAY. Stressful. Any emotional situation is likely to add extra pressure to your already pressured schedule. Get in touch with your feelings early in the day and stay true to them. Don't let your need to impress or fit in allow you to compromise what is important to you, and you will avoid this situation. If you practice meditation, you can balance your mind and emotions. An opportunity for promotion might come at the expense of a coworker and cause you to backpedal. If you are being open and honest, then welcome this good fortune without guilt. See that your coworker may have been at fault. Avoid arguing with a neighbor.

5. SATURDAY. Stretched. Your schedule could be overloaded as you try to pack more than is possible into your day. Being popular means your friends, siblings, and neighbors will want a piece of you, but you may need to learn to say no. Consider what is a priority and then leave some time for relaxation as well. The events of the day will show some surprises and spare time will allow you to make the most of them. A car trip might be on the cards, and if you put on some relaxing music it will add to your traveling fun. Take a good friend or lover so that you can share a laugh and explore interesting places and make it a trip to remember. With forethought you can turn any chore into fun and adventure.

6. SUNDAY. Stimulating. At some point there will be a shift of attention toward your emotional life or to the business of home and family today. There may be urgent matters demanding your attention, or it could simply be a change of mood. Give loved ones the care and concern they need and get on with the domestic tasks that need doing. If you're a little moody yourself, you need to get away from the busy world outside and focus on looking after the inner Lion. Joint resources may need to be reviewed, and if you have the time, sit down with your partner and put your finances on the table. The decisions that arise from such a discussion will put you in a good situation for the future.

7. MONDAY. Powerful. Traditions from the past can be a source of strength. Ask an older and wiser relative for advice if you are unsure of what to do next. Acknowledging family ties will open doors through influence and common bonds. A commitment in love may become necessary for a relationship to keep going. But if you are having second thoughts, look within and make sure your inner feelings are harmonious with the reality. As Mars, the planet of war, travels through your house of open enemies, you may experience more than your fair share of confrontations. Be true to yourself and you will find resentment and anger disappear. You can then practice compromise in a fair and just manner.

8. TUESDAY. Enthusiastic. The Moon visits your fifth house of creativity, romance, and children today. You can expect a surge of energy to give you enthusiasm for life's pleasures. Don't sit at home watching the television; now is the time to go out and play. Even if the weather is bad, you can find a way to bring enjoyment into your life. With so much to see and do, it may be hard to decide on one activity. Fit as much recreation into the day as you can without having to work to get everything done. Fun stops being fun when you feel like you have to do something or be somewhere by a certain time. Be wise when choosing friends and ensure that your trustworthiness can be counted on.

9. WEDNESDAY. Productive. Romantic Venus moves into Capricorn and your house of work and health today. This placement will boost your work social life by improving your reputation and friendships amongst your colleagues. It also hints at the possibility of a new romance forming through work contacts. You might need to watch a strong perfectionism that can make you more critical of others than usual. Above all, don't beat up on yourself if you don't get your work just right. Just watch your workload, as you could easily take on far more work than you can physically cope with. Your desire to help others might also add to your workload, so the lesson here is to know your limits.

10. THURSDAY. Busy. Today the Moon joins the life-giving Sun, communicative Mercury, romantic Venus, and transformative Pluto in Capricorn and your house of work and health. This major emphasis suggests that you should keep an eye on your health and well-being first and foremost. Reflect on your diet and your health problems, then do some research on exercises and foods that will enhance your well-being and help you to avoid chronic health problems in the future. It is hard to change habits at any time, but this is probably one of the best times for doing so. Be prepared for disruptions and you can keep ahead of your competition and impress the boss. It is also a good time to change jobs.

11. FRIDAY. Practical. Today's New Moon in Capricorn and your sixth house suggests your creative efforts will be pressed into the service of some higher good, urging you toward finding a practical use for your creativity. No seed can flourish in sixth house soil unless it serves humanity or the planet. If you find a way to make your art useful, you can combine work and love and enjoy whatever you do. Open up to your inspiration and intuition and you can find new ways to make your work simpler and easier. Some of you might even invent a new method of doing something that spreads across the workplace and beyond. You are special, so believe in yourself and you can improve your future now.

12. SATURDAY. Optimistic. Think twice before acting, as you may have to face the consequences of your actions and you don't want to have to do any explaining right now. Be free but thoughtful and you can't go wrong. There may be a few contentious issues between you and a partner, and if you can organize a sit-down to discuss them in an orderly manner you might find an agreeable resolution. If matters disintegrate into argument then you would be better off finding a mediator. Plans for a holiday escape could move forward, in fact you might decide to head off for the weekend and take in some new and inspiring scenery. An invitation to a philosophical debate could be mind-expanding.

13. SUNDAY. Energetic. Disagreements from yesterday can fade into the background as common ground comes into view. Rather than seeking company amongst friends and acquaintances, you will crave closeness and intimacy with your partner. Be reasonable if they have commitments that take them away from you for some of the day. Instead plan something exciting and enjoyable for the time you do spend together. This is a great time to finish off a personal project or to get training in a practical skill or artistic interest. The development of your creative side is in full swing at the moment, so don't let any self-doubt creep in and spoil your fun. Leo people are ruled by the Sun and need to shine.

14. MONDAY. Intuitive. Pay attention to body language and things that are left unsaid and go with your gut feelings. A business meeting or negotiations will be very informative and could open up a new avenue for business if you are willing to go with your gut. Try not to be fixed about any of your ideas because there are new horizons coming into view and you will want to be open to them. A new romance could bring up all sorts of problems because you both come from different walks of life. Accept the challenge to understand the differences and this can be a very rewarding relationship. An overseas interest can take up a lot of your time; research the customs of this foreign land and you will profit.

15. TUESDAY. Promising. This is a favored time to seek advice from a financial advisor, as you have some very good money-making ideas or investments in the works. But you may need to tighten up your methods and gain more understanding of the opportunities and pitfalls in front of you. For the spiritually minded Lion, this is a fantastic time to go on a pilgrimage or start a spiritual practice toward enlightenment. The people that you mix with now are very influential on your ideas, and if you can, you should pick these people wisely. Don't just follow along with the crowd, as you can end up where you would rather not. A strong urge for independence can cause friction in a relationship.

16. WEDNESDAY. Demanding. Take it slow and steady early and organize your thoughts and desires before venturing out into the world. Some days are more conducive for inner reflection, and this is one of them. Don't be surprised if you are late for a meeting or if another is late, holding up finalization until later in the day. Be thorough when asking for something from another, as they could easily misunderstand and give you something you don't want. Travel plans could be delayed or you may have second thoughts about your travel destination and decide to postpone your trip. If you are worried about a health issue, see a professional right away before it has a chance to develop further.

17. THURSDAY. Important. Matters of the heart need to be acknowledged and not pushed aside. Accept any feelings of inadequacy and face up to those who are important to you with humility. Be true to yourself and your own feelings and problems will find solutions. In fact, love can deepen and understanding will grow. This is the perfect day for a little adventure; nothing too outlandish, simply a change of pace from your usual routine. If you typically only shop in department stores, try a flea market. If you usually only eat burgers and fries, maybe it is time to try sushi. Accept a situation or a person that challenges you. Open your mind and let your soul grow through new experiences.

18. FRIDAY. Challenging. A strong desire to be good at what you do might cause internal distress when it comes to making decisions. Listen to your intuition, and if you find that a little fuzzy, practice ten minutes of meditation and see the difference. Leo writers might receive some criticism from a publisher, but if you are willing to accept what they are saying, it can be used very constructively to produce a successful manuscript. Dissatisfaction with your daily routine might get you down. Plan an evening out to add excitement and interest to the day. It is time to bring change into life rather than waiting around for it.

19. SATURDAY. Thoughtful. Family responsibilities can weigh heavily. If you are worried about an elderly parent or some other loved one, speak to them about it. Now that Mercury, the planet of communication, is transiting Aquarius and your house of relating, it is the perfect time to communicate one on one with those you care about. Be honest and you can bring issues out into the open and dispel the fears that only live in the darkness of silence. If you are having trouble with a housemate, call a meeting and get the problems out on the table. Self-confidence issues can arise if you are expected to talk to a crowd, but swallow your pride and speak honestly, and your self-confidence will return.

20. SUNDAY. Sparkling. The Sun joins Mercury and Mars in Aquarius and your sector of relationships today. This is the time of year when you should try to work with others as much as possible. Even if you find conflict arises in your one-to-one relationships, conflict can be creative, because it forces you to examine your position more thoroughly and thus become more aware of yourself. Single Lions may be more likely to feel the pressure to find a partner. Don't go it alone; join in with groups of people who have the same interests and through doing the things that you love, you will make contact with people you can share with. It's a sure thing that you won't be alone for long.

21. MONDAY. Expansive. The celestial influences are looking positive today and no matter how big a problem you may feel you have, if you let go and relax you will find it will all work out fine. Probably better than if you try to fix it. Good friends will offer you support and may introduce you into a group where self-help is on offer through sharing mutual problems and/or situations. Don't be afraid to step out of your comfort zone, as you will likely meet some very interesting people and add valuable contacts to your network. Business deals are likely to pay better than expected, but watch out for wastefulness. Money that comes in easily can go out just as easily.

22. TUESDAY. Interesting. You have all the energy you need to get everything done this morning, so watch out for procrastination. Communication is big today, and you might spend a lot of time try-

ing to work out new mobile phone applications or Internet programs. If you're not an expert, contact one and save yourself some
time. This is a wonderful time to clear the table and begin a new
chapter in your life; you may want to leave groups you have grown
away from and join new, more promising ones. You may experience
some difficulty as you end old cycles to begin new ones, but you will
find you are ultimately happier for it. This evening enjoy a relaxing
and fun-filled night amongst friends.

23. WEDNESDAY. Diverse. The energy between you and those
close to you could be fractious and things may be out of touch.
Don't try to avoid discord; leaving thoughts unsaid can sometimes
fuel suspicion and distrust. Matters from the past will be at the root
of anything that's wrong today. Go over old ground and ask yourself if there's something you're not willing to confront. You'll come
to a new understanding if you do, you just need time to sort out
the process. Fears around personal security could undermine your
self-confidence. Face up to these fears and watch them disappear.
Remember that fear isn't based on fact.

24. THURSDAY. Involved. Nothing will be as it seems today. Take
a breather from your work and enjoy some peace and quiet alone.
If you take this time to order your thoughts and let feelings rise up
into consciousness, you can then work toward your goals positively.
A workmate could try to influence your decisions or your associations. If they try to bully you, report them, but whatever you do, don't
give in. A legal matter may need to be addressed before it escalates.
Put your cash on the line and see a professional, and you can bring
an end to the problem once and for all. Some of you may be going
through a messy divorce and need to examine your own part in it
rather than blaming the other.

25. FRIDAY. Successful. There are promising aspects in the sky for
Leo today. Take a risk and watch it pay off; go with your gut feeling on
all matters and reinforce belief in yourself. You may want to work behind the scenes to avoid interference, as you are more receptive to the
thoughts and emotions of others right now. A romance can blossom in
the workplace and you will need to keep this private to protect your
workplace relations. If you are already in a relationship, you would be
wise to ignore your feelings and stay loyal to your lover. Any temptation to stray will only lead you into deep water, not just with your
partner but with your personal integrity. Your Leo pride won't allow it.

26. SATURDAY. Emotional. The Full Moon is in Leo, shining its
light on you and yours. You are likely looking for a bit of atten-

tion. Try to avoid infantile outbursts and instead work on your assertiveness. You do count, you just need to find a healthy balance between autonomy and dependence. This is a great time to start a new project and initiate some new creativity in your life. Have faith in your own abilities and pull out those plans you've had secreted away for ages. Act on them and find out what works and what doesn't. Before you know it, you will be on the way to manifesting one of your dreams. Celebrate your existence and go shopping for a new outfit.

27. SUNDAY. Fruitful. Everything is a rush today and there will be a bit of chaos that always seems to go with a fast pace. However, as the day wears on, there will be a change of pace that will see you shift into a more practical and mechanical mode. Don't worry about the hustle and bustle of things; concentrate on simple routines that get the job done. In the end you'll be able to settle into domestic comfort. You may not see eye to eye with your spouse, and even though you might want to criticize, you would do better to praise something they do that you love. The focus of the mind can make all the difference in many instances, so try to look on the bright side and watch gray skies turn blue.

28. MONDAY. Competitive. The moody Moon and action-oriented Mars oppose each other in the cosmos today, making everyone prone to acting on emotions. This is a great time to get away and do your own thing. What people don't know doesn't hurt them, and it works in reverse too. If you find you are annoyed at what your partner or other significant other is doing, you would be wise to withdraw and let them learn without your criticisms. Impulsive actions can lead to accidents also, so think twice before dashing off on a whim, reacting to another's statement, or while driving also. Be kind to your body when working, as the mind might think you are stronger than you really are,

29. TUESDAY. Chancy. All things are likely to be up and down today. Don't pin your hopes on any one thing, but keep a few irons in the fire as a backup. Disagreements over spending could arise between you and your partner. If you are planning to go into business with another person, get the agreement drawn up professionally to ensure you are both protected in your investments, that way disagreements can't lead to one person leaving the other high and dry. Make sure you give your lover a call, especially if you have promised to do so. No matter what crisis might make keeping your promise almost impossible, a promise is a promise. Act with integrity in all matters and reap the benefits.

30. WEDNESDAY. Difficult. Today everything may seem depressing and restrictive. You may want to break out of your rut but find that you cannot because of your duties or responsibilities. You may wish that you didn't have to go to work or school or be with people you don't want to be with. But has it occurred to you to talk to somebody about this, or ask yourself if you are really required to do what you don't want? You may be making assumptions without checking whether they are true. Relations with authority figures are not good under today's influences, unless you can convert your impatience with restrictions into self-discipline. Apply self-discipline and enjoy the difference it makes.

31. THURSDAY. Rebellious. As the emotional Moon opposes impulsive Uranus you can expect the unexpected. You may leap to unwarranted conclusions, especially about matters involving your emotional life, so you should avoid making any decisive moves at this time. In your contacts with others you will seek excitement and stimulation and thus may attract very different people to your usual crowd. You or your partner might act disruptively and cause a fight; consequently, this can be a stormy period in relationships. Computers and electrical equipment are likely to go on the blink, so ensure you have the latest virus protection on your new machine. Expect and plan for disruptions and delays.

FEBRUARY

1. FRIDAY. Busy. There are places to go and people to see. Get on with the plans that need to be made and engage in discussions with lots of different people. There will be banter and laughter among colleagues and there should be lively debate around current topics. Watch that you think on your feet, as things may not go as scheduled. Keep ahead of the game and take care while traveling. If you are thinking about buying a new car, take someone who is mechanically minded with you to ensure you don't end up with a lemon. In fact, you would be wise to seek advice from an expert on any important decisions you need to make today. A good friend may need a loan, but only lend what you can afford to lose.

2. SATURDAY. Domestic. Important concerns in family life come up today. No matter what you have planned, ensure you have time for those most important in your life. If you said you would call someone, make sure you do so, otherwise resentment and distrust can creep into the equation. Give your folks a call, as you will probably have dealings of some kind with an older family member and you will want to be the first to call. Be patient with problems and take a measured perspective. If there are repairs or improvements needed at home, then make sure you plan to get them done. Talk your plans over with family so that everyone gets to have some input and feels loved and included.

3. SUNDAY. Exciting. This is a day when nothing is likely to go to plan but whatever happens will be lots of fun anyway. Venus moves into Aquarius and shines her beautiful light on your sector of relationships. This influence will help to put harmony and balance between you and all you meet, which will help all your encounters to work out smoothly. In marriage or other love relationships, expressing affection will come easily, allowing for a deeper understanding and romance. Singles may meet a new love at this time. Also, with Mars, the action planet, moving into Pisces, you can expect to encounter someone who has a powerful effect on you that can bring about a personal transformation.

4. MONDAY. Beneficial. The Moon moves into Sagittarius and Jupiter's expansive influence. The urge for freedom is very strong and you might not agree with everybody today. If your temper is ignited, try not to chew anyone's head off. Instead put your thoughts and feelings down on paper and you can find out something very useful about yourself. Also, you may find that your passion is ignited by someone special today; if you are single, the need to connect strongly with another is there. Your appeal is at a high level, so go ahead and send clear signals to the one who makes your heart beat faster. Leo parents might need to keep an eye on your children, as they are likely to get up to mischief.

5. TUESDAY. Creative. As the Moon glides through your house of fun, lovers, and children, you will notice a new sensitivity in your relationships that can cause some upsets. Try not to read too much into another's actions and you can avoid those disturbing doubts. Instead, try to tell it how it is for you and get what's left unspoken out on the table. Your mood will be more conducive to an artistic endeavor as you can put music into your words, expression into your drawing, or feeling into dramatic work. Avoid covert business deals, as somebody is not telling you the whole story. Too many influences will mean the profit has to be split too many ways. Withdraw and wait for the right time and you will profit.

6. WEDNESDAY. Sensitive. The Moon joins nebulous Neptune in Pisces and your house of other people's values and psychic phenomena. This aspect will touch everybody with a certain amount of oversensitivity, but will allow you to understand what is going on beneath the surface. In all matters that involve groups of people, you can smooth over the misunderstandings and help people to feel more comfortable. One word of warning about avarice: it can be overpowering but comes with a very high price tag. Some of you might become aware of a sixth sense and want to develop this further.

7. THURSDAY. Influential. Stay on your toes when dealing with business colleagues and partners. Know what it is you want and how much you are willing to compromise before you start any negotiations. There are strong forces of influence that can override decisions and desires. This is a wonderful day for artistic pursuits; you can draw out the essence of a thing and make it available to all. This is not a good day to go shopping with your credit card, as you can get tricked into a level of debt that is far out of your depth. Romance will deepen in a love affair and bring another level of commitment along with it. If you are living with your lover, you may well decide to tie the knot now.

8. FRIDAY. Unusual. Unexpected visitors can impose on your goodwill just as you are starting a personal project. But instead of putting you behind, they may end up showing you an easier way to do what you are doing. Many hands make light work, and instead of getting one job done you are likely to achieve much more with the help of others. Your local community will be a good place to meet new friends and hear interesting news and information. A public gathering might be fun for all the family. If you have a neighbor who is not well or seems lonely, ask them to come along and brighten up their day too. You might be surprised at what you can learn and how much fun you can have.

9. SATURDAY. Cooperative. The need to merge with your lover and the need to be independent can force you to seek some level of compromise within yourself. Try not to take this internal battle into your relationship with your partner. Remember, he or she is not doing anything; it is all within you. Instead of listening to the voice in your head telling you what you don't have or can't do, listen to what the other person is saying. If you apply this principle to all your affairs, you might find that everything you do comes off beautifully. Harmony can be achieved with cooperation and you can learn how to do it successfully now. Surprisingly, you are sure to have time for you, as well.

10. SUNDAY. Variable. This morning's New Moon in Aquarius signals a new monthly cycle with the focus on relating. Issues around sharing could arise, as part of having a loving relationship is usually sharing joint resources. Whether you combine your incomes or keep them separate, there is always a point where you have to contribute to the bills and other expenses. Coming up against other people's values can often be difficult, and you might have to negotiate with another who has different values. Now you must look for the common ground from which to negotiate, as what you have might not be what they want, and vice versa. New ideas and understandings can bring life-changing revelations.

11. MONDAY. Interesting. With the Moon passing through Pisces and your solar eighth house of sex, money, and power, you are likely to experience a depth of intensity in your relationships today. This is a wonderful day to spend increasing your knowledge and understanding of psychological issues, which will help you in both your personal and business relationships. Take a trip to a bookstore and back up your theories with facts. There is a competitive edge to the Lion today, and you can sway the minds of your contemporaries. You might visit a psychic or medium, seeking answers to a problem on health or the spirit.

12. TUESDAY. Expansive. An opportunity to take up further study could open doors you never knew existed. Try not to let rigid beliefs lock you into your situation. Remember that beliefs are not facts; they are usually developed within a culture and often don't apply if you look at it from another cultural perspective. As the global environment takes over, the ability to adapt and broaden your thinking will put you in a better position to succeed and take advantage of the new opportunities that change brings your way. If you can't see the forest for the trees, you become a victim of your situation. Networking is very important, and you can succeed in your endeavors through the power of your contacts.

13. WEDNESDAY. Spontaneous. Intuitive thoughts could inspire your thinking and put you at the top of the class. Trust your instincts and you can't go wrong today. Plans are likely to go out the window because of unexpected factors that can't be helped. Students might decide to change your stream of study as new influences lead to exciting new ideas and avenues of endeavor. Some of you might win a ticket overseas and unexpectedly start packing your bags and saying your good-byes. An opportunity to work in the information technology industry could come your way. Think twice before making the switch, as the excitement and inspiration could pass as quickly as it arrived.

14. THURSDAY. Problematic. Your usual reaction to a problem may not work anymore, forcing you to start looking for an alternative. You are being pushed to broaden your thinking at the moment, and this will occur regardless of how amenable to change you may be. A health issue, either in regard to yourself or a loved one, may not be responding to regular treatment, forcing you to look at other methods and philosophies around health and well-being. A change of diet or way of life will introduce you to new people and associations, broadening your horizons in a roundabout fashion. A desire to travel will benefit Leos also. Consider taking a voluntary position and experience life from another angle.

15. FRIDAY. Fair. Dealings with authority figures and official communications will give you a chance to shine. Your organizational and creative talents will come to the fore and show your employers what you are worth. Some of you might even receive a promotion to a leadership position. While you are enjoying your work, don't neglect the home fires, as there are sure to be some responsibilities you might avoid through overwork. Ensure you strike a healthy balance between your work and home life to maximize all benefits that come your way. If you are feeling dissatisfied with your job, don't hesitate to look for a change.

16. SATURDAY. Tricky. Conflict between your career and your relationship can surface. You may be so busy pursuing a career that you don't have time for your partner. Or perhaps you were attracted to your partner because of their status and career, but are unhappy about playing second fiddle in their life. Whatever you do, don't get your mother involved. She has your best interests at heart, but on the other hand, she is also your partner's mother-in-law, and it will be difficult for her to be fair. Be honest with yourself and list your values in order of their priority, and you might discover your relationship isn't at the top of the list. A social affair will put you in the public eye; be on your best behavior.

17. SUNDAY. Stressful. As much as you may desire to sleep in and relax on this day of rest, you are likely to have appointments or social arrangements that you cannot avoid. Get up early so you have time to practice morning meditation and eat a good breakfast. This will put you in good spirits to cope with whatever comes your way. A public gathering could influence your thinking and inspire your activities for the rest of the day. If you are involved in a spiritual group, you may end up doing charitable deeds for the rest of the day. A disagreement with your partner is better left at that. Accept that you don't have to agree on everything and it will renew your interest in each other's ideas.

18. MONDAY. Positive. Friends and associates will play a large part in the day's proceedings, and the opportunity to add to your network of contacts will be a great benefit to you in the future. Don't be afraid to contact a friend or relative in a power position to add their influence to your cause. They will be happy to help and it could be the start of a productive relationship. The shining Sun joins communicative Mercury, energetic Mars, healing Chiron, and nebulous Neptune in Pisces, stacking your sector of sex, money, and power with a wealth of activity and opportunity. There is also a greater than usual chance of misunderstandings and rip-offs, so watch out for greed and dishonesty.

19. TUESDAY. Breezy. You'll start out full of good intentions, with a buzz of interest or a group of good friends; there's lots to do, and you'll be the Lion to do it. Whichever way things go, a sense of cooperation is all around you. You can gain through the efforts of others. You can really put in and help others move toward a goal. A healthy dose of teamwork does wonders for the Lion, so you should be able to sit back contented at the end of a pleasing effort or a good day's work. However, as the day wears on, your mood may change. You can feel a little somber or withdrawn, and you might opt for an afternoon nap. Just let this rhythm take its natural course and don't push yourself too hard.

20. WEDNESDAY. Intense. Behind-the-scenes work will be right up your alley. In fact, work as a private detective would be perfect. Some of you might apply for a job in this field, or start a course in criminology and be assured of success. Fantasy can play a strong part in your life today, either as a creative channel or an escape. Listen to your favorite music or express your feelings through artwork for a truly therapeutic activity. Yoga and meditation would be another wonderful activity to help balance the different sides of your nature and bring about physical and psychological healing. Practice empathy and forgiveness as much as possible and watch your own emotional wounds disappear.

21. THURSDAY. Fortunate. Look, listen, and learn should be your motto for the day. If you remove yourself emotionally from all your dealings, you will have the benefit of clear sight and understanding. A commitment from the past may return to haunt you. Don't try to avoid it, but deal with it head-on and be done with it once and for all. Magic can happen now, even if you don't think you can afford to repay a debt; if you try, the dollars are likely to come to you from another quarter. Believe in miracles and they will happen. Discussions or negotiations regarding jointly owned assets or property can go well. If you are unsure about the worth of the thing, seek an independent assessment from a professional.

22. FRIDAY. Relaxing. Take it easy this morning and enjoy the unexpected holdups that are likely to occur. Grab an extra hour in bed and review your day before you get started. If you can spend extra time with your significant other, do so. This will be a great time to talk about the things that matter to each of you and synchronize your plans. Don't be afraid to address an issue that has been a bone of contention between you. You might be surprised to find that your partner feels differently now. A sexual relationship might represent an intense and transforming quality that you seek to take you out of the ordinary and into the transcendent. Just remember, this is a big ask for a frail human being.

23. SATURDAY. Emotional. The fiery Leo Moon puts the focus squarely on you and your ego. Pride and self-confidence go together, but whether you have them both in the same amounts is another question. Too much pride might make it hard for your self-confidence to grow as you set your standards on nothing but perfection. Revise your standards and place reasonable expectations upon yourself and enjoy what you are doing. You are likely the center of attention and could receive an invitation to an influential social gathering. Dress to impress but don't go over the top, Be prepared to share as there is plenty to go around.

24. SUNDAY. Reflective. Mercury, the planet of the mind, started a retrograde yesterday. If you can spend the next three weeks redeploying your debts and reallocating resources, you will not regret it. In fact, it may simply be a necessity to pick up loose ends and take a second look at whether you are unnecessarily overextended. Joint resources especially will need your joint evaluation. With a little tweaking, you could be sitting pretty, but you'll need to test the wind to get some height. Pick up on assets you've neglected or forgotten about, and you'll have all you need. Make new friends, but keep the old; one is silver and the other's gold, in ways you hadn't even thought about.

25. MONDAY. Auspicious. Conflict is sure to arise between you and those close to you. Issues around what is yours and what is shared might cause problems. Somewhere along the line you are going to have to give a little and find the middle ground or else you'll end up on the outside—something a Leo doesn't enjoy one little bit. With the Full Moon in Virgo shining into your sector of money and values, your self-worth is tied up in whatever it is you are doing today. Buy yourself a piece of furniture, an antique, a painting, or any other object that will boost your self-esteem. The cost might be high, but the ultimate lesson will be worth it. No object can outshine your inner worth. Value what's on the inside.

26. TUESDAY. Valuable. Venus, the planet of love, glides into Pisces and joins the Sun, Mercury, Mars, Chiron, and Neptune in your sector of joint resources and other people's values. Love relationships are bound to become more intense at this time, and any relationship that starts now will be intense for the whole duration and have a greater impact, for better or worse, on your life than other relationships. You can attract money to yourself through other people, especially your partner, and have a better chance of borrowing from a financial institution over the next four weeks. Subconscious issues can come to the surface, and mediation or counseling can help you recognize and learn to deal with them.

27. WEDNESDAY. Interesting. Just breeze along with the communicative Moon today as she moves through Libra and your sector of communication. Listen to what people are really saying. Say what you really feel while being sensitive to the feelings of others. Negotiations are likely to become heated, and you will need to be in possession of all the facts if you hope to come out on top. Leo salespeople will have your skills sorely tested by some very obdurate clients. Look at whatever challenge raises its head as a gift, as you are only ever as good as your opposition or experience. Today you will get the chance to grow and learn.

28. THURSDAY. Artistic. There are magical vibes in the air today. A chance encounter with an attractive stranger could sweep you off your feet. Be sure to get his or her number, as you may be floating on cloud nine and forget all about tomorrow. Group work will be interesting, but be careful how far you take criticism, as everybody is going to be a bit more sensitive than usual. This can make for a deeper understanding though, as everyone will be able to talk about their feelings more than usual. A business meeting could turn into a deep and meaningful gathering. Be careful what you divulge, as it might get back to your partner.

MARCH

1. FRIDAY. Confident. Multitasking is the best way to get through your workload. If you can do as much as you can yourself, you won't have to worry about the communication barrier. If you do delegate, don't expect everything to be done to your expectations, but rather accept that it will be done to the best of the other person's ability. Be kind and understanding to yourself as well as others. Memories of a loved one departed can bring up grief. If you notice you are feeling the pain of loss, take time off to cry and acknowledge the grief. Whatever emotional process you are going through is easier with understanding.

2. SATURDAY. Positive. Enjoy the comforts of home if possible. Renovations could be under way, leaving your living quarters akin to a construction site, but put in the effort and make it comfortable. Ensure that safety is paramount and put away electrical wires and tools that can be hazardous in thoroughfares. Home entertaining will be fun, especially if you have family members that you haven't seen for ages coming around. Share the work by asking everyone to bring a dish. Some of you might be setting up a business from home and would be wise to separate your office from your living quarters and keep work separate from home.

3. SUNDAY. Lazy. Your day could be full of social dates, but the last thing you feel like doing is going out. Some of you might hold a position at a social or sporting club and want to avoid your duties this morning. There is nothing wrong with taking a sick day and doing what you want to do, which may simply be nothing. An important emotional issue can arise and you will need time alone to understand what the underlying matter is, otherwise you might end up blaming those close to you just because they happen to be there. Don't be afraid to speak up about what is on your mind. Better to put things politely on the table than wait until you explode and say things you wish you could take back.

4. MONDAY. Indulgent. It's easier for you to relax and enjoy the pleasures of existence today. Don't let someone close to you lay their judgments on you about what you should be doing. Everyone is different. You might remember this fact when you are indulging others, as you could unthinkingly do them a disservice by expecting them to be the same as you. If you can look after yourself and let others look after themselves, your day will go smoothly. A friend may ask for your shoulder to cry on, but in reality is only looking for an ally in their domestic situation. Children may need a little extra discipline.

5. TUESDAY. Magical. Trust your instincts when it comes to business deals. Above all, don't listen to the gossip of your colleagues. You can see the beauty in others and instinctually know whether you can trust them. There is an opportunity for you to change the system and make a leap forward, adding to your sphere of influence and social prestige. A creative frame of mind will help you to think outside the box. Whatever problems come your way, don't be afraid to try something new. Romance could push your buttons and it might be time to end a relationship and make way for a new and loving one.

6. WEDNESDAY. Compulsive. Strange urges can force you to do or say things you might want to take back. Spend some time on your own to examine these deep-down emotions honestly and you can learn quite a bit of valuable information about what makes you tick. Once armed with this inner knowing, you can make wise decisions and avoid needless argument. Market forces could make your working life untenable, but with a bit of insight you can move into an area of growth and start to build a business for yourself. Consider taking up a course of study that will help you combine your talents and interests with a marketable resource.

7. THURSDAY. Active. Health matters are very much dependent on lifestyle at the moment. Take a look at your daily routine and ensure you are getting a reasonable amount of exercise and balanced meals, not just snacks. Also make sure you are putting some enjoyment into your day. Remember that all work and no play will make anybody dull. Communications and business matters will need special attention. Things can get mixed up and cause all sorts of problems. Actively working with a plan will be invigorating and enable you to be clear and concise. Try cooking an ethnic recipe for interest and nutrition.

8. FRIDAY. Problematic. Love and friendship go hand in hand. Any problems that arise today will come from communication mix-ups and breakdowns. If you are having a problem with your significant other, the stars suggest getting help from a mutual friend or seeking mediation. An objective third party is more likely to be able to see the problem than either of you. A romance with a friend could start to blossom as you make plans for your evening's entertainment. Many of you may be mixing with people from different cultures and will enjoy the differences. A lecture on culture, religion, or economics could be informative and give you new direction.

9. SATURDAY. Retrospective. Something or someone from the past may come back to haunt you as the day gets under way. Focus on partnerships and cooperation. Work things through and don't resist any reasonable requests; after all, Leo is very fond of fun and creativity, and the best way to achieve this today is through negotiation. Keep things simple and instead of hanging with the group, concentrate on one-on-one relationships. It will give you far more enjoyment to talk from the heart with a friend or lover. Be prepared for an unexpected opportunity to get away for the weekend for a refreshing break.

10. SUNDAY. Moody. The Moon joins up with retrograde Mercury and influences rational and logical thought with emotions. A lot of communication can go around and around and get nowhere, so instead of trying to make a decision or find a resolution today, just enjoy expressing your emotions and learn a lot about each other. A family get-together could be insightful and bring back memories and understanding of your family dynamics. This can also show you how you go about dealing with the world as a whole and give you the ability to change where necessary. Plan to have fun, get into your hobbies, mix with friends, or go to a concert.

11. MONDAY. Invigorating. Your appetite may be stimulated by the sensuous New Moon today, and whatever you feel is likely to be passionate. Psychic energy is strong while the Moon moves through Pisces and your eighth house of death and rebirth. Dreams you have now can tell you more about yourself as well as give you a glimpse into your past lives. Be open to receiving messages from beyond. A business colleague could show a sexual interest and either turn you on or turn you right off. If you are already in a relationship, then this person is only interested in using you either for their passion or for furthering their business influence. Stay clear of all greedy people and maintain your own peace of mind.

12. TUESDAY. Impulsive. The Moon joins up with active Mars and erratic Uranus in Aries and your solar ninth house of travel and adventure, ensuring Lions will be ready for a change. After a longs day's work, find a way to break your routine. Whatever you do, don't do what you always do, as Mercury is retrograde in your eighth house of sex, money, and power, creating trouble for you over the next week. Travel could be problematic, so make sure you have plenty of time to get where you need to go. Matters of inheritance and insurance are delayed, so have patience. Learn meditation skills and enter the higher mind.

13. WEDNESDAY. Interesting. With Mars, the planet of action, now in its own sign of Aries and your sector of travel and the higher mind, you can do more creative intellectual work than usual. Whenever necessary, you will assert and defend any beliefs that you consider true and important. The key is to avoid identifying your ego with what you believe. Instead of focusing on what you believe to be true, put your energy into expanding your mind. This is a great time to take up study and to travel to broaden your experience and understanding of the world. Over the next two months you might be more inclined to enter into legal disputes, but not at this time.

14. THURSDAY. Disadvantaged. Start the day slowly and get organized before you head out. Don't try too hard to get what you want. Instead, relax and watch the shenanigans as others all vie for their own ends in vain. Business meetings are likely to be full of talk, and no one is listening. Don't hesitate to take the day off if you have a few sick days saved up. Have an adventure and do something out of the ordinary. You can meet some very interesting people and learn new things. If you are unemployed, get together with a few buddies and do things as a group that singly are out of your league. There is always power in numbers.

15. FRIDAY. Testing. Balancing your work and your family life could seem nearly impossible today. If your boss is making unreasonable demands on your time, don't let your fears about losing your job stop you from talking openly to them. There may be a compromise that you can both live with. Facing up to your fears is the best way to overcome them, so look at those areas you would rather avoid and shed light into the darkness. A family meeting could be the quickest way to remedy dissatisfaction. Just make sure that everybody gets to have their say and is listened to. Change is in the wind, and nobody enjoys stepping out into the unknown. Be willing to change, and you might be surprised with the outcome.

16. SATURDAY. Constructive. The Taurus Moon places you in the public eye as it moves through your tenth house of status. Be sure to mind your manners and follow protocol. Although it may be hard for the regal Lion to follow all the rules, you might find your life is easier when you at least pretend to be somewhat conventional. A family outing can put you on display, so watch your moods, especially if the young ones won't do what you want. If you find a disagreement with your lover can't be ignored, then take it home and work it out behind closed doors. Otherwise, your reputation could suffer from a public emotional display.

17. SUNDAY. Diverse. Opinions can be influenced and sway with the wind. Don't rely on others to support your claims or intentions. Instead use inspiration personally and work on developing a pet project without involving anyone else. Recognize the different aspects and needs of your own personality. You are likely to be feeling more independent than usual and may dislike the rules and regulations set down by your employer or the powers that be. Instead of complaining, start becoming active. Join with other people who share your philosophy on life and help change outmoded aspects of society. You do need to watch for impulsive behavior, as there is a higher than usual chance of accidents occurring.

18. MONDAY. Beneficial. Surprising events can change a problem into a solution. Be open to different viewpoints and your understanding of a situation will grow. Show compassion to a workmate who is experiencing pain and trouble. Instead of judging where they have gone wrong, try to see how they might feel. Listening rather than talking will be very instructive and could put you in a place of power in the workplace. Lions might be asked to take control of a situation that you feel is out of your depth. Be brave and have a go. You can find that you instinctively know what to do when under pressure to perform, and you may impress yourself. A workplace romance might need to be kept separate from work.

19. TUESDAY. Confronting. Conflicts could arise between your own humanitarian, political, or social ideals and those of your partner. Although you might want them to feel the same way you do, allowing them to have their own set of ideals and values could be very rewarding. This way you can both learn something from each other as well as accepting that beliefs and views are not facts but simply beliefs and views. Spend more time listening rather than speaking and learn which friends are true blue and which friends are fair-weather. As the day wears on, you may feel yourself turning inward. Arrange for a peaceful evening at home.

20. WEDNESDAY. Healing. Keep tabs on your inner emotions and you will better understand your motives for doing something. This is a good time for psychoanalysis, as your subconscious mind is closer to the surface than usual. Start a dream journal and chronicle your nightly exploits for further understanding of the other half of your life, because when all is said and done, half of our lives are spent sleeping. Nurture yourself and allow your creative side a free rein. Renovations could take a surprise turn as you come up with something completely different from the norm. Don't be afraid to explore your ideas, as some of them are likely to be ground breaking and improve your outlook considerably.

21. THURSDAY. Inspirational. The shining Sun joins action-oriented Mars and intuitive Uranus in the pioneering sign of Aries and your sector of travel and the higher mind today. Grab hold of those thoughts that inspire you and take a risk on following them. They may take you to new heights and opportunities. An association with people from another culture can introduce you to a new understanding of the possibilities on offer to you. Don't miss a chance to travel overseas. Instead of a dead-end job, why not gain work experience and join volunteers abroad. Take a risk and start a course of study that will open doors in the future. Don't be afraid to follow your dreams.

22. FRIDAY. Improving. Loving Venus joins the Sun, Mars, and Uranus in Aries and your sector of the higher mind and adventure today. This emphasis ensures you can start to learn new ideas and gain valuable understanding in areas of interest. Your in-laws can be a great help to you now. Consider discussing some of your problems with them to gain the benefit of their experience and engender good relations. An adventurous spirit can make travel to exotic destinations far more romantic than the reality. Before you head off impulsively, be sure that you have the correct visa and a good understanding of the political relations with your own country.

23. SATURDAY. Valuable. A new romance may force you to re-evaluate who you are and what you expect from others. Don't let your pride get in the way of a humble attitude and a chance to grow in self-awareness. Leo is a fixed sign and likes to be the center of attention, making it hard for you to accept anything different. Be open to change and watch your life expand and blossom. Be compassionate and understanding of others' positions and opinions and make your path in life that much easier. A spiritual gathering could be very interesting and give you contact with people who can help you in many different areas of your life.

24. SUNDAY. Romantic. The chances of waking up in the arms of a gorgeous lover are high. A new romance can sweep you off your feet and make it hard for you to make any important decisions, so don't try. Be careful of your budget if you go out to the shops. An extravagant and generous turn of mind can put you in the red on a whim. Even worse, you can end up with an expensive white elephant that serves as a daily reminder to you and those you live with of your wanton wastefulness. If you've been keeping track of your income and expenditures, you'll be well prepared for making the most of the coming transits. Do your homework and you can move ahead and gain wealth over the coming month.

25. MONDAY. Challenging. An altered fiscal picture will call for a revision of your budget. There may be fluctuations of fortune. For some, there's a windfall or a well-earned reward, while others may have to tread a frugal path. Whatever the development, skilled management is the solution. A change in living quarters might be warranted, and if you spread the word amongst your business and social contacts you may hear of something much more affordable than your present home. If you can cut costs on your living expenses, you will have more to invest or to spend on a hobby or favorite pastime. But the savings won't compensate for any lack of home comforts.

26. TUESDAY. Variable. Discuss any important matters with partners or associates and get some feedback. A second opinion could help to clarify a problem. If you add up the figures, you may find that you can afford one thing, but only at the expense of another. The beginning of the day might find you uncertain of quite which way to jump, and uncertainties about other people could be at the root of this. However, as the day progresses, you'll swing into action and be yourself again. After a slow start, you can get a lot done if you keep abreast of important communications. This is a good day to make peace with a sibling or a neighbor if you have been at odds lately. Be willing to take advice.

27. WEDNESDAY. Exciting. This morning's Full Moon in Libra pulls in the harmonious vibes of Venus and the erratic vibes of Uranus. Expect the unexpected and you'll be well prepared. An exciting new love affair can put you on cloud nine. A new neighbor could attract your attention and have you peeking through your curtains all day. Try to live life without worrying about what others think. While you are trying to accommodate everyone else, your own plans will suffer. Artistic Lions could have a win with your talent and gain recognition in the public eye. This success comes with a few problems, not to mention the jealousy of another. Be kind to all and diffuse any possible animosity.

28. THURSDAY. Lively. Romance, fun, and adventure are all on the cards today. If you are already in a relationship, why not take off together and have an adventure. This change of pace will allow you to revive the romance and interest that often dissipates with familiarity. An unexpected invitation can take you away from your comfort zone. But if you don't go, you will be left wondering what-if. Weigh the pros and cons first and you can enjoy the fun and excitement. What you expect to be a bland business meeting can turn into a lively exchange of interesting ideas, introducing you to new associations and opportunities.

29. FRIDAY. Inhibited. Breaking with family traditions could get you into hot water. Talk to your elders before you do anything rash and gain the benefit of their wisdom and experience. If you do decide to go against their wishes, at least you will have explained yourself and given them fair warning, as sometimes the shock of something unexpected is worse than the reality. On the other hand, someone close to you may act unexpectedly. Try to find out their reasoning before you judge their actions. Accidents are likely, so be sure to think before you rush into anything. Home buyers could come across the perfect property but would need to borrow more than budgeted for.

30. SATURDAY. Promising. Home entertainment will give you an opportunity to impress those important to you. Some of you might go out of your way to turn out a lavish dinner and invite important guests. Others of you may ask your close friends and ensure you have a lot of fun instead. Whatever turns you on is the way to go today. Home renovations can provide a wide scope for creative endeavors, and a simple interior paint might brighten up your living space. Allow the artist in you free rein and enjoy being with your own tribe this weekend. Leo parents could want to please the kids and build a playhouse for them. Start cooking nourishing meals.

31. SUNDAY. Difficult. Something in your family or emotional life may be stuck in a recurring pattern, and now's the time to deal with whatever it is that keeps going wrong. If there are problems, try not to argue. Talk about it rationally and get to the heart of the matter. Don't treat the symptoms; treat the cause. Cosmic energies urge you to make a choice about where your life is going. Work is at the core of it, but the life you want or the cause you're devoted to may become mutually exclusive. In order to gain something of importance in your life's work, you may have to set aside something you want. If you choose emotionally, a door on the path may close.

APRIL

1. MONDAY. Refreshing. Take time out today and enjoy having fun or getting into your favorite recreational pursuits. Sports Leo could have a serious training schedule to keep up for an upcoming event and your mood will make it a fun workout. Make the most of your mood and attack those projects that you've been itching to get at for weeks. You can get some great artistic and original work achieved if you do. Student Lions are likely to miss a few classes and socialize with your in-crowd. There may even be a budding romance that takes up most of your time. Try to keep a balance and ensure that your responsibilities aren't neglected. Then you can enjoy the party with a clear conscience.

2. TUESDAY. Intense. A large workload can make this a day of stark contrast to yesterday. Perhaps you missed something important and now have double the amount to catch up on. There is a likelihood that you have to cover up a mistake or some such from your superiors or authorities, and this may cause you some grief. Some of you could be working a job that you know isn't going to last and you need the cash, so you're out to impress the boss. Just remember that you are only human and can only do so much. Otherwise you might get sick and lose a few days' pay completely. Efficiency is the key today, so don't flit here and there. If you change gears at the right time you can get a lot done.

3. WEDNESDAY. Tense. There are important choices or decisions to be made shortly which may involve family, relationships, and money. The issue of what you believe in and how far you're prepared to go to express that belief is a crucial one. You may even have to give something up or break ties with someone who's been a fixture in your life. Problems with the Internet can cause unnecessary worry regarding a loved one abroad. It would be worth having any problems with your communications equipment fixed before they become serious. Your workload may be interfering with your social life. Take a note of the demands you put on yourself. You might find that you are your hardest taskmaster.

4. THURSDAY. Interesting. Chances are your social skills mean that you are popular with the public. Invitations to all kinds of interesting events will take you away from your loved ones far too often if you are not careful. If you start to notice those looks as you leave home, it might be time to take a rain check and let your nearest and dearest know how you feel. Your ability to drop what you are doing to focus on them will give you many extra brownie points. Besides, there might be some interesting news you need to talk about. Don't let your partner play coy; instead, love them into laughter and go out for the night. A problem with joint resources can be solved simply if you can both compromise.

5. FRIDAY. Assertive. At your charming best you can be most persuasive. The problem you are facing today is that you will come up against competition that may be more persuasive than yourself. How do you out-charm the charmers, you might ask? Trust yourself, be natural, and stop trying too hard, as you are one of the best charmers on the planet. Try not to bend the truth either, as any lies will come back to haunt you. A strong desire to travel might influence your future plans. Talk to your partner before you book anything too extravagant and make it a joint venture for best results. Even if you think your dreams are out of your reach, working with another will bring them closer than you think.

6. SATURDAY. Dreamy. The Moon joins forces with nebulous Neptune and will make it hard to find clarity in anything you do. If your memory deserts you, leaving black holes where the information should be, write yourself plenty of notes before entering important discussions or negotiations. Even in love, whispering sweet nothings in a new love's ear may seem distorted or exaggerated once the heat of the moment dies down. Watch out for deception, as Neptune is one of the greatest chameleons there are. What sounds like a fabulous deal could be the biggest ripoff of the year. It might be a good idea to lock your house securely before venturing out and to leave your plastic cash in the drawer.

7. SUNDAY. Promising. Family ties will bring much enjoyment to any of your endeavors today. Don't be surprised if relatives turn up unannounced and create a party atmosphere, bringing memories and insight regarding your heritage. You have a lot of support, and if you are planning to start a new business venture, involve your family and friends and ease your burden a little. With contacts in propitious places you can pull strings you never knew you had. A blossoming romance can enter a stage of intimacy that's quite addictive. Be careful not to cancel too many engagements, as you need to have some time apart to maintain your own independence and thereby avoid the possibility of codependence.

8. MONDAY. Hot. You may be surprised by the heat of your passion as the celestials twist and turn today; be sure to find a positive outlet for this energy. You can meet problems head-on at work but you are likely to stay in high stress mode. Take a brisk walk right before lunch so that you can relax enough to digest the food that you eat. Pay attention to your instincts, as they will not lead you astray. Listen to your inner voice, especially what it tells you about others. You may need to keep information about your personal life to yourself because there are people in your environment who are not as friendly as they would like you to think. Pay attention to duty and avoid gossipmongers.

9. TUESDAY. Demanding. Get into work early and you won't miss anything important. There are likely to be some unexpected changes to your plans or workload, and if you are up-to-date, you'll be able to come out on top. Your intuition is sparking, and if you are willing to be inventive you could make a good impression on your employer and colleagues—enough to push you up the ladder and ensure your job security. Some of you may be craving a career change and should start looking. Staying in a profession that doesn't give you any inspiration or satisfaction is ultimately bad for your health. Consider going back to school to gain skills that will help you attain a job that does satisfy you; you won't regret it.

10. WEDNESDAY. Illuminating. Leo is likely to be future-orien-tated now. Focus on your dreams and aspirations can push you to make the changes you have been thinking about for a while but haven't had the necessary drive to carry them out until now. Watch an impulsive streak, as you might bite off your nose to spite your face if you get carried away with the mood. Today's New Moon is in Aries, starting a new lunar cycle from your sector of travel and the higher mind. This is an opportunity to explore who you really are, to search for meaning in life and bring your actions into a better perspective. Focus your attention on philosophy, higher education, and travel for the most fun.

11. THURSDAY. Practical. Responsibilities can pile up and put a damper on your mood. But if you take a practical approach and do one thing at a time, you won't feel swamped and your progress could be quite impressive. Leo is meant to be in the limelight, and your good work could be noted at this time. Remember, it is better to do one thing well than try to juggle too much and get nothing done. With this attitude you might be home early and able to keep a promise to a loved one that is more important than anything else. Practice relaxation techniques; then, if you have to cut everything close, the stress won't end up causing any arguments, especially when you want to be your loving best.

12. FRIDAY. Ambitious. Pay attention to rules and regulations and you won't end up having to explain yourself. Your determination to push ahead with your plans or goals at any cost might not be the best way to go. Consider others and be helpful, and you can gain valuable support and assistance from your peers and loved ones. Above all, listen to what others are saying before you speak and you will be able to tell people what they want to hear; adapting your goals to suit the situation. Interesting news regarding a family member could be cause for celebration. If they are away at the moment, get on the computer and have a family get-together over the air-waves while the moment is right.

13. SATURDAY. Social. A business meeting could be finalized to your satisfaction this morning. Take the time to socialize with your clients and colleagues before disappearing, as you can hear some interesting information that will set up another successful deal. Your friends should be pleasant company as the Moon sails through Gemini, your sector of friendships. Communication will be easy and you may be able to unexpectedly help someone you care about. This is a great night for a party. Single Leo may meet someone special through associates, so don't turn down a blind date. Married Leo will find that stepping out with your significant other is just what you need to get the fires burning hot tonight.

14. SUNDAY. Beneficial. Enjoy a relaxing day in good company, as there is no need to push yourself on this day made for leisure and recreation. If you do have work to finish, gather your friends around. Hand out the paintbrushes and order pizza for the gang. Not only will your job get done faster, you just might have fun doing it. This is also a great day for team sports. If you don't play, go along to a local game and enjoy letting out the week's frustrations while rooting for your team. You may run into someone new while you are out and about, so dress to impress while you're at it. This person may be an important connection for your business networking, or a new lover and best friend.

15. MONDAY. Lucky. Venus, the planet of love, moves into Taurus and your sector of career and reputation, creating favorable circumstances in your business and professional life, attracting persons and circumstances that facilitate your work. People in authority will be favorably inclined toward you also. You may become involved in artistic matters, such as design, layout work, office redecorating, even public relations for the purpose of making your workplace more attractive. A new love relationship with someone quite a bit older can help you learn more about getting ahead in life. Perhaps you will fall in love with your employer or supervisor. Watch out for ambitious motives.

16. TUESDAY. Retiring. Be willing to rest and recuperate over the next day or so. Lighten your workload and give yourself a break from your hectic social schedule. Just sitting and listening to the sounds of nature and letting go of inner stress through relaxation is gold. If you live close to the coast, take a walk by the ocean and benefit from the spiritual infusion this brings. Prayer and meditation can bring serenity and peace of mind to a stressful lifestyle. Review the past month and gain insight into your progress. Inner reflection always helps to put our lives into perspective and get in touch with our underlying feelings so that we can stay true to ourselves.

17. WEDNESDAY. Independent. This is a perfect day for starting a new project, particularly one that you can work on by yourself without having to take orders or coordinate other people's actions. With the life-giving Sun and energetic Mars together in Aries, you really do need to be physically active today. Whether you get out and go for a long walk or run, work out at the gym or stay at home and practice yoga, you will prefer solitary exercise to team sports. Look after your health; if you feel that you have an infection of some sort, see a doctor or natural therapist now before it flares up into something much more dangerous. Debate over philosophical issues could deteriorate into an argument.

18. THURSDAY. Dramatic. The moody Moon swings into Leo bringing the ups and downs of emotion with her. It may seem as though the people around you are more moody than usual, but you do need to take a look at yourself before you start pointing the finger. It could be that they are just reacting to you. With an excess of your dramatic artistic flair, disagreements could take on the shape of a real Greek tragedy if you are not careful. Use this influence to take advantage of your popularity. Dress to impress and go out of your way to please those you love, then you can enjoy the attention they lavish upon you. If you aren't willing to give a little, the attention you receive might not be so desirable.

19. FRIDAY. Stimulating. New and interesting associations can come into your sphere of influence today. Be open to new ideas and you can broaden your world view considerably. Your situation could be changing quite radically, but although you might feel reticent to change, you are assured there is positive influences if you do go with the flow. Trying to stop the change will only bring problems. People will be drawn to you, as you exude a loving and nurturing nature; so don't be afraid to reach out. You need to maintain your close relationships, as they will be a beneficial resource for you over the coming month. Disapproval from a family member should be ignored, as it is not your problem.

20. SATURDAY. Fair. A reasonable amount of popularity or success can inflate your ego. The only problem with this wonderful fact is that at some point the ego can be deflated again, bringing pain and confusion. Put yourself in your competitor's shoes and learn what is driving them, thereby giving you the upper hand when it comes to negotiations. Watch out for greed and avarice, in yourself as well as others. Try to be happy with a satisfactory profit rather than wanting it all, that way you will leave everyone feeling satisfied rather than ripped-off. Pride is another one of the seven deadly sins attributed to Leo, and this alone can bring you undone. Practice humility and gratitude to all.

21. SUNDAY. Industrious. An idea for a home business could sound like a great little moneymaker, but consider how much time you will need to put in. If you are thinking about running it as a second job, you might not have all that much time and energy for it. You do need time for play and relaxation, too. Work on budgeting your time as well as your money. There may be a crisis over money, especially where children or creative projects are concerned, and you'll have to set a limit for what can be spent. The important thing is to work from the figures rather than allowing impulse to take hold. Don't get into quarrels over money. If you have to deal with financial institutions, think calmly and clearly.

22. MONDAY. Useful. A social outing may have to be canceled due to lack of funds. Focus on your spending at the moment. Even if you are not experiencing financial difficulties right now, your prudence will serve you well in the future. Those Lions who are experiencing difficulties might be wise to contact your financial institution and negotiate a payment plan that you can manage. This will eliminate the stress from your daily existence and allow you to enjoy life while you are alive. Remember that while you enjoy having goals and plans for the future, life is happening in the present. A conflict of values between you and your partner may need mediation to help you find the middle ground.

23. TUESDAY. Manageable. Stay away from the gossip around the watercooler. If nothing else it can cause dissatisfaction and disease. Someone may be trying to pull the wool over your eyes on a money matter, so keep your own counsel, and if unsure, get professional advice. A local community event could involve you in a series of meetings, and instead of going to plan, you find that some of your neighbors are very difficult to communicate with. If you are thinking of pulling out simply because of this, don't. Instead contact other neighbors whom you do see eye to eye with and see if you can work something out. At the end of the day you will have to go with the majority. Which side are you on?

24. WEDNESDAY. Uncertain. Check your office equipment, as faulty machines can cause miscommunications and confusion. Double-check all your facts as they come to hand and you can avoid this problem. There may be a tendency to fantasize about your career and goals in life. If you find that you don't enjoy your day at work and your colleagues rub you the wrong way, reevaluate what you do like. Write a list, as this is helpful to assess the facts. You might realize that what you like belongs to a different profession entirely. Don't quit right away though. Give it some thought and you may be able to put in for a transfer within your own company and easily attain the working life you truly desire.

25. THURSDAY. Competitive. Amicable discussions may seem impossible today. Try to let it go and leave it for another time. As the day progresses you can come to the conclusion that it isn't that important anyway. There is high energy in the ether and energetic pursuits will suit best. If you play a sport, this is a great day to do some training or play a game. If you don't then look for something which you love doing that demands high concentration and you will be in your element. The Full Moon is in Scorpio, shining its light into your sector of home and personal security, so you may be more inclined to take what another says personally, when you really shouldn't. Spend time beautifying your home.

26. FRIDAY. Renewing. Check whether your parents may need your help today. They might not want to bother you, but you would rather be there for them and know they are okay. Some of you might avoid seeing your parents because of their judgments, but consider whether that means you can't help them if they need it. Issues of partnership, money, and your spiritual life could be elements in an important decision you need to make. Are you really going in a direction that serves your inner self? What role does someone close play in your life? Some Lions really need to make a commitment now while others need to break free. If you really want to develop and get more from life, sow the seeds of change.

27. SATURDAY. Chancy. Any opportunity to have fun and get out with your friends will take priority today. Don't let your responsibilities hold you back. Leo parents may take your kids to a fun park and let your hair down together. Later, drop in at the home of a friend who has children the same age as yours. You can take some food and make your visit fun for all. Artistic Leo could enjoy visiting the local art gallery, or you might travel to see an interesting exhibition. Either way the inspiration you gather will give you new and fresh enthusiasm and ideas for your own projects. A public gathering can offer the chance to make new friends, and singles might meet someone very attractive this evening.

28. SUNDAY. Expansive. Luck is on your side today, although you do need to watch an urge to splurge, as you could blow your budget as well. New associations are opening up for the Lion. A new love affair can introduce you to pursuits and hobbies. Some of you might start teaching a hobby in which you have gained a fair amount of skill. Home renovations could also enter the creative realm as you decide to knock down a wall, paint the interior using the principles of color therapy, or design the bathroom around an original mosaic to replace the tiles. Itchy feet could see you planning to take your holidays overseas. Listen to your friend's travel tales to get an idea of the best destination for you.

29. MONDAY. Industrious. Home improvements or health matters can take up most of your thoughts. It might be time to do your yearly spring cleaning and you've decided to take on the task of emptying out the attic or the basement. If this hasn't been done for a long time you can find lots of old memorabilia and things you can revamp and reuse. There may even be a family heirloom that comes to light, or something thought lost or stolen. This is a prime time to start a new diet or exercise routine. Be careful that you don't overdo it though and end up with muscle aches and pains that mean you can't continue with it tomorrow. Also stay away from fads when it comes to dieting and ensure proper nourishment.

30. TUESDAY. Pleasant. Today you might find yourself minding your own business for the early part of the day, with just the usual things to be done and you to do them. However, as the day progresses, you will find that your time and effort will go more toward meeting the needs of others. You'll gain insight into tricky people or difficult situations if you just go with the flow. Be careful that you don't try to be all things to all people and you won't overextend yourself. Get out of the house for some part of the day, as the fresh air will do you good. Ask a friend or your lover to go for a walk with you and enjoy the benefits of exercise while you laugh and converse together.

MAY

1. WEDNESDAY. Productive. Communication on the job may assume greater importance than usual, but be careful not to get tangled up in red tape. If you have been thinking about advancing your career, now is a great time to talk to your employer or superiors about how you can advance in your present job. Your enthusiasm can open doors and there could be an offer for extra training to learn new techniques, or a subsidized course in management skills. Some discord between you and your partner or lover should be discussed. Talk about your individual goals and how best you can both work together to achieve them. Having a plan together might be the glue you need to cement your relationship.

2. THURSDAY. Thoughtful. Friends and loved ones are important to you today. Go out of your way to do something special that will let them know your feelings. You don't have to do a lot or spend large amounts of money; something simple is enough. Divorce proceedings can be finalized amicably now. You may both be able to accept your individual responsibility for the breakup without having to blame each other. A new relationship may come with a ready-made family and introduce you to the world of stepparenting. Just remember that you don't have to assume the role of the missing parent. Simply be a benevolent adult in the child's life and nurture the relationship so that you can grow together.

3. FRIDAY. Creative. Many opportunities to expand your life's experience could make it very hard to choose which direction to go in. Tertiary education would give you an advantage, as you would get the opportunity to switch subjects if you discover that your first choice doesn't agree with you. Some of you might decide to travel overseas to gain the skills and the experience you need without having to pay a small fortune for it. Voluntary work is another avenue that will give you experience and put you in touch with potential employers. An opportunity to start your own business could encourage you to purchase a home as well. Gain the agreement of your partner, as full cooperation is necessary for success.

4. SATURDAY. Healing. This is the perfect time to apologize to a family member if you feel that it is warranted. Perhaps you have been a problem child and feel the need to make amends to your parents. Even if you have been estranged from someone you love, now might be the time to make up and find common ground. If there is love between you, anything is possible. A business deal that seemed lost can be revived at a profit. Some of you might have to call a family get-together to discuss the division of an inheritance. Accept that some people won't be agreeable with any decisions, but ensure that all things are fair and equitable and avoid any further legal proceedings.

5. SUNDAY. Private. A feeling of restlessness this morning may lead you to list the variety of things you want to accomplish now. You can accomplish quite a lot around your home once you become focused. Cleaning, preparing for the workweek, writing letters, and making phone calls all add up to the feeling of control. Be careful; too much intensity will create the inclination to spoil your own nest. Your many responsibilities and obligations may keep you away from those who would offer you much-needed emotional support. Time shared with friends and loved ones will add to the support that you feel from time to time; a sense of goodwill prevails. Take any opportunity to spend time alone with a loved one.

6. MONDAY. Challenging. Stepping out of your comfort zone will test your skill and ability. Although you might be stressed, it will also be exciting. Accept what challenges come your way and you won't be left wondering what-if. You may crave a change of pace more than usual now. Take a break at lunchtime and get out into the fresh air. Ask a friend to have lunch at your favorite café and enjoy indulging yourself. There is an indication that you are going to hear some valuable gossip that will aid your cause. Watch your impatience and the impulsiveness of others, as there is a higher than usual probability of accidents occurring. This cautions you to take extra care on the roads especially.

7. TUESDAY. Good. Being with your loved ones or favored friends today is a rewarding, fun, inspiring experience. There are quick answers, great wit, and a surplus of insights and solutions at the ready. The events today could revolve around a variety of social gatherings. Whatever the case, be it a garage sale, a shopping expedition, or an outdoor picnic, the joy of interacting with others is as stimulating as it is satisfying. Not to mention the type of artifacts and exotic foods for you to buy. You are likely to come across a collector's item that your intuition tells you is an antique of some value. If you can get it for next to nothing, what have you got to lose? Trust your instincts and take the risk.

8. WEDNESDAY. Responsible. The focus is on your career and reputation sector today, as the Moon joins the Sun, Mercury, Venus, and Mars in Taurus. You might ask yourself if you are doing enough to provide for your loved ones, and whether you are stretching yourself as much as you could. If you have a parent who is critical of your choice of career, you may want to leave home and find your own place to live. Young Leos are likely to be looking forward to moving away from the protection of the family and testing the waters out in the world. If you feel that you need to find more work in order to provide for your loved ones, be creative. What can you do that might give you a home-based business?

9. THURSDAY. Outgoing. There are powerful energies protecting your ambitions today. Take care with assertiveness, as there are some pushy characters in your path. What you think is a reasonable statement might cause an argument or a misunderstanding. Stick to your own resolutions and don't let others influence you to change your plans. With the New Moon in Taurus and your sector of career and ambition, this is the perfect time for quiet preparation. Check your motives and ensure you are honest and true, and you will succeed in your endeavors. Venus, the planet of love, moves into Gemini and your sector of friends and associations, bringing good vibes and the possibility of romance.

10. FRIDAY. Positive. This is your time to shine in your profession and be recognized and appreciated. The thing to watch is your emotions. You may be overly attached to your work and could come across as dictatorial with your workmates. Try to listen to others and working together won't seem so hard. You are also in danger of burning the candle at both ends, as you feel passionate in all areas of your life. Find a balance between your home life and your ambitions. Rearrange your daily schedule to include times for rest, relaxation, and most important, reflection. Without this opportunity your life will go by while you are busy trying to meet all your deadlines. Practice being in the moment.

11. SATURDAY. Friendly. A smorgasbord of social events to choose from could be your biggest problem on this fine day. Try not to spread yourself too thin so that you can enjoy whatever it is you chose to do. Get around to some local events, as you are likely to bump into people you haven't seen for a while and can catch up on the local gossip. Enjoy philosophical and political debates as well as the valuable feedback you only gain from your contemporaries. You may get a view of how your efforts have been received over time and a long-overdue success can finally come your way. The advice and efforts of friends have been pivotal in your journey. Acknowledge your efforts, and also what you've been given.

12. SUNDAY. Advantageous. Look, listen, and learn today. You are open to absorbing new ideas, skills, and facts, and can develop and open up new possibilities in more than one area of your life. New associations can inspire you to learn a new sport. Perhaps through debate you can see the world from a new angle or find entertainment and fun in a different way. Inspiration is your driving force, and if you're lying around at home, pick up an interesting book or start a creative project that will feed off your inspiration. Jump in the car and take a road trip somewhere out of the ordinary, or visit friends who live far away. You are sure to have some interesting adventures wherever you go.

13. MONDAY. Retiring. Although you are likely to have a demanding schedule today, don't be afraid to ask for space if you need it. Everyone needs to be alone now and then, and this may be your time for solitude. It could surprise you to find you get more done by taking regular breaks. The fresh air and chance to reflect can allow you to see where you can do better, or where you can cut corners successfully. Prayer and meditation can be especially healing for you, so make an effort to block out the world at some point this afternoon or evening. Some of you may experience spiritual or psychic insights that are uplifting. Life's mysteries may deepen, so make sure you have any legal issues straight and tied into place.

14. TUESDAY. Variable. Expectations may be too high for you to live with. If you are feeling that it is too hard to keep going, then take a break. Consider that your frame of mind is not conducive to peak production at the moment anyway. Avoid malicious gossip, as you may hear something you wish you hadn't, which will upset your equilibrium for the rest of the day. If you are not feeling well, take the day off and get the rest you probably should have had on Sunday. Remember that burning the candle at both ends, while it may be fun and exciting at times, still means we run out of wick twice as fast. If you are struggling with a resentment, then look for someone you can help and peace will return.

15. WEDNESDAY. Questionable. Business or personal negotiations can challenge you on moral grounds today. If you are having doubts about what you are doing, then stop. This is your intuition telling you not to go ahead. Take the time to reflect and allow your inner knowing to give you the guidance you are seeking, and you won't be sorry. A disagreement with your partner might highlight differing values. Talk to them about how you feel and listen to how they feel, otherwise neither of you will be able to compromise productively. If you find that you can't listen to each other, try professional mediation. Otherwise you might have to consider that even though romance bloomed, compatibility was lacking.

16. THURSDAY. Subjective. Avoid getting caught up in your own personal issues. You can go around and around in your head on matters of the heart or the world and get absolutely nowhere. This also goes for feelings of resentment toward others. You are sitting pretty at the moment, so start thinking of others and change the subject. Broaden your horizons and talk to workmates you usually don't talk to and go out with some different friends for a change. Changing jobs might not go as smoothly as you would like, so it would be wise to put up with the one you have and perhaps see if you can't do what you do better. It is all in your approach today, dear Leo. Look on the positive side and benefit.

17. FRIDAY. Diverse. The demands of work and family life can leave you feeling like the meat in a sandwich. Orders from the boss and the responsibilities of your home life might not gel, and only you can do something about it. Talk to friends and associates and get the benefit of their insight. Sometimes it is easier to see what the issue is when you are looking at it objectively. Don't act blindly on this advice, however; take it and use it to help give you options and insight so that you can come to your own understanding and decisions that suit you. Talk openly and honestly to those who are important in your life and have faith that a positive solution will become clear with time and devotion.

18. SATURDAY. Imaginative. Your dreams are likely to be important to you now. Planning a practical budget so that you can do the things you dream about is the perfect way to start. If you are planning to buy a home or property, start looking. Even if you don't have a deposit at the moment, you might be surprised with what is available. Leo parents should start valuing your own parents and in-laws; see if you can lessen the cost of your childcare and let them enjoy their grandchildren. Health issues may arise for some, and a clear course of action for a cure can be elusive. Rather than spend a lot of money on doctors and drugs, look to your food as medicine and set up a diet plan.

19. SUNDAY. Confronting. Remember that Leo is a fixed sign and not all people are wrong. Arguing with friends and loved ones over a sticking point is just a waste of time. Be open to change and you may broaden your outlook considerably. If you can't do that, then allow other people to have different viewpoints and maintain healthy associations. Your home is important to you, and you may spend more than you can afford in an attempt to beautify your environment. Look at creative projects that you can do to keep your costs down and give you a form of cheap entertainment as well. Families can paint the house together and end up spending quality time talking about issues you wouldn't usually talk about.

20. MONDAY. Profitable. Recognition for your skills and hard work can come through some form of public acknowledgment. Your employer may see fit to give you a pay raise, or maybe you will be successful if you talk to them about one. An assignment may go so well that a bonus comes your way, and if you have your own business, you are sure to receive a windfall now. Communication figures highly in your day, and you should talk about your plans to those who count and gain valuable feedback from those in the know. Contacts and connections will also come in handy, so don't hesitate to use your network, if needed. Whatever you do, don't let pride hold you back from asking for assistance.

21. TUESDAY. Expressive. The shining Sun moves into Gemini and joins communicative Mercury, loving Venus, and expansive Jupiter in your sector of associations and intuition. It's time to take a gamble on your dreams and start initiating the process to bring them into fulfillment. No matter how unattainable you may think they are, start trusting in the universe and you might be surprised. Romance is possible for those who are looking. Don't say no to a blind date because you think it won't work. Give it a try and see what happens. Start experimenting with life and you will gain new experience and have a lot more fun. Volunteering with a local charitable group could be very rewarding.

22. WEDNESDAY. Testing. Job seekers may find that the best way to get into the work force is through education. Be willing to do hard work for a while to gain the skills that will get you into a well-paid position. Even if it takes a couple of years, then you will be comfortable for the rest of your life. New drivers need to be aware if you are taking your test now. There is the chance of unexpected phenomena, and if you are paying attention, you can turn it to your advantage and show off your skills. A group gathering could be informative, and if you are interested in gaining knowledge, then getting together with others can open doors that otherwise wouldn't be accessible to you.

23. THURSDAY. Supportive. Although you may feel that you are on your own, you have family and friends you can turn to if needed.

Talk to your parents about any issues that are causing you pain or worry. Even though they may disapprove of some things, they will be able to give you the benefit of their experience. You may be worried about a parent's health, and again you should talk to them about this. Do your research on how you can help and you will feel so much better because you are doing something. Those of you sharing a house might need to call a house meeting to air your problems and find that the others also have problems. Because of your common needs you can find solutions.

24. FRIDAY. Idealistic. If you've been trying to take a new path and change the way you relate to people in general, you now need to see some real results. If you've been persistent despite delays or disappointments, the fruit of your efforts begins to ripen now. Circumstances may force you to make a complete break, but not before it has been confronted and dealt with openly and honestly. Childhood conditioning may be undermining your efforts, and, counseling may be invaluable. Issues and events that have been buried will not stay buried. Your personal status within the family is a likely focus, and control of family property and resources may become an issue of intense interest.

25. SATURDAY. Entertaining. The Full Moon in Sagittarius brightens your fifth house of romance and creativity, urging you to get out today. It's time to reconnect with your friends and seek their opinions and advice on certain subjects. You may be able to gain a great deal of support by reaching out now, as people are more inclined to listen to your dreams and ideas. Reading can offer you an avenue for adventure if you need to relax, otherwise lying around won't sit right with you. Romance is there for Lions on the prowl. Go out to different venues and start mixing with new and creative people for fun. Leo parents may need to watch your children, as they could be restive and troublesome.

26. SUNDAY. Pleasurable. The waning Moon combined with your imagination can create worlds of wonder today; don't hesitate to express your creative ideas. Mixing with creative people will inspire you to reach for goals you normally wouldn't try for. Stretch your talents and skills and you can create some marvelous works that surprise even yourself. Children can bring great pleasure, so spend some time with the young ones in your life. Some of you might be trying for a baby, but don't let your desires override the romantic aspects. Love and romance are sublime, but possibly bittersweet and elusive. No matter; the greatest love stories are about love found, love lost, and the painful pleasure of longing.

27. MONDAY. Intense. Your mood will reflect the outcome achieved. Remember to smile at others no matter how worried or upset you may feel. The physical aspect of smiling can influence your internal mood also. Be kind and try not to blame others for anything that goes wrong. Write out a gratitude list and watch your mood recover. As you reap, so you will sow today. A competitive workplace could put you off your game and make it hard to be creative. Let go of pride and perfectionism and you might just enjoy the fun of the chase. Laugh at adversity and your competitors may start laughing with you. Health matters are also affected greatly by our moods. Fresh air and exercise is the best medicine.

28. TUESDAY. Optimistic. Get going early and make the most of the morning's high energy, as the early bird will indeed catch the worm today. Deals can be finalized with authorities that will make your job so much easier. Don't look for the easy way out, but do what needs to be done and you will get the best outcome. An ex-colleague could approach you with a job position that offers much greater room for advancement, and you may need to make a snap decision or miss out. You know what you really want, and if it fits the bill, you can't go wrong. This is not the best time to seek advice, as you will only hear what would suit another, not necessarily what would suit you the best. Take a walk and think on it.

29. WEDNESDAY. Unique. Partnership is on the agenda, so devote some time and attention to your loved ones. If there are thorny matters between you and those you love, then today is the day to put them to rest. Choose the right time and place to address outstanding issues, as the mood will play a large part in coming to a practical understanding. Put your partner or significant other first before you get involved in social activities also. They may not tell you what they want, and therefore you will do well to show them how much you care. If your partner is having career or financial problems you may be able to pull a few strings and get the ball rolling in a positive direction.

30. THURSDAY. Compassionate. Good communication will help any problems or issues among loved ones and friends. Your social network figures highly in today's events, so make contact with someone in the know. One of your friends may need a shoulder to cry on over a broken relationship. But if you are also good friends with their partner, you will need to use discretion concerning what you are willing to talk about. Acknowledging their feelings without blame will be the most helpful approach for all. If you are going through a relationship breakup there is the possibility of reconciliation through mediation, if you and your partner are interested. Just remember both sides need to be willing for it to work.

31. FRIDAY. Active. Mars, the action planet, joins the Sun, Venus, and Jupiter in Gemini and your sector of associations, turning your focus toward your social network. You can expect to receive more invitations than usual and may find that the demand of others on your time could impose on your own private time. With Mercury, the communicator, moving into Cancer and your sector of privacy and solitude, you will need to look inwards more. Try to plan your day so that you have time for others and time for yourself. Prioritize your time and eliminate those engagements that don't serve your purposes. Of course you will want to help out loved ones and friends, but otherwise you do need to serve yourself too.

JUNE

1. SATURDAY. Intriguing. It's not a day to be taken in by appearances, especially where money is concerned, so consider any financial decisions carefully. Put them off for a little while if you can. You will be inclined to abandon alliances and joint ventures that fail to add to your status and influence. Manipulating or gaining control in a partnership is in the stars. Don't be used by a more powerful partner. Don't go on a spending spree, as you might buy things out of boredom rather than genuine need. Take stock of the inner Lion. Give your psyche a workout and try to glean what it is that will satisfy you. A spiritual gathering may present a forum for the sharing of ideas and understanding.

2. SUNDAY. Rebellious. Plans and expectations will go out the window as you look for adventure. Whether you are interested in art, fashion, animals, or hiking, the list is endless. Stop window shopping and just thinking about your dreams. Get out into the world and start living, because today will give you that little bit of extra magic that can make things happen. A fear of commitment can be overcome now, as a strong impulsive mood will force the issue. Arguments are highly probable, so tread carefully around the in-laws or anybody else you may have cross purposes with. Check out local events in your neighborhood. A visiting celebrity could bring excitement and interest your way.

3. MONDAY. Caring. Loving Venus joins Mercury in Cancer and your sector of solitude now. Your home and family are likely to be important to you, and if you have a loved one at a distance, schedule an online chat and bring them back into your life. The need to think and reflect should be acknowledged, and if you can take some quiet time for yourself, it would do wonders for your health and sense of well-being. Volunteering or charitable work is highlighted in today's energies. If you have never thought about getting involved in your local community in this way, start now. The rewards are well worth the effort, not to mention the opportunities to learn new skills and make valuable contacts.

4. TUESDAY. Changeable. A high level of commitment and dedication may be necessary to move up in your job. If you are finding the challenge too much and it is destroying your home and private life, you may have to rethink your direction in life. Adjust your lifestyle to suit your income and downsize into a more comfortable way of living, with plenty of room for love. Look after your health by eating simple home-cooked food. Instead of eating fast-food and watching TV, you might start growing your own greens and cooking up tasty and nourishing recipes from exotic faraway places. Join a hiking group and get your exercise as well as your entertainment and friendship for free.

5. WEDNESDAY. Important. It's time to revisit your secret fears and discover what is holding you back. For some Lions it will be onward and upward. For others it may be a case of revising plans. There is an unexpected development, as factors that you have not taken into account reveal themselves. Prepare to do some serious reevaluation. Power plays at work are potentially destructive, even if you resent anyone who tries to control your fate. If you allow or are forced to allow others to make important decisions for you, the results will not be favorable. If you can wrangle a holiday, do so. Any time you can find for fun and relaxation will improve your whole outlook and allow you to be you.

6. THURSDAY. Insightful. Communication in all forms is likely to be more complicated than usual. Workmates may insinuate something without actually saying it. Hidden messages can come along with off-the-cuff remarks. Dishonesty is another aspect that can leave you wondering when what is being said doesn't seem to add up. Watch, listen, and learn is the motto of the day. Observe and you will start to understand the inner motives of others, even if they don't recognize these motives themselves. Reflect on your own motives and you might get to understand yourself better. In order to balance the inner and outer worlds we do need to be conscious of them. Wake up and accept who you are, warts and all.

7. FRIDAY. Energetic. Interaction could be tricky, so think twice before you say anything. Try to coordinate your goals with your colleagues and you can develop good teamwork. Business meetings will need to be well organized, so ensure you have all the information and facts necessary for the business at hand. There are likely to be some underhanded motives at play, so peruse all the paperwork, especially documents that you need to sign. Workplace bullying could be an issue. If a colleague confides in you, you may have to act as their advocate and take their complaint to supervisors. If you are experiencing coercion from a colleague, bring it out in the open and watch it disappear.

8. SATURDAY. Social. The New Moon in Gemini and your sector of associations, hopes, and wishes puts the focus on your networking and group contacts during this lunar cycle. This gives an opportunity to work on your personal goals, your feelings about friends, and your future. Friendship, fellowship, and contact with like-minded people will help to give your life purpose. You could become politically active and strive to raise the social consciousness by participating in group activities. Magical work or meditations regarding your hopes and dreams can offer you a greater sense of purpose and help you to integrate the many facets of your personality and desires. Be open to new opportunities now.

9. SUNDAY. Intense. Be honest with yourself this morning and start the day on a positive note. If you take time to meditate on your inner feelings and motives, you won't be at the mercy of your childhood complexes that can operate beneath the surface of your conscious mind. Watch out for drama in real life; if it starts to play out then you can bet your boots your inner motives aren't in line with your conscious actions. This may be true of someone close to you. If you are stuck taking their flak, then talk to them about it. If they are not interested in understanding your side of the argument, then it might be safest to stay away from them. Violence is a product of fear and awareness dispels fear.

10. MONDAY. Communal. Your community spirit may come into play today. There is a drive to work with others on projects that concern humanitarian interests. An urge to make your dreams a reality needs to be acted upon while it is strong. There is a feeling of being a part of the bigger picture which encourages you to move forward with political issues. You are very communicative and conversations come easily. Study, research, and investigations of all kinds are possible as you search out answers to your questions. Family is important to you, and you may find yourself planning a get-together for the evening or setting time aside for being with the family in a group gathering soon.

11. TUESDAY. Low-key. A need to escape from the noise and hustle and bustle should be acted upon. Get outside and go for a walk in nature if possible. Even if you only take a half hour it will give you time to think and reflect on where you are going and what you want. You may have a difficult time voicing your disappointments and failures, especially if you feel the knives are out. But you will have to confront them within yourself anyway. Engaging in self-pity and guilt and playing the martyr are not only unacceptable ways to manipulate others, they don't work. Instead they bring about seriously unhappy consequences. Enjoy pampering yourself; have a massage or facial and let go of the rest.

12. WEDNESDAY. Bright. The Moon cruises into your own sign of Leo today and shines its loving light on everything you love. Your popularity is on the rise and someone may make a fuss over you. Getting an ego boost is wonderful, just be careful it doesn't inflate beyond an acceptable level. Those close to you may seem a little moody, and it could be because of your lack of attention. You've got to give a bit to get a bit, so spread your warmth and charm around. After the last couple of volatile days, life can start to settle back down again. Just be sure that the changes that have occurred don't also move to the back burner. Keep your resolutions and learn your lessons so you can move on toward your goals.

13. THURSDAY. Fruitful. Family and friends are the source of your personal security. Cultivate your network and look after those close to you for a truly loving day. A close friend may return from an overseas trip and shower you with mementos from their travels. Inspiration comes from others also, and you are likely to start planning your own trip abroad now. Getting down to the business of work could be very hard, especially as your workmates may tell stories and jokes and keep you laughing. Organize a lunch at your favorite café and escape the confines of your work while on your break. A secret romance can make it hard to think straight, so be careful of the urge to reveal all.

14. FRIDAY. Deep. Your inner world is far stronger than the outer reality, and what you perceive in others may simply be true for yourself. The superficial social realm will be distasteful to the Lion, as you would prefer to have deep and meaningful conversation in a one-on-one situation. You could hear a workmate's life story over lunch ,and if you are at home, keep the kettle boiling, as friends may drop by for tea and sympathy. A secret romance may become intense, and there is a chance that you could blow your cover if not careful. Be watchful of dangerous situations and employ workplace health and safety techniques and guidelines wherever possible, as accidents on the job are highly likely.

15. SATURDAY. Interesting. Explore your emotions early, as they will point you in the right direction. Think about the things that are important to you, not the things you think should be important. Sometimes in our efforts to please others we lose sight of our own ideals and values, and you can get back in line with your true desires and intentions now. A disagreement between a friend and a lover can make you the meat in the sandwich. But this will only happen if you allow it. Avoid playing mediator or rescuer, and you'll discover a new sense of freedom. A health issue could spark an interest in natural health and healing. Some of you might even consider going to medical school to become your own physician.

16. SUNDAY. Sensitive. Look after your karma today and do something nice for a family member or loved one. If you feel torn between social expectations and family needs, pay attention to the latter. You may not receive the attention at home, but a full heart will be your reward. Being overworked and underpaid can make life difficult. Look at cutting costs by cooking your own meals, substituting legumes for meat, and growing your own herbs and greens. Consider quitting expensive addictions and riding a bike to work. If you take a look at these alternatives you will notice that they are a much healthier way to live. Ask friends over for a game of cards and save on social entertainment as well.

17. MONDAY. Surprising. Nothing will be quite as you expect it today. Throw your plans out of the window and go with the flow because you are unlikely to want to buckle down to anything and therefore won't do much of a job at it anyway. Distractions will be far more interesting than the job at hand and you are likely to drop everything on a whim. New associations, a desire to travel to exotic shores or a public gathering are all on offer. If you are planning to travel you might bring your departure date forward now. A move into a new neighborhood could open up a cornucopia of opportunities for friendship, fun and learning. A short course in a subject of interest can open up a whole new world.

18. TUESDAY. Entertaining. Although you may have a situation that is causing some stress in your life, today could be far luckier and more exciting that you expect. On a purely mundane level, you should feel very good physically and psychologically and enjoy an optimistic outlook. This sense of hope and expectation means that you can find the positive even in a very bad situation. All sorts of challenges can inspire and push you to heights you never expected. An acquaintance whom you have desired to have a friendship with could show more than an interest and ask you out. A workplace meeting may give you the opportunity to show your expertise and boost you toward a promotion.

19. WEDNESDAY. Reserved. Considering that Leo is ruled by the Sun and loves to shine, you will want to stay away from the lime-light while you work on achieving your goals. Don't be shy about canceling an appointment if it will give you the extra time you need to do your best. An elderly parent may need assistance with daily living, and if you can, you might want to have them move in with you. If it is your partner's parent who is coming to live with you, en-sure you set down some guidelines to protect your own needs. That way you will ensure that resentments won't rear their ugly head further down the track. The desire to save money might inspire you to find a smaller and cheaper residence.

20. THURSDAY. Enjoyable. Maintaining your friendships and family status quo assumes more importance than usual. This is an excellent period to increase goodwill and trust with others. Give someone in need a hand and enjoy getting away from your own problems. Try not to scatter your energies too far though. Focus on a few good deeds and receive rewards for your actions; if you try to please too many people, you are likely to get nowhere fast. The chance to unload a secret and clean away a sense of guilt or remorse could surprise you. A caring friend or relative may be a great boon to you now. Someone from the past is likely to reappear, or perhaps you may spend time sorting out your photos and reminiscing on the past.

21. FRIDAY. Beneficial. The shining Sun moves into Cancer and your sector of the unconscious mind today. This signals the final month in your solar cycle and suggests it is a good time to enter therapy and look inward. Reflect on your progress over the last year and focus on the things that brought you true inspiration. In-spiration comes when we are being true to our spiritual purpose, and as such gives you a valuable guideline to the course you should take into the future. Concentrate on finishing off any personal proj-ects you have lying around and put in extra time on your plans for the future. Practicing prayer and meditation over the next month should bring insight and self-understanding.

22. SATURDAY. Extraordinary. As usual, when we get a taste of the good things we assume they will last forever. The alarm clock just went off. There are things to deal with in the world, and these issues also must be addressed in the ones you love. Avoid the destructive tendency to manipulate and control, to view them only as extensions of your own influence and identity. Children as well as romantic attachments are the focus of intense concern. The positive approach is to form more powerful bonds by giving up our needs and focusing on the other. Some of you might join a charitable organization and start giving your time for the good of the planet and the faceless human beings who suffer daily.

23. SUNDAY. Unpredictable. As the Moon sashays through Capricorn and your house of work and health, it's a get up and get on with it kind of day. There could be disruption to daily routines and problems in your emotional or domestic life. Watch out for intense workmates who might want to take their bad mood out on the first person they see. You have a kind heart but you don't need this excess baggage. Remember, it is none of your business. Beware of accidents or clashes in the home. Be especially careful to clean up after yourself. Something hidden may come to light, bringing a realization that will affect your spiritual life. There may be a crisis or change with regard to a health matter.

24. MONDAY. Quiet. This is a great day to hang out at home and get your odd jobs done. If you aren't feeling quite up to scratch, stay in bed all morning and enjoy the weekend papers. Look for bargains at local garage sales and stay away from public places where you might be seen. Gardening is always good for the soul. Set up a window box with pretty colored flowers and uplifting herbs if you don't enjoy the luxury of a backyard. Team sports will give you a great outlet for your pent-up frustrations. But release them with skill to enhance your player performance; don't aim them at your teammates. Spectators will enjoy roaring with the crowd as you collectively ride the ups and downs of the game.

25. TUESDAY. Cooperative. It will be shifting sands with your nearest and dearest. If you must air a disappointment or disagreement, be sure to balance it with gratitude for the special things they do for you. There may be unexpected developments or changes of plan. If so, go with the flow. Be willing to talk about the situation and be honest about all your feelings without expecting your partner to accommodate you. By listening and acknowledging each other in this way your relationship will become interdependent rather than codependent. Someone in your life may be in a foul mood; just ride

things out if you can. Any change that affects one of you will affect
the other too.

26. WEDNESDAY. Reflective. Planet Mercury starts a retrograde
now. For the next three weeks you may feel like you're waiting
for things to come together, but you don't know exactly what they
are. Kind of like watching a row of seeds you've planted, you hope
something is happening, but it's hard to tell. Events for you are, in
fact, restructuring themselves behind the scenes, and you may be
in for some surprises when all is resolved. Your best course is to
make as few assumptions as possible and don't bet on the same
old horses. Be open to your own intuitive hunches and be ready to
jump aboard a new bandwagon when it suddenly materializes. It
may come from closer than you think, and from those you might
have taken for granted.

27. THURSDAY. Beneficial. Expansive Jupiter joins the Sun, Mercury, and Venus in Cancer and your sector of solitude and the unconscious. At this time you have a great capacity to learn a lot about
the spiritual and religious dimensions of life. You can also learn a
great deal about yourself without encountering the fear or resistance that you often experience when you come face-to-face with
the aspects of yourself that you consider less desirable. The urge to
help others is stronger now, and charitable work would be very rewarding. An interest in health can lead to further studies and even
to an eventual career in medicine or naturopathy. Avoid a tendency
to isolate whenever anything goes wrong.

28. FRIDAY. Excellent. Venus, the planet of love, is now in Leo,
adding attractiveness and creativity to your attributes. A love of
luxury also comes along with this transit, so watch your budget if
necessary or your expensive tastes can put you in the red, big-time.
Use this three-week period to make peace where necessary and
cement important new relationships. Venus ranks pleasure above
work, so this is also a good time to take your holidays or have fun
with your friends. This is not a good time to start home renovations,
as you are likely to pull down the wall with gusto but run out of
enthusiasm or funds to finish the job. Living in a construction site
definitely won't appeal.

29. SATURDAY. Artistic. Give free rein to your creative instincts
and allow your dreams to find form. You can produce a masterpiece
of style in whatever medium you wish to become involved with.
Take up art, design, fashion, music, or theater studies and enjoy the
inspiration that comes with artistic expression. A decision to follow

your dreams no matter how little security they may offer will build your faith and open doors to remarkable options, if you have the courage to simply let go of your fears. Contact with a friend or relative overseas could keep you busy for much of the day. An Internet romance may deprive you of sunlight. Unplug your mind from the machine and go outside for a while.

30. SUNDAY. Testing. Put principles before personalities today. Accept that individuals are all different and get on with life. Group work can enhance your studies and your understanding of life. Philosophical ideas might inspire your mind and draw you toward a spiritual, humanitarian, or environment group. Your ability to bring people together and take a position in the limelight makes you an invaluable member of any organization. Something unusual is likely to steer you toward another direction in life. Make all decisions consciously and don't let others influence your ideas, otherwise impulsive actions can upset future plans, not to mention your loved ones waiting for you at home.

JULY

1. MONDAY. Problematic. As Pluto opposes the Sun in the heavens, you can expect many confrontations of various types and seriousness to plague your day. For Leo in particular this aspect suggests you would prefer to isolate and shut the world out, but work or family responsibilities are going to force you to deal with everything. Remember to smile and you will feel better as well as send out peaceful signals. Take what time you do get to yourself and go outside for a walk, take a swim, or your enjoy your favorite hobby, sport, or other pastime. Work within an institution might not suit you at the moment. Bureaucratic rules and regulations can make you feel as though all humanness has gone out of your work.

2. TUESDAY. Optimistic. After the problems of yesterday, today should be a walk in the park. Career matters are likely to figure high on your agenda, and some Lions might receive a promotion that gives you more room to work to your own standards and express your talents and creative potential. Work behind the scenes as much as possible, as the space will give you a chance to think without having other people's problems to sort out. You are likely in a very kind mood and could take on someone less fortunate than yourself and try to fix their problems for them. This is okay to a certain point, but be sure that you are helping them to help themselves and you are not just playing the role of rescuer.

3. WEDNESDAY. Accountable. Energy is such that you are more visible and accountable for your actions today. Others tend to look at you for what you've done, good or bad, instead of who you are. It can be an annoying influence if you're not in the mood to explain yourself or to keep up appearances. On the other hand, you could also enjoy some appreciation and recognition, particularly for your more unique qualities. Problems around communication can cause misunderstandings. Instead of getting upset with another, ask them to explain themselves. It could be you mishcard what they were really saying. Dealing with authorities could be difficult. Leave these matters until tomorrow and avoid the headache.

4. THURSDAY. Emotional. Moods are likely to be oversensitive, yours included. Keep to yourself as much as possible, otherwise stay with your close friends with whom you have a mutual ability to understand and forgive. For those of you celebrating this holiday, there may be some upsetting news that comes your way, perhaps an outing being postponed. Before you make an issue about it, ask other people how they feel. Just putting on an emotional display will not get you anywhere today. Make sure you look your best, even if you are just going to a picnic. The chances of running into an attractive stranger are higher than usual, and you'll have more confidence if you know you look good. Also, you may have competition.

5. FRIDAY. Friendly. Your social life begins to pick up pace. Today's events tend to bring to the surface your need to be part of a group or team. You're not in this alone, Leo. Reach out to others, especially those who are more likely to be considered friends, acquaintances, or associates, as those very close to you may not be as available or forthcoming today. An exercise program could isolate you from others, so why not join a sports team. If you like to run, join up with a group of runners who like to travel around and you'll get to see more of your country as well. Otherwise, isolated Lions might look at a self-help or interest group and put some excitement and interest into the dull moments.

6. SATURDAY. Independent. Discussions with an old friend can fall into a blame game and send you packing. Don't start feeling sorry for yourself, as no one likes a whiner, and you'll lose even more friends and company. Asking for advice on a personal problem might not give you the answers you are looking for. Instead, take your own counsel. Use a pen and paper and write down your questions, then jot down all the possibilities you can think of. It won't take long for you to realize what your inner self is trying to tell you. Group efforts could be marred with personal perfectionism. Perhaps you should accept that there is more than one way to skin a cat.

7. SUNDAY. Affectionate. Be sensitive to the needs of others and think about what you can do to help. Join in with a charitable organization and you can enjoy the camaraderie while gaining the benefits of giving. A spiritual retreat would also do you a world of good. Look around for a meditation group if you can't go on a retreat and enjoy the revitalizing effects of this natural therapy. Clarity of mind will dispel your worries and improve your health. If you are stuck at home and feeling bored, get out in the garden and pick up the healing vibes from the plants. Go for a walk at a local park and you'll probably run into a neighbor who will chat with you while you walk.

8. MONDAY. Reflective. With the New Moon in Cancer and your sector of solitude, this signals the start of a new lunar cycle where the focus is on the past year, specifically on what you've been able to achieve and what you could have done better. Some soul-searching is in order now, and the urge to find a level of emotional peace of mind will be apparent. This is a more sensitive position of the New Moon, and it is best to find some sort of peace for the soul in preparation for the New Moon in the first house, a period that is more active and busy than this one. Take your time with any important decisions and don't let anybody push you into something you are unsure of.

9. TUESDAY. Supportive. Opportunities abound today. Take your time and choose your direction wisely. If you are out searching for a job, you might go to your local educational institution and take a look at the courses on offer. A short course might be right up your alley and get you into a job quickly and easily. There are positions in health service and social work that are good moneymakers. Of course Leos love to shine, and a part in a local play will give you confidence, contacts, and fun if you have nothing else to do. Cultivate any artistic talents that you have. The creative Lion is further inspired through creative pursuits, which could also lead to a lucrative cottage industry.

10. WEDNESDAY. Pleasurable. With the Moon joining loving Venus in your own outgoing sign of Leo, you will feel like partying. Dress to impress. Make sure that your personal appearance and grooming are at your usual high standard, and people will flock around you. Choose the circle that you move in and ensure you rub shoulders with the best of the best. You can sell your talents and business credentials now and give your career a boost in the right direction. Having the right contacts always helps, too. Romance is sure to follow you around at the moment. If you have more than one suitor calling you, be kind and consider their feelings. If you let the attention go to your head it might not last long.

11. THURSDAY. Chancy. There are moods and intentions driving all deals, and a situation can change at the drop of a hat if someone gets their nose out of joint. Look, listen, and understand what people are saying with their body language and mood, and you can respond to your advantage. If you try to control a situation it will quickly become uncontrollable. Be happy to play your part and be another cog in the wheel that gets oiled. A strong desire to escape the boredom of your usual routine might encourage you to take the afternoon off. Make tracks to visit a distant friend or relative, but let your loved ones know where you are.

12. FRIDAY. Financial. Money matters are on your mind today as the Moon and nebulous Neptune meddle in your financial affairs. Neptune's presence suggests you should avoid any underhanded deals and stay away from anything illegal. You are not in full possession of the facts and therefore don't really know what you are getting yourself into. Joint resources could become a bone of contention between you and a partner. If you are in business with another, make sure you have a legal agreement to protect your rights first and foremost. Disagreements over spending can flare up between you and your significant other also. Perhaps you should get some financial advice before doing anything.

13. SATURDAY. Imaginative. Mars, the planet of action, moves into Cancer and your sector of the unconscious mind and makes an aspect to psychic Neptune as well. Unconscious behavior patterns could influence the way you assert yourself. Some Lions may experience insomnia during this phase, especially if you are not allowing yourself the chance to recoup or not letting your intuition serve you. Other Lions may enjoy a more active dreaming life, including daydreaming. If allowed to run free, the imagination can serve you very well, especially with regards to goals and new concepts. For those who struggle against drug or alcohol addiction, this is a good time to enter a rehabilitation center.

14. SUNDAY. Hectic. A generous attitude toward friends, neighbors, and family alike will give you a reputation for being kind and loyal. But today you need to say no to the demands of others and treat yourself. Give yourself a reward for being the person you are. Ask your favorite person to lunch with you and spend the afternoon laughing. Romance would be a good way to pass your time and a new lover could be on the scene. For longtime lovers, put some mystery back into your romance and do something different. Talk about your fantasies and explore uncharted erotic territory. A business deal could give you a few headaches, especially when you find you're not the only one with a hidden agenda.

15. MONDAY. Helpful. Social and business communications may require tact and diplomacy. Do your homework and find out all you need to know about a business proposition and the people involved before you get into any deals or contracts. Short trips will be pleasurable, and you might take someone along with you. A new lover might fit the bill and you can find out all about each other while you sit in traffic. Some of you might be putting in the footwork to sell a new business idea and may work on your own advertisement. Talk to your local radio station and get your message out now.

16. TUESDAY. Variable. There are signs suggesting you have extra responsibilities around your home. Home repairs could be in order, and unfinished renovations may need to be completed to eliminate a safety issue. Some of you could be moving and find yourself up to your armpits in all sorts of memorabilia that has piled up in the back of all your cupboards. What to keep and what to discard can play on your emotions. For any major family decisions, get everyone involved and make it a group decision, shifting the weight safely off your shoulders. If you have disapproving parents, don't avoid the problem. Talk to them about it, and you'll find that once you've voiced your fears, they'll disappear.

17. WEDNESDAY. Confusing. Listen to what other people are saying to avoid senseless misunderstandings. You will have to put some effort into paying attention, as your mind is likely to want to wander off continuously. If you have the time to devote to a work of art or other creative pursuit, this day should be one of satisfaction. But if you are trying to do business with the outside world and successfully make your way through the maze of expectation, then it will be more trying. Nevertheless, trusting your intuition can allow you to act on instinct and get it right the first time. Don't be surprised if you enjoy a passionate encounter with a gorgeous stranger along the way.

18. THURSDAY. Changing. Shifts in belief will start to come to a head now, manifesting through a break from or change with people you've been dealing with, or with your current environment. You are likely looking for something that you feel is missing. Although you may take on many different responsibilities, jobs, or relationships, what you seek is more likely within. Make sure you stick to the old adage and give yourself time for rest and recreation. Pursue your favorite recreational activity or immerse yourself in a study project. Take time away from duty and do the things that will sustain yourself for the rest of the week.

19. FRIDAY. Sensitive. Investors beware, as we are in for the same aspects that caused the financial instability two years ago. Trying conditions in the workplace will make your day that much harder. Use your mediation skills and stay in the good books with everybody. When it comes to business deals, keep your money in your pocket and you can't get burnt. Romance is a far safer bet for the Lion. Plan a weekend away with your lover, and if you are hoping to expand your family, this weekend might be the time to do it. Go out to the movies or the theater this evening and enjoy watching the drama on the screen instead of in your life. Take in a meal at a foreign restaurant and give your taste buds a treat.

20. SATURDAY. Excellent. Energetic Mars joins expansive Jupiter, suggesting lots of physical activity. There is also a hint of the spiritual, the compassionate, and the adventurer thrown in. All activities that help those not so well off, such as the disabled, would be very rewarding and give you the opportunity to do something completely different from your usual Saturday activities. You may be working with people of other cultures and have to put up with different brands of prejudice, perhaps even have to break up an argument. If you notice your thoughts becoming judgmental, take a break and walk away. Partygoers need to curtail your drug and alcohol intake to avoid a lesson in guilt and remorse.

21. SUNDAY. Penetrating. Issues around greed and envy can impede open communication. Mercury, the planet of communication, turned direct yesterday, freeing up all forms of holdups, delays, and misunderstandings. But there could still be a lack of clarity around an important issue simply because somebody isn't being honest. When exterior sources fail to provide the information you need, you may have to rely on your inner resources and come to your own conclusions without external input. Try not to tie yourself down on any matter that still isn't clear either, as it might not be as you perceive it to be. Shop at a local market or the secondhand stalls for some great bargains.

22. MONDAY. Personal. Care in spending is advisable. You are especially susceptible to beautiful clothes, jewelry, and art objects to beautify your home, or entertainment to make life more pleasant and enjoyable. The Sun moves into your sign of Leo today, putting you center stage in your own life—and everybody else's, for that matter. Be careful not to bulldoze over the feelings of others, as you are quite possibly much more subjective and forcible than usual at this time. Venus moves into Virgo and your sector of money and values, setting up favorable circumstances for financial negotiations. Borrowing money should not be very difficult either, but don't borrow more than you can afford.

23. TUESDAY. Difficult. Although everything may seem to go along smoothly, Leo is likely to feel dissatisfied deep down inside. Look for inspiration and develop a creative outlet through which to express yourself in a fun way. You have original ideas and should act on them. Business plans can get the go-ahead, and if you have a plan for a business of your own, start talking to those in the know to get an idea on where and how you should start. Listen carefully to people's stories of failure, as you can learn what not to do. Discussions over future plans with your partner could become so watered down with compromise that you are no longer interested. Don't give up; improvise rather than compromise.

24. WEDNESDAY. Rewarding. Hard work will bring results and put you on top of your game. Your ability to impress those in powerful positions will help you win their support and favors. You do need to watch your ego though. With your creative flair it is understandable that you feel a little bit more special than others. But doesn't everyone have something uniquely special about them? Start to notice this in others and you will add to your attractiveness. When all is said and done, you can't fail today unless you expect too much. Take note of what your partner is telling you, as they are familiar with those aspects of yourself that you don't see. Let them know how special they are.

25. THURSDAY. Cautious. Today is not a day to be taken in by appearances, especially where money is concerned, so consider any financial decisions carefully. Put them off for a little while if you can. Don't go on a spending spree either, as you might buy things out of boredom rather than genuine need. There is the possibility that you'll have an argument with your partner over spending habits. Before committing to any long-term agreements, make sure you speak to them first. Even if they are happy with your decisions, the fact that you involved them will make a world of difference to personal life together. Take stock of the inner Lion. Give your psyche a workout and find what it is that will satisfy you.

26. FRIDAY. Disconcerting. Joint business ventures could offer great returns but demand so much time and energy you may start to wonder whether the results are worth the effort. Warring factions within your family could embroil you in all sorts of gossip and intrigue. Stay out of it as much as possible and you will be able to be everybody's friend. A compensation case might necessitate the proof of your injuries beyond the point of truth. The more you start to bend the truth, the worse things might become. Today's lesson is to stick with the strength; honor your own truth.

27. SATURDAY. Unique. Get out and head down the highway today if you can, as you need fresh air and wide-open spaces. If you give yourself a dose of freedom, you will settle more easily back into the harness when it's required. If you can't get across the physical horizon, then head for the horizon of the mind. Open the vistas of your thinking with some new ideas or contemplate doing a course. There is a tendency toward rebellion coupled with impulsiveness in the skies, so watch those spur-of-the-moment ideas. What seems like a streak of genius today can look quite foolish later on. The trick is to choose your company wisely. Take note of an old adage: If you lie down with dogs, you'll catch fleas.

28. SUNDAY. Risky. Stick to your plans regardless of your mood. A tendency to feel like isolating yourself should be avoided if possible. Once you get out and about and mix with others, the stimulation will pick you up and bring with it inspiration and creativity. On the other hand, if you stay stuck at home, depression could set in. A political rally could be very interesting and incite you to become active yourself. Keep it low-key at the start until you know what you are getting yourself into. You don't want your boss or your parents reading about your escapades on the front page of the newspaper. An Internet site can introduce you to people with similar interests from the comfort of your own home.

29. MONDAY. Buoyant. Career, work, and finances should all get a boost today. Some Lions could receive a promotion, which puts you in a position of independence and pays better. Job seekers can find a position that offers the security of a regular income. A new relationship may bolster your sense of personal security, especially if you are moving in with a lover who owns their own home. Emotional issues could be aired publicly, so don't go talking to anybody you don't trust. An older and wiser family member might act as a secret benefactor and pull strings for your benefit from behind the scenes. If you are planning to set up a business of your own, use everybody who's anybody to achieve success.

30. TUESDAY. Brilliant. An extraordinary or unusual spirit of enterprise and great creative powers imbue this day with the possibility of great success. You are capable of tackling big projects and following through on innovations to improve standards and output. Plans to get married could start with announcing your engagement to family and friends. There is the chance that plans can overtake reason and become larger than life, so be realistic with your guest list and ensure whatever you are planning comes in on budget. A promotion might enforce a move interstate, and you will need to talk to your family before you accept the position. Be sure to let everybody have their say and go with the consensus.

31. WEDNESDAY. Tricky. Lions may have trouble balancing the needs of others with needs of your own. Perhaps you're giving too much or focusing on one person rather than another. The pursuit of dreams or goals may have taken you too far away from the people who care about you. Romance is in the stars. Lions who are single and interested in a special colleague should take the initiative; a casual lunch date can't hurt. If you are finding it hard to get your work done, try delegating tasks to those who know how to complete them. Group work will be much more satisfying today. Besides making light work of the task, the discussions that go around can stimulate interest in new and different things.

AUGUST

1. THURSDAY. Busy. Whether you are out and about or relaxing at home, your mental interference can drive you nuts. Telephone calls with hearsay conversations are useless and go nowhere, so make your excuses and hang up. Do something productive with your time and gain a sense of satisfaction at the end of the day. Visit a friend in need and make their day. Take a bunch of flowers to someone you know recovering in the hospital. If you belong to a club of some sort, you are likely to be nominated to a committee position. Be careful of office politics, as it may be hard to stay impartial. Once you air your position you could make a few enemies, regardless of your intentions.

2. FRIDAY. Individual. Use lateral thinking and solve problems effectively. You have the ability to intuit what is going on beneath the surface and come up with unique and inventive solutions to problems. An associate who you've always thought a little strange, can impress you with their thought processes and turn your opinion of them around. You'll be more attracted to the unusual and can do something completely out of character. Insights abound and students will grasp the finer points of a subject and manage to achieve top marks on an assignment. A chance encounter might revive a broken relationship and give your romance new life without the crippling expectations. Travel plans can come together now.

3. SATURDAY. Secretive. Although you love attention and being the life of the party, you are liable to be more reserved than usual. A power struggle between you and a colleague or a friend can cause you to close up for your own protection. Some Lions could be involved in a secret love affair. Regardless of the passion between the two of you, if you have to be dishonest you can be sure that, sooner or later, someone will be hurt. Be honest about it early and leave while relations are good and your reputation is intact. A competitor in the love stakes can test your mettle. If your partner allows this to continue, you should consider that their intentions are based on ego, not love, and look elsewhere.

4. SUNDAY. Low-key. Reserve this day for rest and relaxation. Whatever you plan to do, ensure you don't have to rush and it will be pleasant. Everything points toward the great outdoors for health and rejuvenation. Perhaps you will go on a picnic with those close to you and take in the joys of nature at a local park. Large animals are indicated, and you may enjoy horse riding, a trip to the zoo, or a day out at the race track. You are not likely to make a fortune though, so be frugal with your gambles. Indulge in sharing a massage with your lover; cover yourself with sweet-smelling oils and get lost in the sensual touch.

5. MONDAY. Nurturing. Indulge in a slow start to the day and put yourself first in the scheme of things. Enjoy getting organized, writing in your journal, and being in your own space. Practice creative visualization and picture yourself as you would wish to be. If you remind your subconscious often enough, it might get the idea. The Moon moves into Leo later in the day and, along with the Sun, makes you a real charmer. Fantasy and romance can cloud your better judgment on important matters, so leave decisions until tomorrow. For now, enjoy romance and fun and try not to break your budget as you indulge in your extravagant whims and romantic revelry.

6. TUESDAY. Powerful. The New Moon is in Leo today. It's a time to reinvent yourself in some personal way, such as with a new look or manner of expressing and presenting yourself. This is a personally busy time of year, when you feel energetic and enthusiastic. A project you've had on the drawing board for some time should be initiated now. Regardless of your confidence levels, if you push yourself to new heights, they will rise as you succeed. This is an emotional time as well, so go with it; feel the fear and do it anyway. This is a year of change and now is the time to get started. If you've been planning to go back to school or apply for a passport, put in your application and get the ball rolling.

7. WEDNESDAY. Influential. There is an expression of richness in the celestial sphere. Because the focus is still on Leo, you have the ability to sway others through an appeal to their feelings. An interest in politics can arise from the desire to bring about social aspirations and improvements. Your charisma may be such that you are appointed as the candidate for your group or party. Challenge yourself to be the very best you can be, avoiding pettiness and ignoring the bad behavior of others. You can always change the way you respond to others, even if you cannot change them. Enjoy the attention; you deserve it.

8. THURSDAY. Optimistic. Mercury, the planet of communication, moves into Leo, suggesting an especially fruitful time for any endeavor that requires dealing with words, ideas, facts, and figures. Your demeanor is more youthful, perhaps mischievous, lighthearted, and nonthreatening so that others may be more inclined to turn to you for advice or pleasant conversation. Using the power of words to attract what you want or to further your interests will work best now. There could be someone within your orb of influence who is trying to pull the wool over your eyes, so stay alert. A romantic attraction to one of your business associates can make doing business with them harder than it should be.

9. FRIDAY. Healing. Money matters can go in your favor today. Regardless of the type of negotiations you may be involved in, you should come out on top. This is one of those times when you will get what you need regardless of your situation. Your bank balance may hit rock bottom and then you receive an unexpected refund. A lottery ticket may not be the winner but may still make runner-up and pay a good dividend. Be sure to stand up for the things you value and don't let yourself be swayed by an attractive friend, colleague, or neighbor. A sibling could turn to you for support, so use your connections wisely.

10. SATURDAY. Sensitive. Pay attention to your dreams, as there could be an important message in one of them. Be sure you have a map if you have to travel to an unfamiliar place. Don't trust your GPS unless you have the most up-to-date maps installed. Even then the sky warns of technological mix-ups and communication breakdowns. Check your battery on your mobile phone also, because you could get lost and find your phone doesn't work. The Leo artist will be capable of writing some beautiful poetry and prose. Perhaps you'll write a love letter or receive one from a secret admirer. This is an excellent day to go shopping for a gift.

11. SUNDAY. Receptive. You can use your skill at drama to assume the right mask for whatever situation you find yourself in today. As you are likely to be out and about, expect some surprising situations in which to test your repertoire of personas. A philosophical or spiritual gathering could inspire you to stand up and express your own ideas and understanding. Public speaking will come naturally to you, and even though you may suffer some nerves, they'll disappear once you open your mouth. You may even try acting in a local theater company, as being up on stage comes naturally to Lions. Running a market stall could be up your alley as you put on a show to attract customers.

12. MONDAY. Interesting. Implement time management and enjoy your day without rushing. If you have every move planned, you'll be able to play with your target rather than chase it. Try to avoid getting sidetracked, as your imagination can take you on a wild-goose chase just because something appealed to one of your fantasies. Love and attraction could take up much of your thoughts if you don't stay focused. A family matter will demand your attention later in the day, so you do need to ensure you get your important matters out of the way early. Stay in this evening and spend plenty of quality time with those nearest and dearest.

13. TUESDAY. Positive. Take time out to enjoy the little things that bring you pleasure. As the Moon travels through Scorpio and your sector of home and family, you could be more sentimental than usual. If you have lost a loved one in the past, their memory can be strong now. Allow yourself to feel the pain and grieve your loss. An anniversary could be cause for celebration and can take you for a walk down memory lane, too. Lions living in shared accommodation might decide to move away from petty squabbles and the perfectionist demands of the people you live with. This can be your lucky day to find a place of your own and privacy.

14. WEDNESDAY. Uneven. Conflict between your creative desires and your personal security needs could become obvious today. Perhaps you are staying in a relationship because it feels safe, even though you have to deny parts of yourself to do so. Or you may put on a brave front and accept a position or responsibility because you don't want to hurt another's feelings or let them down. If you start to become aware of personal sacrifices, you may need to talk to a counselor to sort out what is the most important thing for you to do. Some may prefer to look after others first, but if you don't, there is another way. While the Sun is in Leo, it is time to step up to your own plate and enjoy being you.

15. THURSDAY. Fun-loving. Regardless of your responsibilities you can feel footloose and fancy-free today. Perhaps there is a new romance on the horizon and your heart is beating a mile a minute waiting for the phone to ring. A love letter from a secret admirer can give your ego a boost, but don't let the compliment put you off your guard. There are also dangerous types looking out for their own interests in the relationship game. A vacation could be needed, and if you can afford it, now is the time to head overseas and experience other cultures. The desire to broaden your worldview and understanding should be strong, and if you aren't traveling, studies in travel, philosophy, or politics might be a good substitute.

16. FRIDAY. Artistic. Creative juices are flowing through inspiration from friends, family, and your environment. Get out the paper and paints or go to a jam session, whatever your favorite medium for art may be. Home entertainment is also on the cards and you may want to impress your employer or supervisors and have a work party at your place. With the delectable Venus sweeping into Libra and your sector of communication, you are most attracted to wit, cheerfulness, and verbal rapport. You are especially good at mediating conflicts. Smoothing over differences using your diplomacy skills will be one of your strong points now. A love affair with a neighbor is also possible.

17. SATURDAY. Revealing. Important meetings or discussions can produce positive results that are valuable to your future. The exchange of ideas can stimulate your own views on a subject. But you do need a word of caution when it comes to a heated debate on cul-

tural or religious matters. Good friendships can be lost in these idealistic debates. Job opportunities can arise in the mining sector, in
research, in health care, in the army, or even in detective work. Psychological issues can arise for those freshly returned from armed
service overseas. If this occurs, seek help immediately. An effective
treatment for post-traumatic stress disorder is group therapy.

18. SUNDAY. Surprising. Watch your temper at work, as someone
could push your buttons. Instead of blaming this person, look at
what those buttons are. If you honestly assess the fear, pain, or
dishonesty that is creating them, you can be free of them once and
for all. Pace yourself at work because you may have the tendency
to push yourself too hard and even play the martyr. Look after
your health because, after all, you only have one body. Relations
with women can be especially difficult, so stay under the radar if
you have a female supervisor. Trouble at home can be a reflection
of a problem that has been boiling under the surface for some
time.

19. MONDAY. Promising. Let a partner take the lead today. It's not
the best time to act entirely independently or to make executive
decisions, Lions, as you'll find life all the more interesting with two.
You are projecting a warm, approachable manner now, and this can
attract positive circumstances to your life. Any problematic issues
between you and your partner can be discussed openly now. You
should be able to make yourself heard as well as be able to appreciate and understand your partner. Business negotiations also will be
profitable. Problems with a neighbor can be ironed out, but if you
find someone particularly aggressive, you may have to simply agree
to disagree and stay safe.

20. TUESDAY. Restless. The moods of those around you may appear to go up and down today, leaving you confused about where
you stand in their world. This is your number one problem for
today. Don't gauge your value on other people's moods, but gauge
your value on how far you have come toward your own goals. Don't
be surprised if there's excitement or even tears around your loved
ones as the Moon comes to the Full in your opposite sign. The tide
of feeling may carry you along or even away altogether. For some
Lions, there could be a significant development in a partner's life.
For others, you may have dealings with a mother figure or an unusual woman. Watch out for minor accidents.

21. WEDNESDAY. Constructive. Important truths are coming to
light now that can stir up all sorts of unusual feelings, and generally

mixed ones. However, know that what's happening is designed to pave the way for personal changes that truly improve your life. Pay special attention to your intuition, and don't be afraid to pay attention to things you normally sweep under the carpet. A little honesty with yourself goes a long way. An unexpected inheritance or windfall can come your way and help you pay off your mortgage, buy a home, or renovate and beautify an existing one. An elderly family member may need medical attention and you decide to foot the bill. Perhaps you could pass the hat within the family, too.

22. THURSDAY. Variable. Today marks the last day of the Sun touring your sign of Leo, and the Sun will move into the sign of Virgo late this afternoon. Negotiations and business transactions can be disrupted as secret dealings come to light. Ensure that your side of the street is clean and tidy, and an inquiry won't affect you adversely. Someone is out to influence your opinions on an important deal and you need to keep your wits about you. Don't ever underestimate your competition and you won't learn the hard way. The outcome of a lawsuit might disappoint and leave you to rely on your own resources for an upcoming move or possibly some elective surgery.

23. FRIDAY. Adventurous. Your emotional energy runs high today, as long as you feed it with interesting experiences and interactions. If not, you could be feeling a tad restless. Routine tasks will not satisfy you now. You might also find yourself attempting to attach meaning to what you do or to your life today, as a higher purpose is something you're seeking now. Illumination comes through learning, the fruition of a project, or deals that have nice payouts. An idea that you've been working on might blossom now. Advertising or promotional efforts can be successful. The only thing to watch for is a tendency for some to be devious or envious. Overall you're in a friendly and curious mood.

24. SATURDAY. Motivating. The Sun and Mercury both touring the sign of Virgo are lighting up your sector of values and money. Watch out for a tendency to value yourself by what you possess. This attitude leaves you prey to the unsatisfying attempt to keep up with the Joneses. There will always be someone better off than you, so gauge your self-worth on your internal values. Write a gratitude list and suddenly you might feel incredibly rich. Mercury rules the mind and is often called the trickster, simply because the mind can lead us down the garden path. The journey from the head to the heart takes dedication. Once you find love and compassion, you will find peace of mind.

25. SUNDAY. Attentive. Be there for your family today and enjoy the emotional bonds between you. Knowing that you have their loving support will add to your self-confidence to succeed with whatever goals you have chosen. An elderly parent will enjoy a visit from you and give you peace of mind for your efforts. Professional matters tend to work beautifully for you today, as if everything is falling into place. The same is true of personal finances. You have a chance to show your competence in a quiet, understated way, and people in authority will either give you the space to do what you want to do, or they'll show their approval in more explicit ways. Well-meaning flattery will get you everywhere.

26. MONDAY. Good. Your daily routine is the key to achieving your goals on time. Structure your daily chores and relaxation to allow you enough time to comfortably get your tasks done. Pushing yourself too hard will only lead to a breakdown, and life isn't worth living if all you do is eat, sleep, and work. Ensure you balance out your family and professional life for a rich and healthy existence. A personal project could reach the public arena. Leo artists might have the chance to put on an exhibition and finally make some money from your talent. Leo performers may get the opportunity to be seen by talent scouts.

27. TUESDAY. Heartening. Hard work and dedication can pay off with an unexpected pay raise or bonus. Don't let the urge to splurge diminish your profits, though. Although you might think you need something, consider that you have been going without and that perhaps there is a more expensive prize that is worthy enough to save for. You are out to impress the best, and an invitation to a gig where you'll be mixing with the movers and shakers of your industry will give you the opening you've been looking for. Don't let your nerves and senseless fears hamper you. Trust your intrinsic worth and talents and simply be yourself, that way you will know that you can maintain an honest face to the world.

28. WEDNESDAY. Dynamic. Mars, the planet of action, is now visiting your sign of Leo, imbuing you with the impulse and energy to get personal projects off the ground. Mars spends two months in a sign, and during this period your ambition won't desert you, allowing you to cover quite a lot of ground on the way to achieving your goals. Some of you might be dissatisfied with your social life, feeling that your work takes this enjoyment away from you. Try negotiating a different schedule, and if this is not possible, perhaps you need to look for another job. Ask around amongst your friends who have their own businesses. If they don't have work for you they may give you some great ideas for your own business.

29. THURSDAY. Rebellious. Lions are not likely to want to do what they are told. If you are having trouble with your parents, you need to approach them with an open mind. Think outside the box and you might even come to the conclusion that their reasoning is sound. Stop worrying about those cool people you want to emulate and start thinking about yourself and what it is you want. The in-crowd might not like you, but that doesn't mean there aren't a lot of other interesting and amazing people that do. Consider that these other people are happy being themselves and don't need to push their ideas and views on others or set themselves apart. Enjoy being you and discover a new reality.

30. FRIDAY. Rejuvenating. Don't chase the clock this morning. Take the time for the things that are important and start the day on a positive footing. A chance to work behind the scenes will give you the space to do your own thing. Once you let your inner flair take over you are likely capable of some amazing new ideas and designs. Start working on one of your dreams. Set up a drawing board and write down your goals in large letters. Then begin brainstorming ideas and possibilities, you don't have to do anything else. You have started the ball rolling and the momentum will do the rest. Treat yourself to a massage or sauna and enjoy the relaxation and glow of health that follows.

31. SATURDAY. Introspective. It's time for quieter activities and perhaps some personal space or privacy, dear Leo. Now and tomorrow, you are in the final stage of a lunar cycle, and although it generally points to lower energy levels on an emotional plane, it's also a good time for tuning in to your feelings as well as for reviewing the events of the past four weeks. There may be some outside pressure to talk about something that you're simply not ready to speak up about. Let others know that you're not answering because you need time to sort things out first. With your own space you can research your ideas and read up on travel destinations or spiritual ideas that interest you.

SEPTEMBER

1. SUNDAY. Difficult. You'll need to protect yourself as the Moon in the realm of the unconscious brings illnesses and enemies out into the open. You may find trouble brewing with a coworker. Do what you can to help, but do not risk your health, your job, or your sanity in the process. Sometimes you just have to back away after you have made every possible attempt to assist another. Retreat into the company of a trusted friend and enjoy sharing deep insights and inner truths that always surface in times of struggle. The practice of meditation will be helpful, as it allows you to relax and turn off your mind. Go outside and smell the roses. Become one with nature and leave your worries behind.

2. MONDAY. Assertive. Nothing will stand in your way today as you instinctively know which course to take to achieve your goals. A strident supervisor could rub you the wrong way and you will have to bite your tongue if you want to be able to get on with the job. Be careful if you start to exaggerate your abilities or what you can achieve. If you expect more than is humanly possible, you are going to end up losing confidence in yourself and the confidence of those around you. Be honest in all your affairs and watch the satisfactory outcomes that this brings. What you are unable to control, you are likely to ignore. At some point you will have to put an end to the vacillation and make a choice.

3. TUESDAY. Ambitious. You will perform at your best when you have a structured agenda to work by. Athletes and sportspeople might start a new training program with a new coach and find the change gives you a boost of energy and renewed interest. If you are feeling stale today, it might be worth looking for a new course of action to revitalize your inspiration. Focus on your money matters and bolster your personal security. Knowing you don't have to worry about your financial situation will give you a chance to enjoy whatever you are doing. Don't let threatening letters from your bank upset you. Get on the phone and find someone who can help you get back on top. Perhaps an assistance package might help.

4. WEDNESDAY. Persuasive. Indecision over a financial matter, business deal, or large purchase should be cleared up as soon as possible. Speak to someone in the know who can give you trusted direction. New ideas and interests can boost your energy and ambition, but consider those nearest and dearest before doing anything drastic. Assure someone important in your life that the changes you've been making are things that have furthered your growth and that they are still an important part of your life. You may need to do a lot of reassuring and possibly some negotiation today, and luckily you're well-equipped for the task. Listen, respond, and make sure the conversation is going both ways.

5. THURSDAY. Lively. This morning's New Moon is in Virgo, highlighting your sector of money and values. Attunement to and appreciation of the physical world of the senses is the focus now. This is a time to start fresh in terms of how you arrange your life in order to feel a sense of value and worthiness. Financial issues come to the fore also. Setting realistic financial goals as well as formulating such things as budgets and other sensible financial planning projects will be favored during this time. Discovering ways to increase your income is featured. It is also a wonderful time for taking moments of pleasure through earthy, tactile, and comforting endeavors.

6. FRIDAY. Focused. Your actions are constrained by your commitments. Be realistic with your goals and just take one step at a time. If you try to run before you can walk, it seems likely that you will fall. Don't let the remarks of authority figures, such as parents, employers or those you respect, discourage you at this time. Instead just adjust your methods to accommodate any valuable advice you might receive. Remember that everyone is different, and remind yourself of all the famous people who were told they were mad to start with. Lay out your plans, do your research, and wait until the time is right to instigate them.

7. SATURDAY. Exciting. There are sure to be places to go and people to see today. Something you've been waiting on for a while can come about now. A long-awaited party or other social event might be on the schedule, and you've set the whole day aside to ensure you are well presented and prepared for what's ahead. Watch out for expert salespeople, as you might just be browsing, but suddenly they want to give you a discount that seems way too good to be true and you can't let it slip by. Unfortunately, if you're not careful, you can regret this purchase for many months ahead. New associations can introduce you to fun and stimulating ideas. Don't let a chance to be creative pass you by.

8. SUNDAY. Amicable. Warm relations with friends, relatives, and neighbors can make this a fun day. Unexpected visitors can create an impromptu party. Send out for takeout and pass the hat to save you from having to slave away in the kitchen and miss out on some interesting gossip. Some of you might be involved in a local community affair or meeting. This could be about making changes in your local area, such as improving health care, cleaning up toxic sites, or beautifying the nearby parks and gardens. A plan to start a community garden will get the interest of a lot of locals and not only save everyone money on vegetables and health bills, but also beautify your area and bring neighbors together.

9. MONDAY. Domestic. Tending to the hearth, attacking problems from their root, or finding secure and familiar places and people to be with are likely your desires today, as the Moon is in your sector of personal security. You are not in the most adventurous of moods, but others tend to find you nevertheless. Do what you can to find quiet moments and comforting activities to take part in. If you find yourself at home alone, apart from feeling a touch deserted, take this time to get a personal task completed. Leo students will want to be alone anyway to work on an assignment that might be overdue already. Make sure you let the appropriate person know that you will be late to avoid unwanted consequences.

10. TUESDAY. Sentimental. Thoughts from the past can come flooding in as you clear out your old junk and memorabilia. Have a laugh with family and friends as you reminisce on days gone by and take note of how the fashions have changed. If you are harboring a resentment toward one of your parents or another family elder, talk to them about it. Approach them in a rational manner and discuss the problem. If you are willing to listen to their side you might find a middle ground that resolves the problem. Or you might end up receiving an apology that changes you relationship forever. Keep smiling, dear Leo. Expect a positive outcome to all things and watch your expectations come true.

11. WEDNESDAY. Varied. The loving Venus sweeps into intense Scorpio and adds a deeper dimension of commitment in relationships. This is not all good or bad, and it will be wise to understand that some less enjoyable aspects to commitment are there for a reason. Make sure you do what you say you are going to do today. Saying sorry won't fix anything or renew the trust that is lost. An impromptu gathering can bring your friends and ex-lovers together. Although this may seem a little daunting, hold no judgments and you could be pleasantly surprised, as old hurts are eased, disagreements resolved, doubts replaced by laughter.

12. THURSDAY. Easygoing. An opportunity to socialize at work, or with people you normally look up to and think of as out of your league, is an opportunity too good to miss. Dress to impress and don't be surprised if romance comes into the mix. Be open to what people are saying and a very lucrative business proposition can come your way as well. An important meeting or get-together might mean traveling a fair distance. Take a friend or lover with you and turn the monotony into a party. You must avoid being led astray, though. Your friend may want to bring someone else, and suddenly you will have to fit in with others. Be firm with your plans and enjoy the outcome you most desire.

13. FRIDAY. Preoccupied. Strong influences affecting your personal security can take up most of your thoughts. It is important that you do not presuppose a negative outcome and let your fears dominate your behavior. It is quite likely you will be pleased with the outcome, so have faith and take one step at a time. A job interview could have you chewing your nails and sitting on the edge of your seat. Approach this interview as good experience for your next interview and your fears can turn into curiosity and interest. Watch body language and ensure you have your resume in order, and you might be pleased with the result. Someone may try to bully you, but if you simply ignore them, they might go away.

14. SATURDAY. Interesting. New ideas can control your thoughts and entice you to do more research. Visit your local library for most of the resources you need and avoid having to pay for books or magazines. Of course the Internet is another option, but when it comes to empirical evidence it might fall short of the mark. A health matter can influence your diet as you try to find out whether you have an allergy or not. Talk to the naturopath at your local health food shop for advice also. Exercise is the most important aspect of healthy living, but how much and what sort might be your questions. Start a course in yoga and you'll be amazed at how quickly and gently this exercise routine works.

15. SUNDAY. Amorous. A strong attraction can unexpectedly turn into a full-blown relationship today. Don't turn down any invitations, no matter how little time you have. The usual tasks of daily living will wait, although you mustn't neglect your children if you have any. A child could be very demanding, necessitating the use of tough love. This doesn't mean a punishing response; it simply means allowing them to experience the results of their actions. Those of you coming out of a relationship might need to avoid falling for someone on the rebound. Although it will boost your self-confidence and dispel a sense of loneliness, it won't allow you time to heal and may cause it to end prematurely.

16. MONDAY. Fair. Focus today is again on partnership, dear Leo. Intimate partnerships provide emotional sustenance. You might feel a temporary need to have your partner mother you, or vice versa. If you don't have a significant other, you could be yearning to share yourself with someone special. Today, you tend to want to have someone at your side, even if it's just about a trip to the store. For those of you living alone, attempt to have a relationship with yourself. Start thinking about what you can do to please yourself.

Go out of your way to take note of how you are feeling. There may be a creative interest that you've never had time for. You can now do what you want without having to compromise.

17. TUESDAY. Positive. Issues that have been plaguing you on a psychological level can be addressed today and possibly even purged. Now you are more aware of some of the subconscious issues that have you behaving in ways that may seem difficult to control. Self-improvement endeavors are highly favored, and don't shy away at the cost. Anything that makes you a better and more effective person should justify the cost. Relating cooperatively with a significant other in your life figures strongly also. The goal is to interact as equals and to see someone as a whole, rather than focusing on the flaws. It's an excellent day for talking about a private or personal matter so that you both can benefit.

18. WEDNESDAY. Chaotic. Too many people all trying to have their say and do their bit can confuse the matter at hand to the point that nothing is achieved. Delegate responsibility and coordinate efforts for the best results. Many hands make light work when they are working cooperatively. Contact with a distant relative may renew a family matter, as emotions are ignited again. If this person insists on airing the skeletons in the cupboard, you may have to tell them to leave you alone. Your parents can help you out financially and assure that a loan application is approved. See what you can do for them to contribute toward solving any of their problems. Don't lend money unless you can afford to lose it.

19. THURSDAY. Tense. The Full Moon has the effect of illuminating matters that have previously been hidden or suppressed. Today's Full Moon in Pisces and your sector of other people's money and values can play out on the level of finances and shared resources for Leo. Intimate matters might come to a head. Emotional energy is a little bit tense also. Keep your wits about you and avoid undue stress over money, or differences in values with your partner. This applies especially to investment decisions. If the investment belongs to both of you, then you need to be in agreement before a decision can be arrived at. Neither of you should act without the approval of the other.

20. FRIDAY. Unexpected. The moody Moon joins impulsive Uranus, which will give this day a fairly erratic edge. Accidents are more likely at this time, so extra care should be taken. Unfortunately with this aspect, impulsive behavior is the norm, and so to be safe it might be wise to avoid any dangerous pursuits today. Differences of opinion upset the status quo wherever you are, and if you keep your opinion to yourself, you might enjoy watching the interaction of those around you. Disagreement can trigger fear around self-worth, and all rational decision-making might disappear, too. Inventive ideas can come to you, and if you are a student, insight and understanding could blossom under this influence.

21. SATURDAY. Encouraging. Your pioneering spirit is triggered today. Any opportunity to head into uncharted territory, whether it be in a social setting, an educational or intellectual medium, or simply travel to distant shores, you won't think twice. A social gathering can inspire you with debate on political, philosophical, or spiritual matters. The more you learn, the more you might want to learn, encouraging you to go back to school or study online. A chance to work as a travel consultant can sound too good to be true, especially if you will be traveling outside the country as part of your job. Don't get sucked in by clever advertising, as you may be more gullible now.

22. SUNDAY. Motivating. Communicating your ideas may be harder than usual, but instead of putting you off, it might inspire you to learn more about your topic and how you communicate. Gaining clarity of mind can open up new vistas of thought and get you chasing new ideas. You are eager to investigate new things, whether scientific or technical. Today the Sun moves into Libra and joins Mercury in your sector of communication. Siblings, neighbors, relatives, and friends may play a more important role than usual now. You are more interested in exploring your own neighborhood than you are a different country. This is not a time for big adventure-seeking. Rather, it's a time for little adventures close to home.

23. MONDAY. Structured. If you do what is expected of you, you can't go wrong today. A backlog of work could weigh on your conscience, especially if you have promised your boss it will be completed tomorrow. Remember, the more you procrastinate, the worse you'll feel. Get going on whatever jobs you are facing, and later in the day you'll have time for fun. You and your lover may decide to start living together and reorganize your living quarters to suit. Your long-term goals could be changing lately, making you wonder what it is you really want to do in life. Start a journal and jot down your thoughts and ideas as the new you starts to develop. It will be an invaluable reference for you in the future.

24. TUESDAY. Inspired. Leo is well known as a very creative and regal sign. While you are artistic, you do like to be known for your ability to achieve your goals and be successful. Don't let either of these aspects of your personality be your main focus at the detriment of the other, or you will suffer the consequences. Look at the type of people you are attracted to, and if they express either of these characteristics, then you'll know what aspect of yourself you need to work on. A romance can bring out sides of yourself you didn't know existed. Don't be surprised if you become attracted to someone from a totally different walk of life whose exotic personality acts as a powerful aphrodisiac.

25. WEDNESDAY. Tricky. Your plans may have to be changed as hidden facts come to light. You may find that your finances are more stretched than you imagined, causing you to postpone a long-desired holiday abroad. Work together with your colleagues on a business matter and gain a broader understanding of the whole deal. Workplace meetings will give you a chance to air your opinion. Just be careful not to push the establishment too hard, lest you get earmarked as a troublemaker. Even though the Constitution clearly states everyone's right to freedom of speech, you may discover differently now. Get together with friends this evening and let your hair down with other like-minded souls.

26. THURSDAY. Diverse. Divorced or separated Leos may find yourselves on the outs with your partnered friends. Likewise, single Leos may lose a friend to a relationship. Don't let your mind work it up into something bigger than it is. Over time everything levels out, but it is a fact that a common situation aids friendship. Give thought to your hopes and wishes. Try writing them down and sticking them to your fridge, as this is the time when they can start to take shape over the coming month. Juggling funds to keep a new business afloat could be scary but well worth the risk. If you don't take the chance you'll be left wondering for the rest of your life; but if it is successful, you'll never look back.

27. FRIDAY. Secluded. The desire to get away on your own can be strong today. Perhaps you live in a crowded space and need to find another place to live to allow all members of your family a chance to escape from one another. Any outside activities should soothe your nerves and bring peace of mind. If you can get to the beach, the fresh air will clear your head and help a lot of health problems as well. This is an excellent time for study and research, as your mind can delve into all sorts of subjects and tease out the essence of them. Practice makes perfect, and if you are learning a skill or developing a talent, you might gain great satisfaction from your endeavors now.

28. SATURDAY. Relaxed. The comforts of home and good friendship are on the agenda today. Work around your home and on your own self-awareness will bring the most pleasure. Avoid having to go out, especially to crowded and noisy places. If you have a garden, buy some seeds and start planting. This will bring peace and relaxation and give you a hobby that is good for your health and one that saves on your budget. A fantasy novel or a trip to the movies will give you the excitement you crave without the stress. Romance will blossom behind closed doors, and if you can get away for the weekend with your lover, do so. The privacy will enhance your intimacy and refresh your interest.

29. SUNDAY. Dreamy. Mercury moves into Scorpio and your sector of home and family today. Your memory is more retentive than usual, and your thoughts often turn to personal matters, family, and loved ones. It's a great time to open up conversations with loved ones relating to personal matters. A romantic turn of mind suggests you are more sensitive to the moods of others. An interest in spiritual healing can bring out your own psychic abilities and get you interested in tarot cards and astrology. If you are suffering from an ailment that can't be cured, you can alleviate the symptoms guided by an expert in the field.

30. MONDAY. Important. The Moon joins action-oriented Mars in your sign of Leo, which can cause irritability. It may be hard not to fly off the handle if someone wants to push your buttons. You'll be equal to any challenge, and in fact will probably enjoy it. On the other hand, you may come up against quarrelsome people and have to react as calmly as possible and be willing to compromise to defuse the situation. It is a great time to initiate a new project, as your energy levels are high and you are likely to have a high profile in your field. A passionate love affair can upset the equilibrium of your family life, especially if you are a single parent. Bring your lover and your children together slowly.

OCTOBER

1. TUESDAY. Opportune. There are many influences at work today. Mixed messages can confuse the issue, and if you're not clear about your job you could end up with egg on your face. Luckily, a thorough preparation will give you the upper hand and add to your confidence levels. Opportunities can open up in many different aspects of your life during the day, so be clear on what you want and you can make the right choice. Shop for the right outfit, or get your hair done to suit your new image. Popularity can make you far more noticeable than usual and you will want to look the part. Avoid a desire to tell another your problems. Save this until you have the ear of a close and trusted friend.

2. WEDNESDAY. Practical. Get right down to business today, especially in the financial department. Count your dollars and scrutinize your budget. There is a lot of activity in many areas of your life, and although you might only be paying a few dollars here and there, those dollars can add up to a lot. Prioritize your spending and cut back on those things you can do without, if you need to. Issues around the home might add to your costs. Instead of putting up with a problem, why not fix it and then that cost will be out of the way. When buying appliances or other big-ticket items, look around for secondhand products that you can pay for in full and save yourself the monthly repayments and interest.

3. THURSDAY. Positive. All the focus is on the home front or your personal security. Whether you are grappling with debt, unsatisfactory living arrangements or simply having a problem with your personal boundaries, don't keep the cycle going. The more you worry and think about your problems, the worse everything gets. Resentments build up, the fear factor can become crippling, or depression can set in. See someone who you can talk to. A good counselor will help you to find a solution and develop the right attitude to see it through. You are not alone, although it may feel like that sometimes. If you are having problems with your lover, again, counseling will help, as you need an objective adviser.

4. FRIDAY. Energetic. Being on the go, you probably have a million and one things on the boil at the same time. Ease up a little bit today and give yourself some time to reflect on what you are doing and where you are heading. Sometimes we can get off course without realizing it, and now is an excellent time to get back on track. The New Moon is in Libra and your sector of the mind. This heralds the start of a new lunar cycle, which is favorable for learning something new, feeling at ease in social situations, taking care of the details of daily life, and developing a mental rapport with others. It is a time when you will be more aware of your environment, and when you experience increased alertness.

5. SATURDAY. Balanced. With a chance to reflect, you can put your work, home, and social life into some state of order that allows you time for yourself. This is a time of global change, and these changes in the order of things have an impact on the individual. Take what comes one day at a time and deal with what is in front of you and it is sure to just work out. Solutions will arise surprisingly, and further changes can cause some problems to simply disappear. The upshot of this discourse is to tell you to forget your worries and go out and have a good time. Everything will still be there when you get back home. Would-be parents can receive positive news or the birth of a creative project can bring cheer.

6. SUNDAY. Domestic. The Moon joins communicative Mercury, loving Venus, and responsible Saturn in Scorpio and your sector of personal security. Any problems in your domestic life will become more critical now, and anything you have been putting up with but not really handling will have to be dealt with. Whether this requires a simple reorganization of your domestic environment or a total reshuffling of a personal relationship that will affect your domestic life; this is the time to do so. With Venus in this sector, whatever readjustments occur should be positive and healing. The experience of closeness and warmth within family relationships is strengthened also, pointing to a positive outcome.

7. MONDAY. Optimistic. You're filled with creative energy today, especially if you want to change situations for the better or make some radical alterations to your life. You'll soon be looking around for other improvements that you can make. But don't get carried away and impose your ideas on others without consulting them first. A personal or humanitarian interest, or work within a volunteer organization, can lead to overseas travel now. Consult your family about your plans so they can get used to the idea well in advance of your departure. Some of you may be looking at moving away permanently and should take the time to make peace with all the important people in your life first.

8. TUESDAY. Creative. The Moon and lovely Venus move into Sagittarius and your sector of fun, lovers, and children today. This influence creates calm and good relations with friends and family, engendering a strong interest in art, music, nature, and spiritual pursuits. You will want to surround yourself with beauty and may decide to redecorate your home. With delusional Neptune in the mix you do need to be realistic about your dreams. You can't afford champagne tastes on a beer budget, but your creative flair will allow you to improvise and turn secondhand and budget materials into designer goods. You are likely to be critical of a lover too. Be kind; what's bugging you now will be gone tomorrow.

9. WEDNESDAY. Unrealistic. With romantic Venus in hard aspect to illusory Neptune, a strong romantic imagination settles over all, not just you. This idealistic view of love can cause disillusion with the reality of life. Daydreaming is a characteristic of this transit, so be on the lookout for people who are not paying attention, especially when it comes to working machinery and driving on the roads. Turn your attention to the arts and enjoy this romanticism without expecting your lover, a mere human being, to live up to such perfection. If you find that your lover is expecting this of you, find a reason to be unreachable for the day. Pleasure may be more expensive than you expected, too.

10. THURSDAY. Helpful. Pay attention to your health as the Moon joins Pluto in Capricorn and your sector of health and service today; it might be time for a checkup. Escapist tendencies can lead you into bad habits that will undermine your health at this time. If you feel stressed out, reach for your athletic shoes instead of a double martini and you'll be happy with the results. Coworkers could be snappish, but you'll get more work done if you stay away from the water cooler. Let people know that you are busy and will get back to them later. Fortunate developments are in the wind at work, so keep your head down; with today's intensity, you can't fail if you keep your eye on your main goal.

11. FRIDAY. Stimulating. This is a good day to do something different. You are probably bored with the daily routine and would prefer a change of pace. You may seek this not only in diversions but in your relationships as well. Consider joining a club or interest group that will introduce you to a sport or activity you have always wanted to get into, but never had the time or confidence. Then you can meet new people who will stimulate your mind and renew an interest in socializing. Don't desert your job to get out and have fun, no matter how unhappy it might make you feel. You will be glad of the money when it comes to payday. The day promises to finish on a high note with a fun-filled evening.

12. SATURDAY. Frustrating. Be diligent about sticking to your diet or exercise routine today. You need to pay attention to your body's health needs. You'll also need to cover all your bases at work. Don't overlook any details unless you want to pay the price next week. Your friends may be urging you to come out and indulge in excess with them tonight, but if your diet is important, then you might need to revise where you can go and with whom you should go. Stick with those who are like-minded and you can have a good time and look after your health. Relationships become more important this evening, so why not wine and dine your lover at home where you can control what's on the menu.

13. SUNDAY. Involved. Conflicting emotions can tie you up in knots. If you are trying to please your partner, make sure that it isn't at the expense of your own pleasure. Be willing to talk about your feelings also. Don't let the fear that they will react adversely to you speaking your truth stop you from doing so. If you do, you will become a slave to your fears and deny yourself any enjoyment in life. You can have your cake and eat it, too. Just be honest and willing to compromise. A spiritual gathering could inspire you to go on a pilgrimage. The desire to travel can become a reality now that you have a reason and a destination. A home renovation project may need to be simplified to avoid divorce.

14. MONDAY. Idealistic. Your dreams can undermine your plans because they are unrealistic. Don't get depressed because you can't get what you want. Revise your wants and be practical. Look at today and don't go too far ahead, because what's true for today can change tomorrow. A new romance can turn your head around. If you are already in a relationship and you can't get this new romance off your mind, then you need to come clean with your partner. If it is just a passing fancy and nothing happens, then you don't need to hurt your partner with your fantasies, but you do need to reevaluate your own desires. It might be time to move on and let your partner do the same.

15. TUESDAY. Good. Action-oriented Mars moves into Virgo and your sector of values and money today. This can be a very resourceful time when you'll make the most of what you have. You have an abundance of energy for new moneymaking projects or for stepping up existing ones. You may be over-identifying with what you have and own, and you could be trying to prove your self-worth to others, using money and possessions as the means to do so. If conflicts occur during this transit, they are likely to be over issues of ownership. This is a time when impulse buying is at a peak. You probably should avoid using credit right now, simply because your spending habits may be excessive and impulsive.

16. WEDNESDAY. Intuitive. Trust your intuition and let go of old and outmoded behavior. A relationship may no longer serve you, but the thought of letting go may cause you pain. Talk about it with your partner and get counseling if necessary, as with love and understanding you can start to become honest and experience more freedom to be yourself. In fact, you may find that you don't need to leave the relationship if it starts to change for the best for both of you. Growth can be painful, and perhaps you need to acknowledge your inner pain and learn to love it as part of who you are. If pain is merely the absence of love, then loving your pain may alchemically transform your pain into love.

17. THURSDAY. Exciting. You may feel intense pressure as planetary energies clash today. There is no way to please everyone, so don't even try. You may be challenged to put out fires in both your personal life and your career, but the underlying energy is fortunate for partnership. So if you stay calm and communicate clearly, you should have everything under control in no time. Get cracking on creative projects today because they'll go really well. In fact, you could surprise yourself. Whatever you do now, it's time to put your heart and soul into it. If you get sidetracked behind the scenes or need to work alone, make up for it later with activities that require your complete involvement.

18. FRIDAY. Illuminating. The Full Moon is in Aries, creating havoc in your sector of travel and the higher mind. What you believe, or want to believe, and what others believe could be two different things now. Instead of trying to persuade everyone to see things your way, start to look at the different views. You don't have to give up your beliefs, just accept that while they are true for you, they don't suit everybody. Leo students might start a new subject that you find very hard to comprehend. Talk to your teacher and get references so that you can explore it further. With time and attention to your studies, top marks are achievable. A chance to get away for the weekend shouldn't be missed.

19. SATURDAY. Deceptive. Mars, the planet of action, opposes nebulous Neptune across your houses of money, values, and joint resources today. Encounters with others can be discouraging. Be sure that the people with whom you have to deal now represent themselves truthfully. Don't let your desire to have things your own way cloud your ability to see what is really happening, especially with people. Watch communications, as they could be poor with a close partner, your spouse, or a business partner. Look after your health, as your immune system could be weak and there is a possibility for infection. Practice safe sex, since this is an area where infection can be particularly nasty. Solitary activities are favored.

20. SUNDAY. Diverse. Think laterally and you won't get hung up on logistics. A social outing with your family could turn into an important event. You may find yourself rubbing shoulders with the rich and famous and someone might make you an impressive offer. Consider your future goals and ensure that any decisions you make now will fit in with your ambitions, otherwise you will just create another obstacle in your path to success. Worries regarding a parent can be alleviated with a visit. If they live at a distance, then get going early. If you have to fly, then get a cheap flight. Once you can look them in the face, you'll know what to do. Insight into your inner world can be gained as well.

21. MONDAY. Challenging. Mercury starts a retrograde in the sign of Scorpio this morning. The wheels of bureaucracy turn slowly. If you are having a problem with an authority figure, be prepared to go through the process. A legal matter could try your patience, and it might be worth considering settling out of court to save the expense. A conflict between two priorities may cause you to reevaluate what is important. Responsibilities of home and family can tie you down but also give back so much. Show your appreciation to those you love. Once you start to think about others, your own problems will disappear.

22. TUESDAY. Communicative. The Moon is in Gemini and your social sector, so get out and about and swap ideas and gossip. You can start setting up a new venture, or get a new project underway, as your contacts will be very supportive now. It's a day for activity, and you can do everything you want to do while on the move. Take care later on, though. You may hit an obstacle or simply wear yourself out. Negotiations or discussions may be confrontational, but if you are willing to look at yourself, they can be productive. Creating your own opportunity to show off is also likely to lead to success. Don't hedge your bets or pull the wool over anyone's eyes.

23. WEDNESDAY. Intimate. The shining Sun moves into Scorpio and joins chatty Mercury and serious Saturn in your house of home and family. A sentimental approach is more likely now. You will prefer more intimate relationships and want try to avoid those superficial conversations that go nowhere. This is a great time to look inward and get in touch with your feelings. It is also an auspicious time to go on a retreat and spend time in contemplation and meditation. An opportunity to purchase a home of your own could be very inspiring and get you out into the world to drum up your finances and a deposit. Parents and other elderly relatives may be able to help you in your endeavors, too.

24. THURSDAY. Profound. Your imagination is strong and can be very useful in any kind of artistic work or creative effort. Stay behind the scenes and give yourself the space to feel your own feelings and think your own thoughts, as you could be an emotional sponge. If you haven't been feeling well lately, take the day off and enjoy relaxing with a good book or some interesting movies. Escape from the usual and mundane will do you a world of good. A relationship with a woman could be unusually intense and you should not trust what she says without first testing it. Watch out for feelings of possessiveness, jealousy, or guilt. They'll do your head in and destroy any chance you have to heal.

25. FRIDAY. Generous. Positive and lucky vibes hold sway. You can move forward in your endeavors and know you'll gain the support you need. Remember that you will get what you give today, so be kind, tolerant, and friendly to all. The need to be noticed and gain the approval of others could hamper your progress. Trust your own instincts and be true to yourself regardless of another's opinion. Be careful if you plan to sneak out of work to meet up with your lover. There are eyes in unexpected places and you might regret your actions later. Plan a romantic evening and give yourself a treat at the end of the day. Spend a little extra and ensure you both enjoy some luxury to enhance the love.

26. SATURDAY. Easy. Take it easy this morning and make the most of this quiet time to relax. If you have children then get them a movie to keep their attention away from you for an hour so you can do something just for you. If you enjoy cleaning up, that's fine, but don't do the housework if it just seems like more work. Wait until later and get everyone involved in the chores and make your job easier. Your ideas and plans can be put into action now, and the ease with which everything flows might surprise you. Your popularity is on the rise, so get out amongst your friends and associates and don't miss out on anything. You may be lucky enough to be in the right place at the right time.

27. SUNDAY. Productive. The more open and receptive you are to what is going on around you, the more you'll learn now. If you're serious about making big changes to your life, demonstrate your knowledge or expertise in the financial field. You'll get a better idea of what to aim for in the future. There's a strong sense that destiny is holding you in its hand, yet you're also able to call a lot of the shots yourself. There is a glow about you that will attract the attention of others, so discuss your ideas and get the benefit of a variety of opinions. A romantic date should be lots of fun and the start of something big. Don't expect it to get too serious too soon, and you will be certain it is right for you.

28. MONDAY. Determined. Regardless of what you are faced with today, you'll be able to push through and get what you want. Of course you do have to fit in with others, and if you try to override them they will react and quite possibly upset all your good work. Use your social skills and be thoughtful of others and you can avoid these mishaps and still get what you want. Lions could be concentrating on your image and have a certain style that you want to portray. If you find that the shops don't have what you want, why not see a seamstress and have your own designs made up to order. Then you'll definitely make the impression you want. Students need to be diligent now to keep up with your studies.

29. TUESDAY. Assertive. Be alert to the moods of those around you. With the Moon joining with Mars, there are likely to be far more chiefs and not enough braves. around. If you try to take the lead you could be up against a few tempers. Business negotiations can get out of hand, and if you try to push your product too hard you'll lose your customer. A major contract or deal could be postponed and be in danger of falling through. Don't try to fight the current; let it go and backtrack to make sure your business dealings are in order. That way you can't get caught out and you might learn something that will help you on future deals. Take stock of your finances before you borrow more money now.

30. WEDNESDAY. Manageable. Keep your attention focused on the matters of most importance. Distractions can lead you astray and cause you to miss an opportunity that is far too good to miss. Your love of luxury and expensive possessions can set you back too far today. Tighten your belt and keep your eye on the prize ahead instead. Children could be costing more than you can afford if they have too many activities. Cut out those that are not important. They may not be happy about it, but if you have to do it, so can they. Stick with your decisions and don't give in to those you love because of a desire to indulge them.

31. THURSDAY. Friendly. It's a busy day, as you're constantly on the phone and texting, but don't speak before you think; you may reveal more than you wanted. It's best to avoid confrontations with others, especially when you are tired. There are good bargains to be had in the neighborhood. It's quite a good day for expanding your contacts and renewing your equipment. Negotiating traffic and finding your way could be harder than usual. Make sure you have a map so that you can be sure you are heading in the right direction. This goes for assignments and projects as well. If you are a student, talk to your lecturer and fellow students to be sure you understand the question correctly before you try to answer it.

NOVEMBER

1. FRIDAY. Adjusting. The political environment you find yourself in may not suit your needs. Whether you disagree with the way your workplace or home life is run, it might be time to stand up for what you believe in. Talk to your employer about your concerns. If they are relevant and you have thought them out well, you might be surprised with the response. The same goes for your home situation. If you are living with roommates, call a meeting and bring the issues into the light of day. Your housemates are likely to be in agreement with your argument also. If you find the state of the nation the cause of your problems, then get active. Join a group and start to have your say; after all, it is a democracy.

2. SATURDAY. Problematic. Misunderstandings, delays, and breakdowns can slow your progress today. Double-check the facts, watch the traffic report, and speak to anyone in charge to keep you up to date on all developments. The more informed you are, the better your decisions will be. Visitors might call in and fill your home with laughter and debate. Don't let this camaraderie intrude on your plans with those that count, because this is a good time to tend to a neglected marriage, friendship, or partnership. Spend more time enjoying life with your closest companion, and in the end these are the memories that will sustain you. Sure, there may be work to do, but you can still schedule time for love.

3. SUNDAY. Remorseful. Today's transits can activate a sense of guilt about some past event, particularly if you are around a person who plays on that kind of feeling. The lesson is to be choosy about who you associate with. Do not hesitate to question fundamental values in order to get to the heart of what you believe and resolve inner conflicts that may arise. Small insights can net you large gains, particularly in the future stability of your home life. Rock your own boat before others do, and you'll be better off for it. By the end you may find risk reevaluation highly useful, particularly when you depend on others to evolve into what you will lean on in the future.

4. MONDAY. Testing. Stress and pressure may leave you with a migraine headache before the day is over, so take a few deep breaths and give yourself plenty of time to relax and unwind. Think about making a brand-new start. It can seem like the harder you try to please others, the less satisfied they seem. You may need to just walk away for a while. Watch that old resentments don't come into play and confuse matters even more. Find a quiet spot on your own and meditate for a while. Just be where you are, listen to the sounds, smell the smells, and breathe. You might receive insights that will alleviate your stress. This evening, run a warm bath and let your worries go down the drain.

5. TUESDAY. Industrious. Harmonious Venus enters Capricorn and your sixth house and will journey there over the next few weeks, so work or health will be the focus. Do the right thing in one area and this will contribute to success in another. Be clear and precise with coworkers and focus on the job at hand, not on personalities. You are less inclined to fall in love for the sake of love itself during this cycle. Your tendency is to consider whether it is clever to do so. You're most successful doing tasks that involve cooperation and team harmony. You could find that your talents or skills are especially appreciated. Romantic and social activities may revolve around your work environment.

6. WEDNESDAY. Enjoyable. A female friend could be a great help to you today. She may be able to give you a glowing reference for a job you desire. Work in the arts, design, or public relations sector might appeal now. Why not take up a course of study that will aid your ambition and enable you to find inspiring work? Don't let your situation bind you to any particular work or way of life. Think out of the box and believe in miracles; they can happen. A love affair may start to feel like hard work. If you find yourself always having to be other than what you are to please this person, it might be time to tell them how you feel. Resolve to love yourself and be the things you want you to be.

7. THURSDAY. Confident. Set your alarm one hour earlier and have the time to get properly organized for the day. If you like to practice yoga and meditation, then make it your early morning ritual. Some of you might prefer to go for a run, but whatever you do, the fresh air and exercise will make you feel good and give you clarity of thought. You have the ability to recognize opportunities and make the most of them today. The better prepared you are, the better the outcome. A workplace romance may not last, but it is acting as social glue among your workmates. Build your friendships and most of all treat your lover well, as even little misdemeanors will be noticed by all and affect your reputation.

8. FRIDAY. Indulgent. This is a great day to let your hair down and treat yourself. Pay attention to your aspirations and acknowledge the person you are; a little bit of praise never hurt anyone. Leo parents might do the same for your child. Although parenting could seem like hard work, the rewards of watching your child achieve their goals will be worth stretching yourself now. A business opportunity that promises rewards can also come your way. Don't listen to the hype, but accept that it will be hard work and you will be well prepared for success. Look after your health by developing a healthy diet first. It might take a couple of weeks to establish, but it will last you a lifetime.

9. SATURDAY. Restless. The desire for excitement clashes with your responsibilities. Focus on the responsibilities early and you can get away for fun, without guilt, later on. Leaning on your partner for support might be impossible today, as they are caught up in a personal project. Resentments can build and get ugly if you don't express your disappointment early on and find a compromise together. If compromise is impossible, you may have to accept the results of your choice in a partner. Consider why you got together and the attributes of your partner that attracted you in the first place. Perhaps it was their independence and detachment that tantalized and delighted.

10. SUNDAY. Introspective. As retrograde Mercury joins forces with nebulous Neptune it urges you to look inward and reflect on your recent past. Your dreams could be downright psychic during this time frame also, so pay attention to the language of your unconscious mind. Be sure to give your family members your time and attention throughout the day; by listening to what they have to say, you can avoid future difficulties. Even if life at the office seems more pleasant than life at home, remember that you don't have to live with your coworkers. This evening promises romance and communion, whether you get together with some close friends or enjoy a passionate union with your lover.

11. MONDAY. Improving. Now that Mercury, the planet of communication and the mind, is moving forward again in Scorpio and your sector of home and family, many of the problems you've been experiencing these last three weeks will start to clear up. With a little more fine-tuning, life operations will not only get back to normal but improve. Issues having to do with direction and creative focus begin to resolve themselves and turn out to have been only temporary delays, not fundamental problems. Once you have taken care of the last of the recently arisen distractions, you can put your mind fully on the game and get back to being the person you always thought you were, only better.

12. TUESDAY. Fulfilling. Intense and powerful moments will give you cause to pause and reevaluate just exactly what it is you are expecting. This is a great time to look inside and understand what motivates you to put up with people or things that really aren't worth it. Problems in a relationship might be chronic, and no matter how hard you try, the same old patterns keep resurfacing. If you are both willing to work through this, then see an independent mediator. If one of you isn't, then all you can do is work on your own development and self-awareness. Joint resources may need your extra attention and professional advice could be invaluable. Accept that you may not know everything.

13. WEDNESDAY. Daring. Fortune favors the brave and Leo is a courageous sign. You are sure to be willing to take a few risks during the day. If they are calculated risks, it could be the turning point in your career as you align with your true path in life. Everyone has a calling, and the biggest problem most have is identifying what that calling is. This can become obvious to lucky Lions now. Your desire for adventure is heightened and you may do something that you normally wouldn't do. A social gathering can introduce you to new and exciting people, opening up opportunities to expand your creative talents. Travel plans can get a boost through a foreign friend who offers to take you home with them.

14. THURSDAY. Spirited. As loving Venus draws close to intense Pluto you can expect the sparks to fly in romance. Today's energies are about aligning your dreams and goals with your position in reality. You might be surprised at how a seemingly untouchable dream can become a fact, but it can if you let it. Put the things that interest you into your daily routine and make your day an adventure. Regardless of how boring your job may be, you do get time off for a break. So have an adventure on your break. Affection plays an important part in your day, and there may be meetings or encounters that have a romantic flavor to them. Give where necessary and receive what's given graciously.

15. FRIDAY. Stimulating. A good rapport between you and your supervisors can go a long way toward your success. Be willing to listen and follow their guidelines; even if you have a few ideas for improvement of your own, you can incorporate them in an acceptable way, possibly even winning an award for your innovations further down the track. The trick is to be patient in whatever endeavor you are involved. You can meet an influential person in your business dealings today. Look after your responsibilities and you'll make an impressive first impression. A family affair may need your attention and care later in the day.

16. SATURDAY. Challenging. Finding a balance between your public and private life could be rather difficult at the moment. If you have those nearest and dearest complaining, don't get annoyed; give them your attention. By listening and responding with love you might find you have more time to pursue your own goals and gain their support in doing so. Someone older and wiser can give you advice worth taking. Whether you listen and take heed is another matter. Regardless, ensure you take note for your future benefit. Your reputation could be on show in the community now, so be on your best behavior when out and about.

17. SUNDAY. Bright. The Full Moon in Taurus highlights your sector of career and reputation, putting you in the limelight for good or for bad. Put your best foot forward and don't get led astray by your associates, and you can make headway with your plans. You may cancel your plans because of your concern for a child who is not well. Don't let people make you feel bad and cajole you into doing more than you need to. Put your family first and you will succeed. A political rally or other social interest group could be exciting and enlist your support. Be sure you know what you are getting involved in, as there could be expectations of you that far exceed your own. Demand clarity in all your exchanges.

18. MONDAY. Obsessive. Be kind to yourself, as you may have unreal expectations of your abilities today. Your desires can spur you on to say yes to far too many things and overload your schedule and your sanity. Relax and let go if you can. Broaden your horizons and think about others. Do something for one of your friends without expecting anything in return. Or better yet, challenge yourself to do something for another and not be found out. Your social network can get jammed up with innuendo and complaints. Stay out of the melee and keep a clear head. Everyone will then come to you and get insight into how you cope so well.

19. TUESDAY. Pleasurable. This day looks less hampered with problems and promises a clear path forward. You'll make the most of today by mixing with friends and discussing your goals. Revise your strategies and let others be the objective viewpoint that reveals the flaws in what you're doing. The important thing is to enjoy good company and ride high on what can be achieved through teamwork rather than just relying on your own efforts. There's a lot happening in the finance department but the outcome may not yet be clear. This is not the time to be drawn into a pipe dream that's supposed to make a fortune. Apply your insight and you'll be better off. You can hear some invaluable gossip from a friend.

20. WEDNESDAY. Sentimental. Tenderness and concern for those you love will override your other impulses today. Go out of your way to show your love; perhaps you could buy your lover a gift that will surprise and delight them. Any time you get to yourself will be gold, so if you are amongst a crowd, try to work behind the scenes and at least lessen the impact. Spiritual interests could become stronger than usual, and you may seek out esoteric knowledge from books, DVDs, and spiritual gatherings. Don't hesitate to receive some spiritual healing or have a reading from a psychic. Develop a relationship with your spirit.

21. THURSDAY. Low-key. As the Moon slips through Cancer and your sector of the unconscious, you are less likely to want to start anything new. In fact, this is an excellent time to work on planning a project for initiation in a couple of days. The more you reflect on what you are doing, insight and awareness of how to improve your model will become clear. Romance can blossom behind closed doors. A love affair with a coworker would be best keep secret from those at work, and meeting secretly can add a delicious touch to your intimacy. You might plan to get together over the weekend at an out-of-town destination and enjoy traveling together as well. Whatever you do, embrace the experience.

22. FRIDAY. Favorable. The Sun moves into Sagittarius, a fire sign like yours, and will impact your sector of fun, lovers, and children for the next four weeks. It is a perfect time to plan a fun weekend with the kids. Let your creative talents have a free rein and you can surprise yourself with the results. Prepare for your day in a relaxed state of being. You may decide to start a prayer and meditation practice, and the early hours of the morning will give you the quiet space you need. Parents will also benefit from some time alone before the kids surface. Once they do, your love and enjoyment for their antics can be much increasd.

23. SATURDAY. Inspiring. The impulse to get out and experience something different is strong. You may crave emotional excitement through things that take you away from your usual routine. There is a positive energy for making changes in your immediate personal life or your domestic environment. Home renovation or beautification plans can get under way, although they may depart from your usual approach to design. An unexpected surprise can change your plans for the day and introduce you to new associations and ideas that broaden your understanding of the world and your place in it. Someone close could reveal an aspect of themselves to you that excites the urge for romance and relationship.

24. SUNDAY. Expressive. The need to change your place of residence, while seeming like a nuisance, could bring a lot of fun into your life. Cruising around your neighborhood and looking for new digs can ignite many dreams and fantasies that live in the recesses of your mind. What might sound like a step downward on the scale of success might offer opportunities to express the zany and unique side of your character and talents. Remember that gray clouds invariably hide a silver lining and you can see the fortune in all situations now. Socializing will take you places you've never been. An art exhibition or traveling play will be worth a look, challenging you to examine your life in a new light.

25. MONDAY. Nebulous. The Moon challenges illusory Neptune and can bring your fantasies into reality in some form or another today. Whether it is the fact that your mind will grasp the symbols underlying the issues you are dealing with, or the universe is getting its message across, the chance for some enlightenment is possible. The mundane and business side of life could leave you a little bored, but don't relax your scrutiny. There are likely to be underhanded or illegal dealings going on that you need to be aware of. Research your business dealings and ensure you are safe and aboveboard with your actions and maintain a clear conscience. Avoid borrowing money now and protect your future.

26. TUESDAY. Indulgent. Watch out for a tendency toward excess. This is a day to sit around and take it easy; to explore your interests or indulge in romance and good vibes. Dieter's beware because the temptation to indulge in rich food and drink could pack on the pounds and blow any losses so far. On the plus side, single Leo is likely to meet a new lover and start to dream the dream of love and desire we all so desperately seek. Be aware of your inner motivations and attractions such as beauty or money, because these are qualities that can be short-lived. This is not a good day for shopping if saving money is your object. Play it safe and indulge in a good book full of love and adventure.

27. WEDNESDAY. Pleasurable. Finding a balance between work and enjoyment will go a long way toward improving your daily existence. A strong energy toward ambition can lead your desires to focus on your career and business matters, while an unconscious drive to party throws a wrench in the works. The resulting irritation could cause you to get uptight if anyone gets in your way and you'll be too quick to give someone a piece of your mind. Choose your words carefully, however, as this could be the showdown at the OK Corral, so you won't want to show your hand prematurely. Tonight you should take pleasure in your home, whether you live in an apartment or a mansion. Home is what you make of it.

28. THURSDAY. Surprising. Expect the unexpected and you will be well prepared for today. There are influences for change dominating our celestial sphere that can upset political, financial, and domestic structures. Stick to what is important and protect your interests, whatever they may be. If you have to let go of something, then let it go and concentrate on what is left. Change is never easy, but after the debris is cleared away, improvements might be discovered. A growing dissatisfaction with all routine in your life can change the way you feel and influence your decisions. Someone close might go through a change and affect your equilibrium. Talk about your feelings if possible.

29. FRIDAY. Perceptive. This is a high-energy day that will bring insight and enable your endeavors to be productive. It favors the study of any discipline that can reveal new and stimulating aspects of the universe. Subjects such as science, technical disciplines, astrology, and other branches of the occult might come into play. Get out in your local neighborhood and get involved in group activities. You can extend your network into valuable areas for your future benefit and friendship. Leo writers might come up with a fabulous plot for a novel and convince your publishers to give you an advance to get you going. Travel plans may need to be revised to avoid political unrest in your destination.

30. SATURDAY. Inventive. No problem will get in your way today. Your positive outlook will enhance your ability to improvise and find a solution where normally there is none. Take on a challenge that has always excited you but has been postponed by fear. Fortune favors the brave today, and Lions are famous for it. You will find it is easy to understand others without the need for words. You may even experience telepathy. Even though it is hard to express what you want to say verbally, body language and subtle nuances should be exceptionally clear to you. Listen to what your heart is saying and don't pay much attention to the voices in your head. A deep and meaningful conversation can clear up a problem.

DECEMBER

1. SUNDAY. Beneficial. Go with the flow and accept what is. Luck is on your side and a worrying situation can turn very positive. A friend from the past might reappear and pay back a debt you had given up on ages ago. The less you try to impress others, the more enjoyment there is to be had in social gatherings. You are willing to offer emotional and physical support to anyone who needs it now. People will warm to you and you will get exactly what you give. A romantic alliance may be problematic because you have put your lover up on a pedestal. Try to see them as they truly are: merely human. Relax and accept that perfection is simply a construct of the mind.

2. MONDAY. Entertaining. A delightful day where your desires harmonize with your situation and work will give you great pleasure. What appears to be an ordinary day can bring a breath of fresh air. A new coworker can put fun into the work routine and there may be jokes and laughter to help pass the time. A romantic spark can ignite into full-blown passion over the lunch table in the break room. Watch what you get up to, because it could become public knowledge and also make you the brunt of future jokes. Beautifying your home is a great way to bring a positive change and lift your mood. Hunt around for bargains and combine them with your creative flair for a unique style.

3. TUESDAY. Expressive. The New Moon in Sagittarius initiates a new lunar cycle with the focus on fun, lovers, and children. Over the coming month you may have to redefine your idea of pleasure to suit your situation. Some Leos may become parents for the first time and find the adjustment to life with a baby takes more of your time and energy than you had imagined. A new creative project can get off the ground and force you to put yourself out in the public arena. Artists can get the chance to exhibit your work and grapple with a perfectionist streak that tells you to do better. Pride is the number one stumbling block to Leo self-confidence, so accept that you are only human and enjoy being you.

4. WEDNESDAY. Potent. Tread carefully. For every action there is a reaction, and if you are aware of what you are doing you can achieve much. If you have been ill, now is the time to change your diet and exercise routine to benefit your health and fitness. Exercise is known to be the cure for many diseases, but that doesn't mean busting your gut. Yoga, tai chi and Pilates are all gentle but very effective, and if you are recuperating, these methods are much more suited for a weak system. Love and affection are also good for your health. If you live alone, get yourself a pet. Perhaps a dog that you have to take for a walk. If you are in an unhealthy relationship, do yourself a favor and consider leaving.

5. THURSDAY. Cooperative. Today promises love and success if you are willing to put in the effort to achieve it. The downside of this energy can be an attitude of laziness and expecting something for nothing. Whatever field of art you are interested in or involved in is favored for Leo. Don't put this part of yourself on the back burner and play the martyr. Get into a project you love and reap the rewards. Some of you might go into partnership with your lover, and while you are in the honeymoon phase of the business, ensure you set it up legally and protect both of your interests for a fair and equitable base on which to grow. This evening looks ripe for a romantic finish to an enjoyable day.

6. FRIDAY. Distracting. Your business interests can take you away from your family. Watch that you aren't thinking about your personal projects while involved with those nearest and dearest. Put all thoughts of business aside and be present. Those around you are sensitive enough to realize whether you are there for them or not, and if you neglect their needs you'll pay the price later. If your partner seems detached, talk to them. They may have a problem that you can help them with. Try to work with people rather than against them, and choose options that are for the good of everyone concerned and not just you. Your creative talents will help you in all sorts of complex situations. Trust your instincts.

7. SATURDAY. Favorable. Mixing business and pleasure can be an uplifting experience. The lines between colleague and lover can become blurred as a strong attraction is expressed outwardly. There is nothing wrong with this, just try to keep the business part separate from the relationship part. A social event will be a great way to enjoy time out with your significant other. Agree to leave your domestic troubles at home and just enjoy the fun as it comes today. Helping out a sibling may involve looking after a niece or nephew almost full time for a while. If you have children this is well and good, but otherwise don't let your sense of responsibility stifle the development of your own potential.

8. SUNDAY. Idealistic. Be realistic with your ambitions. As Mars moves into Libra and your sector of communication, it makes contact with nebulous Neptune, clouding your intentions with romantic and imaginative thoughts. This is a good time to get those letters, memos, and faxes out and to make those phone calls. Your ability to express yourself in a sensitive, poetic, and imaginative way will enhance your writing ability as well. Extra energy will be available also for running errands around the neighborhood. If you already have trouble with siblings or neighbors, be careful when conversing so as to lessen the chance of arguments developing.

9. MONDAY. Expansive. Although you are more impressionable than usual, you can take the images and ideas you are receiving from others and turn them into your own unique creations. After listening to your colleagues talking about their ideas, you might get an idea for a surefire business deal that you can sell to all of them. Consider forming a company and your associates will have the incentive to put in as much money and effort as you do. If you are suffering grief from the loss of a loved one, you might decide to go along to a group meeting with a renowned psychic. The message you receive might relieve a portion of your pain and bring some peace back into your existence.

10. TUESDAY. Adapting. Certain situations may force you to moderate your ideals and goals today. Don't worry about this. Accept the reality of the situation and allow your creative flair to make a profit out of a loss. A love affair may come to a close as your lover leaves on an overseas trip. If it is not possible for you to go too, then keep in contact but give them their freedom. As that famous line states, if you love someone, set them free, and if they come back it is meant to be. Work on building good karma and do a good deed for someone in need. By focusing on someone else you can escape your own problems. Volunteer some of your free time to your local community and make a difference.

11. WEDNESDAY. Good. Jupiter and the Moon are dancing for you, so the crazy patterns of the past few days are starting to fall your way. Good news regarding excellent prices for foreign products or travel is in the wind. If you can't focus or concentrate on what you need to do, don't overreact or get too emotional. Humor is the best solution here; try to see the funny side of things. Stress can increase as the day progresses, so you'll need to release energy through a healthy outlet. Take the stairs and walk whenever possible. Sexual tension is also begging for release; the sparks between you and someone intriguing are about to start a fire. Focus on your goals and avoid scattering your energy.

12. THURSDAY. Unusual. The wide-open spaces and the far horizon are calling, so if you possibly can, get out and expand the vista of your life. If you can look to the distance, there's a new light to guide you. If you're bound by routine or work, try to break up the pattern of the day somehow, even if it's just by doing things in a different order. Have a go at a different style of cooking to give the mundane a touch of excitement. Visit a new shopping center or something different such as a bazaar or marketplace when you go shopping. The chances that you'll pick up some unique or hand-crafted gifts for the festive season will be much better. Buy what you can now and avoid the mad rush later.

13. FRIDAY. Conservative. The motivations of others could become clear to you. This will enhance your business skills and enable you take a position as leader. Don't be shy when it comes to pointing out where others can improve production. If you do so in the right manner, people will see it as encouragement rather than discipline. A promotion could be forthcoming, as your employer can see your potential and will want to secure your loyalty for the future. Negotiate your terms and you will both be happy with the arrangement. Organizing a social event could take up a lot of your time, but if it is for an important family celebration, you will want it to be the best. Lions will outdo themselves now.

14. SATURDAY. Unpredictable. Responsibilities clash with fun and creative projects, so get your chores over and done with early. The longer you put things off, the longer you'll feel the stress. Children can be demanding, and you might find their extracurricular activities are stretching your already tight budget further. Call a family meeting and put the facts on the table; even small children can understand what making a choice is all about. Once you know what is preferred then you can focus on that and maybe get them all working on the chores to make everyone's life a bit easier. Nothing is impossible today, you just need to focus on the problem and trust that there is a solution.

15. SUNDAY. Social. Good vibes exist between you and your friends, relatives, and neighbors. Don't turn down any invitations, as you might find your expectations were completely off track. Someone who you have known for a while but never really gotten close with can surprise you and move into a more intimate place on your list of friends. Take the family for a drive if you haven't got anything to do and go see a distant friend or relative. The change of scenery will do you good and put some excitement into the day. Some of you might be selling your home and decide to have an open house. But don't get too excited about any offers you receive until the purchaser has their finances approved.

16. MONDAY. Emotional. Rational logic might be a scarce commodity today. Try not to get into heated debates on subjects such as politics or religion. Instead talk about possibilities for have fun, create art or music, and share experiences. Talking can help someone suffering grief or loss to ease their pain, and everyone can gain by their experience. If you are in the process of organizing a family Christmas, it is not a good day to get a positive response. Instead throw your ideas into the family arena and allow a couple of days for the responses to come in. It could end up being totally different from what you initially planned, but that doesn't mean it won't be as good. In fact it might be better.

17. TUESDAY. Illuminating. Today's Full Moon is in Gemini, highlighting your sector of associations, hopes, and wishes. This influence will disclose the role you play in the lives of those you care about. What you think another needs might not be the case, so be open to listening to those close and learn how best to be a good friend, lover, or parent. A community event in need of volunteers could be a good way for those of you who feel lonely to become part of the community and make new friends. Mutual need is highlighted, and if you would like some help then be willing to be of help to another. A profit from a business venture may enable you to make a donation to a cause you care deeply about.

18. WEDNESDAY. Challenging. Keep a tab on your resentments and avoid conflict. If you don't play the martyr you won't feel used and abused by others. Stand up for your rights and have your say for a fair shot. You are likely to want to stick up for the underdog as well. There may be bullying going on in your workplace and you'll want to put a stop to it. If you feel that your supervisor is turning a blind eye then contact human resources. Objectivity could be a scarce commodity in any discussion, so don't push your point. Better to let a matter slide until later today than lose a friend or a job over it. Meditation is your best medicine today. Get away on your own; go for a walk outside and breathe.

19. THURSDAY. Tricky. Stay under the radar at work and avoid criticism you don't deserve. A colleague will give you a hand when you least expect it and renew your faith in humanity. Be willing to help others and you will receive rewards of another kind also. If you have to take time off work due to illness, make sure you rest so that your recovery isn't hampered. There may be many tasks to get done at home but they can wait until you have recovered fully. If you have had to leave your job due to a health concern, look into studying while you are laid up. Even if your outlook looks hopeless, there is a pot of gold at the end of the rainbow. All you have to do is have faith and miracles can happen.

20. FRIDAY. Improving. The Moon moves into Leo and shines its loving light into your life, bringing nurture and joy. Take pleasure in small things and watch your enjoyment in life expand. You have a particular talent that is worth developing. Look around for a teacher within your neighborhood and you can find someone who is willing to pass on their knowledge and expertise for a small price. A large social gathering might involve you in extra work and activities with others. This will bring luck and chance encounters with beneficial contacts and expand your social network considerably. Love and romance are part of the mix, but watch out that joint resources are distributed fairly.

21. SATURDAY. Important. The Sun moves into Capricorn and your sector of work and health, suggesting an auspicious time to start a new diet and exercise regime. Take pride in your work now and everything you do will be that much better. Venus, the planet of love, turns retrograde and appears to move backward across the sky in Capricorn also, highlighting the everyday care of the smaller necessities in life. You may feel you are not gaining the attention you deserve, but then maybe you haven't asked for what you truly want. Consider taking better care of yourself, eating what truly satisfies, and turning the necessities of the daily grind into opportunities for ever-evolving accomplishment.

22. SUNDAY. Stressful. Too many things to do and not enough time to do them in can make you late and put you behind schedule. Prioritize your activities before you start and once you get the main jobs done, the lesser ones will either get done or they won't. Whatever happens, you won't have to worry so much. A get-together could be fun, but watch out if the drinks start flowing too freely, loosening lips and other desires. Better leave on a high than stay for the low. In-laws could upset your plans and let you down. Make sure you contact them early to confirm your arrangements, as help is in short supply, and you won't have to worry.

23. MONDAY. Exciting. The stress levels are building at this hectic time of year. No one is immune from this collective frenzy, so you might as well accept it and find ways to relax whenever you can. Try getting a massage on your way home from work as a simple way to leave your problems at the office and arrive home refreshed. Leo is the best organizer of the horoscope, and you are sure to be well prepared for the festive season by now. But this doesn't mean you won't have a few upsets brought on by another's disorganization. Someone can stand you up for an important date. Be flexible and ask another; you'll still have a great time. Travel plans can be upset by an airline issue. Just remember to breathe.

24. TUESDAY. Constructive. Spending while balancing your budget can be your main focus for the day. Sit down before you go anywhere and take a look at your financial position, that way it will be easier to stay in the black. If you have gone into the red, don't let that act like a red flag to a bull and spend even more. Slow down and you will be very pleased with yourself later on. There is a very real chance of accidents occurring. Watch yourself when handling machinery, while traveling on the roads, or while playing sports. Arguments could excite your competitive spirit, so avoid heated debates and keep your friends. News from overseas could surprise and delight.

25. WEDNESDAY. Merry Christmas!. Unexpected events are likely to upset your plans, but may improve your day more than you ever imagined. Visitors from a distant place can surprise and delight and make for much excitement and discussion. Family gatherings are likely to be full of high-energy exchanges, affection, and joy, but with a touch of family competition thrown in for interest. Some of you may be traveling on this day and should be prepared for unexpected delays and holdups. Do watch out for the overuse of drugs and alcohol, as interesting discussions can turn into arguments. Delegate the chores and avoid missing out on the fun while playing the martyr in the kitchen.

26. THURSDAY. Mixed. Planetary energies clash today, so ensure you have a quiet place to relax and avoid frustrating communications and stressful interaction. Take the day off and play with your children, romance your lover, help your parents, or just simply indulge yourself in your favorite fantasy. If you are involved in group activities, listen to others and keep your own counsel, that way you can act as mediator rather than victim or aggressor. Misunderstandings are likely unless you are willing to compromise and accept the shortfalls of others. If you have to go to work today, you may end up shorthanded and have double the work to do. Eat a good meal before you leave and practice smiling.

27. FRIDAY. Relaxing. After the buildup of tension over the last few days, the mood is starting to relax and calm down now. Time spent with family members will be supportive and enjoyable. This is the perfect time to get rid of all your leftover Christmas fare and gather the clan for reflection on the past year and the focus for the coming one. A solution to a long-term problem can be found and older relatives are likely to be very helpful. House hunters will be lucky to find a place that suits your family needs and is close to work as well as in your budget. If you are moving, enlist the help of family, friends, and neighbors. .

28. SATURDAY. Positive. This is a marvelous day for making some powerful and long-lasting changes to your life, especially if these will affect your financial arrangements or a close relationship. Changes you make now are important and perhaps rather daunting, but it will be liberating to take charge of situations that have worried you. The home fires could get out of control today and you may find that you are saying all the wrong things to certain family members. It could also be that the emotions of others are getting on your nerves. Get out of the house and do your own thing somewhere else. The chance to do something you've never done but always wanted to do could come your way now.

29. SUNDAY. Spirited. The Sun gets involved in a powerful clash with planetary titans today. This influence can bring global problems into stark relief for all. You might find yourself caught up in a community matter that until now you have managed to avoid. There may be no other option but to roll up your sleeves and get involved. Your electric bill could be off the Richter scale and get you involved in the global warming debate. A family holiday might seem more like hard work as you spend most of your time cooking, cleaning, and driving your kids around. Look after your own health and peace of mind and ask them to do a few things for you in exchange to make sure you have a holiday, too.

30. MONDAY. Analytical. Try not to overanalyze everything and find problems where there aren't any. Use your mental powers to learn about interesting hobbies and skills and be constructive instead of destructive. This is not a good time to talk about relationship problems, although they may seem glaringly obvious right now. Be happy to do your own thing and allow everyone to have the space to do the same. This is an excellent time for would-be writers to start practicing. Perhaps you might find a writer's festival to attend, where you can listen to established authors talk about their experience. Share your problems with a like-minded soul and get some productive feedback.

31. TUESDAY. Significant. Deep thinking is likely today. Instead of just thinking about something, you'll want to delve into the psychological makeup and want to know why. Use this energy positively and turn to research and study. Talk to someone with interesting ideas and broaden your own understanding. Workplace relations are likely to be difficult to say the least. Hidden agendas can cause disagreements and resentments. Watch and listen if you want to understand a situation. Evaluate who benefits and gain a valuable insight. Stay away from dangerous situations tonight. If you are getting together with others to celebrate the New Year, do so with trusted friends and family in a safe place.

LEO
NOVEMBER–DECEMBER 2012

November 2012

1. THURSDAY. Adventurous. An inner restlessness may be due to a subconscious urge to escape your present situation. Reflect on your motivation for getting away and you might be able to address an underlying problem once and for all. Group activities can bring out your leadership skills, as your enthusiasm and energy are bound to be contagious. However, it may be all too easy to get things started without the ability to see it through. Make a plan, set a reasonable pace, and stick to it. An unexpected invitation might be the start of an important love affair for single Leos, although partnered Leos might feel that your love affair is a bit stale. Spice it up with fun and surprise your lover tonight.

2. FRIDAY. Buoyant. Serendipity will turn what's boring into something very interesting for the partygoing Lions. A chance meeting with a friend might change the course of your whole day. Some of you might find the answer to a personal problem while overhearing a conversation on the subway. Be prepared for opportunities to arrive unannounced and you won't miss the chance of a lifetime. Make time to lend your shoulder to a friend in need; even if you have to postpone an engagement, you will be glad you could be there to lend support. Make sure you return all calls and answer important e-mails. A sense of achievement will add to this beneficial day.

3. SATURDAY. Thoughtful. With a lot on your mind, this is a good day to organize a few hours alone. Take the morning off to sort through your private business and reflect on your next move. Although you may feel like asking for advice, your conscience will give you the best advice. But you might not want to listen. Be brave and try anyway. Tune your radio to easy listening while negotiating heavy traffic or making a long road trip, and let your mind drift. Peace will come when the incessant babbling of your mind shuts down for a while and blesses you with a moment of divine silence. Don't avoid a colleague who has disagreed with you. Practice compassion and let go of the need to be perfect.

4. SUNDAY. Relaxed. Although your schedule for today is sure to be pretty hectic, you are more likely to take the easy way out and feign a headache or some such. A personal project or hobby is bound to be of more interest, and you can lose hours while absorbed in an enjoyable creative pursuit. Don't worry about anybody else. Some days you just need to take a break, and now is a perfect time for it. Outdoor activities may also be beneficial. Get your body moving. If you have a family to entertain, a trip to the seaside or the hills could be a great idea. At least everyone will be enjoying themselves, and in the midst of the fun you can let the enjoyment of your happy clan wash all over you.

5. MONDAY. Reclusive. Regardless of whether you are sick or not, you might take the day off and curl up away from the hustle and bustle of the outside world. Be lazy and do whatever takes your fancy. Leo sailors may be planning a sailing trip, stocking up with supplies and ensuring your survival kit is intact and safely stowed away. If you are saying good-bye to loved ones, keep it private so that you will have the time to say what you need to, before it is too late. An elderly relative who lives in a rest home might be glad of a visit; taking the time to cheer them up is sure to have its own rewards. You may have to help a sibling find a job.

6. TUESDAY. Rejuvenating. You can hold your head up high as the Moon lights up Leo and your house of personality, helping to restore your emotional strength and courage. You won't have to say much to express yourself, but do be aware of your tendency to wear your heart on your sleeve. This is a great day for being a little spontaneous and crazy; why not do something you have always thought would be fun. Take a ride in a hot air balloon or go for a picnic with friends for a nice change of pace. By evening your mind will be back to business, so have fun while you can. A decision to move house could be based on many practical reasons, but if you can't find anything better, try staying put and adapting.

7. WEDNESDAY. Excellent. The focus is on your personal appearance and preferences. Take stock of what is no longer needed in your daily life and make the appropriate changes so that you have more time for the things that you now want more of. Enjoy shopping for trendy items to keep you up to date and fashionable. A sporting interest may have moved up a notch into team competition and you now have to purchase your uniform. If you are shopping for a child's sporting clothes, check with their club first, as they often have secondhand uniforms at half the cost. Lions should apply for a promotion. As your charm and magnetism rise, it might get you past a contender with better credentials.

8. THURSDAY. Strategic. This is an excellent day for buckling down and getting back to business. Organize yourself with a plan to get ahead of your competitors and you will have a planned response for anything untoward that occurs. The chances of an unexpected bargain coming your way are high. Be ready, and if you need a big-ticket item at the moment, check out all your local wholesalers, as you might be lucky enough to find one in liquidation. You won't know, though, if you don't go. If you work from home or run a home office, look into updating your computer hardware and software. You might find something that will make your job a lot easier or perhaps enable you to have one less employee.

9. FRIDAY. Slow. Today is one of those days when there is no substitute for hard work, and self-control might not be readily available. Put your head down and tail up and get the worst of it out of the way. If you put it off you will only prolong the agony. Someone may be particularly unpleasant and rude toward you. This may have something to do with issues of finances or ownership, so it would be wise to be honest and up front in these departments, and you will have nothing to worry about. If you have been biting your nails waiting for the right time to ask for a raise or a promotion, do it now. The answer should be positive, or at very least give you hope!

10. SATURDAY. Changeable. As the Moon opposes erratic and electric Uranus, all sorts of upsets can excite you or stress you out. Life is what you make it, they say, and maintaining a cautious and positive attitude will go a long way to ensuring you have fun today. A new interest might take you out of your comfort zone and get you mingling with foreigners and people from different walks of life. A love of philosophy can grow from sharing different perspectives and gaining insights and understandings you would have never had if left to your own experience of life. Watch out for your inner rebel or reactionary, and you won't do something you might live to regret. Otherwise you can expect fun.

11. SUNDAY. Pleasurable. Social outings are likely to put single Leos in touch with someone very attractive and alluring. Partnered Leos might find your relationships deepening with passion and desire as your communication moves to an intimate level that surpasses what you had before. Even a lover's quarrel can have a positive effect by turning a passionate love affair into a blazing fire. Compassion and empathy are also on the agenda, and watch out for someone who might need a helping hand. Community work could take up a few hours of your time and put you in touch with interesting people, sharpen up your skills, and allow yourself to make a difference in somebody's life.

12. MONDAY. Tiresome. Property matters could be problematic, especially if you are trying to divvy up the joint possessions of a deceased relationship. Rather than seek to remain friends and allow emotions to interfere, treat this aspect of separation purely as a business matter and make life easier for yourself. Remember, if you were able to get along and cooperate with and understand each other, you would probably still be together. Childhood complexes could be at play on the domestic front, regardless of age. For those of you who live in a shared house, it might be a good idea to batten down the hatches and stay out of the way of your roommates, at least during the morning hours.

13. TUESDAY. Cleansing. The New Moon is in Scorpio and your sector of home and family, suggesting it might be time to add beauty and revamp yourself, both inside and out. If you have been putting off beginning a regular spiritual practice, now is the time to begin. This lunar cycle is about integration; take what you have learned and find a way to apply it to your own life. This is also a good time to stop and take inventory of your own feelings, needs, and dreams. Meditative practices can be especially beneficial to this process. Make long-range plans for the future now, such as reorganizing or even remodeling your home, and for family-related activities.

14. WEDNESDAY. Imaginative. A dreamy morning can get the day off to a slow start. Emotions might not make your life any easier, as someone or something pushes a button on past hurts or resentments. It might seem a little like déjà vu, but as the day gets underway the craziness will straighten out and you can start to feel human again. If you find this behavior in your partner rather than yourself, give them a wide berth early. Don't get too excited over a love letter in your inbox or mailbox; be cautious until you find out whether this anonymous person is safe. A teenage child may need extra attention; plan activities that encourage communication.

15. THURSDAY. Heartening. The celestial sphere makes happy contacts while the Moon sets off your sector of friends, romance, and children. This is your creative sector as well, and Leo artists and designers might turn out some marvelous and unique work at the moment. Opportunities are likely to open up unexpectedly due to your individual talent, so don't feel shy about taking all the credit. You deserve it. Romance is also highlighted and singles should say yes to any blind dates that someone plans. Remember that your friends know you well and wouldn't set you up with anybody they wouldn't expect you to like. Young couples wanting to start a family might receive good news today.

16. FRIDAY. Busy. Activities that benefit your well-being and efficiency are favored. If you are having trouble staying organized, get out to the office supply store and find organizers, dividers, calendars, and storage compartments to help you get on track. Sort out your timetable for efficiency and factor in time for your exercise routine and other healthy habits so you can maintain a proper balance in your working day. If you have been up against backbiting and gossip in the workplace, why not ask one of your nicer colleagues to have lunch with you and start chipping your way into their heart. You can work through all of them one by one and eventually have a few work friends to make the job more fun.

17. SATURDAY. Energetic. Your ability to work hard is higher than usual, as Mars the action planet now occupies your sector of work and health. You may have to tone down an independent and bossy streak that comes along with this transit, otherwise you could step on too many toes for comfort. Leo self-starters can get a business off the ground with your ceaseless motivation to achieve. Health issues can arise through overwork or accidents due to overenthusiasm. Another cause of disease now may be emotional upsets, as anger and frustration are more prevalent. Emotions are an energy force, and without an outlet the body's chemicals can cause harm. Physical exercise is a perfect solution.

18. SUNDAY. Domestic. There is a significant focus on your home and family at the moment. But whether you are tending to your chores, renovating, or visiting relatives, keep your partner central in whatever you do. Make them feel appreciated and desired and you can enjoy the duet approach. You may be looking to purchase a house and are on tenterhooks waiting to see if your offer has been accepted. Or you need to sell the present house before you can go ahead with the purchase of a new one. One thing is for certain, it won't happen until the time is right. Until then your lesson is to appreciate who you live with and where you live right now. Have a garage sale and get rid of the junk first.

19. MONDAY. Surprising. The intuitive Moon blends well with unpredictable Uranus and generous Jupiter, making spontaneity pleasurable. Romance is aided by your willingness to be flexible, so allow for plenty of leeway in your schedule. Who knows what a romantic lunch could lead to? Keep your options open. Even married Leo should take the opportunity to shock your mate in a pleasant way. Memories can resurface, or perhaps you might experience the consequences of a past situation. Or you may want to explore the role of your childhood in your present life and a counselor would be a good place to start. This is a great time for psychological self-evaluation, whatever the motivation.

20. TUESDAY. Dreamy. Some aspect of your plans that involve another might not seem to work. Examine your expectations of this other person and look at the facts you have about them. It is quite possible that you have rose-colored glasses on when it comes to assessing their character, and this glitch in your plans is a warning. If nothing else, stop pushing and let things happen in their own time. A new job may not be what you had expected, and if you find the wages also are less than your expectations, start looking for another job. Don't let your new employer follow a lie with another one. Repairs to your home need to be examined thoroughly, as does the reason for the repairs; it might save you money.

21. WEDNESDAY. Reassuring. Everyone might seem to want a piece of you. Trying to juggle your career and reputation with your relationships and responsibilities might be a big task, but you can make yourself proud. Just remember to occasionally take time out for meditation or a walk in the park and maintain contact with your inner strength. You are on the right path and good things will happen no matter how stressful it can get in the meantime. Assess the friends and associates who are putting the pressure on you. Could it be that they aren't really the type of people you need in your life? Put yourself first and watch your daily routine smooth out, with more time allotted for the ones who are worth it.

22. THURSDAY. Optimistic. The mood changes for the better as the Sun moves into Sagittarius, upping the ante on happiness, love, and self-expression. At the same time Venus, the planet of love and harmony, moves into Scorpio to smooth over any disruptions of late on the home front. Your attitude toward relationships will lighten up and therefore make any problems seem less. This is a time of

year to kick up your heels and party, so start today. Entertaining
at home might turn you on, and the temptation to shop for extra
furniture or art objects to beautify your home could get out of control. Watch your budget and perhaps try your hand at old-fashioned
crafts and enjoy being creative while saving money.

23. FRIDAY. Purposeful. If anyone tries to pull the wool over your
eyes today, they will have another think coming. Your attention to
detail is a strong point and favors the signing of contracts and profitable business negotiations. If you have to bring up the dirt on your
opponent, then do so in a fair way and be sure you are not just re-
taliating over a past hurt. Keep your activities aboveboard though,
as any illegal dealings will come undone fairly quickly. Watch out
for long business lunches with too much champagne, as you may get
lulled into a false sense of security and give up too much information. A sudden desire to travel might coincide with cheap fares, and
before you know it, you're leaving!

24. SATURDAY. Varied. The planets combine to keep you highly
stimulated. Whether it is love, education, fame, or fortune you are
after, you are inspired to do your best. On the other hand, you could
be feeling dissatisfied with the same old thing and be longing for
a change of scenery. A disagreement with your mother, an elderly
female neighbor, or your sister could get you off on the wrong foot.
Be willing to listen and compromise, and you might learn a few
things about yourself in this exchange. Leo workaholics should start
planning your next holiday; make sure you don't plan one full of
action and work. Instead, give yourself the space to relax and start
enjoying life.

25. SUNDAY. Compromising. Find a balance between satisfying
your needs and the needs of those close to you. This means not
running yourself ragged to please others. A social situation might
put you in an uncomfortable position, as two people you care about
may not like each other. Don't get involved; it is not your fight so
don't make it so, as they may be quite happy for you to take the flak.
If you are helping your parents today, leave plenty of time, as you
might need to do more than you expect and you might also want
to do more. The chance to really enjoy a heart-to-heart with the
people who brought you into the world is worth it. The spotlight
might be on you later in the day.

26. MONDAY. Defining. Professional and business concerns come
into focus, but in a way that will force you to clarify your terms and
conditions. Use this opportunity to define what it is you really want

and need from a career and ask for it. This could be one of the most positive steps you take toward manifesting your dreams. You may be asked to take a leadership position that involves public speaking, something a Leo should have a natural talent for. If not, be assured you can develop the talent anyway. Your intuition and empathy toward those you work with is in your favor and will provide all the support you need. A promotion could also be in the cards.

27. TUESDAY. Ambitious. Socializing with the movers and shakers in your profession will be to your advantage. Let your colleagues get to know you and see your capabilities, and you can go far. Some may want you to take their side in power plays, so tread carefully. You do not want to become aligned with one faction and narrow your future options. Competitive sports might be of interest to you also, and you will have to look out for the same types of factional fighting within your club. Be a team player and enjoy the simple and uncomplicated power of being popular because you are an honest person. A friendship could start to develop into a wonderful love affair, but take it slow.

28. WEDNESDAY. Generous. The illuminating Moon rubs shoulders with expansive Jupiter and brings new associations and opportunities into your life. This morning's Full Moon in Gemini calls upon you to let go of the drama and attachment in romance and personal relationships as well as your willfulness. Learn about the value of the team and be willing to give your lover the freedom you demand. You may also be called upon to stand up for your ethical beliefs. If you are working for a company that produces wastes or products you do not value, then you might decide to leave this line of work. Some of you could be prepared to take a pay cut to work in an area that you believe in.

29. THURSDAY. Opportune. Luck and good fortune will flow from spontaneous and innovative action. Allow the free expression of your ideas without your usual inner censor inhibiting them. Then you will enjoy the success you can achieve simply by being yourself. An important business lunch might give you the opportunity to talk to an influential colleague. Don't hesitate to lay your proposition on the table and you will likely receive very positive feedback. Set aside plenty of time for an evening with your family or lover and catch up on quality personal time. Allow time for discussions over a sticking point and start the ball rolling on free expression and equality in all aspects of your life.

30. FRIDAY. Mixed. Set your alarm so that you can get your work done without too many distractions. The less pressure you have, the better you will perform. Don't push yourself to tackle the backlog of work either. If it has waited this long, another couple of days won't make a lot of difference, but might help you recharge your batteries so you can do a better job when you do get back to it. Take some time out of your day to do something just for yourself. A little pampering will help you relax and put a smile on your face. An interest in genealogy might inspire you to get out your family photos and start cataloging the captured memories. There may be a few that you can finally put a name to.

December 2012

1. SATURDAY. Comfortable. Any trouble that has been brewing on the home front can magically disappear and leave you wondering if you have imagined it. Perhaps in part this might be true. What we concentrate on gets our power, so it is very important to be conscious of what your thoughts are focused on. A relaxed family get-together, full of stories from the past and reminiscences about your predecessors and their arduous journeys, might give you an idea for a creative work. Many Leo people are sure to enjoy cloistering in your workshop or office to dedicate your full attention to an artistic task. This may seem selfish at the moment but is likely to have favorable repercussions on your work.

2. SUNDAY. Demanding. A large social gathering may demand more than you can give today. Don't hesitate to delegate tasks and take a load off your own shoulders. You may need to let go of the delusion that you have to do everything yourself to get it done properly. Yes, it may not get done the way you would do it, but who says it won't get done well? If you don't have any commitments, enjoy the luxury of doing nothing. Lose yourself in a novel or watch movies all day long from the comfort of your couch. The break will do you a world of good. Some of you might be inspired to go on a spiritual retreat. Research all your options on the Internet and you are likely to find exactly what you are looking for.

3. MONDAY. Vibrant. Creative ideas are likely to inspire lots of activity today. Lions might not have a lot of energy though, so be practical with your time and allow plenty of space for a break here and there. If you have not been feeling one hundred percent, seek some expert advice to get you back on track as quickly as possible. You may simply need to change your diet or add extra vitamins and minerals. There are healthful nutritional supplements that can bolster your immune system, but these should be taken only under the advice of a trusted medical practioner. A coworker might seem to have a grudge against you, but you may simply be overreacting to their depressed mood. It won't hurt to have a chat with them.

4. TUESDAY. Restless. Examine a strong desire to get away from your routine and boredom. Ask yourself if you are subconsciously trying to avoid a familiar problem, one that has always been at the bottom of previous moves. If this is your motivation, consider addressing the problem. Then you can organize a holiday or a move because it suits you. Your popularity is high and numerous invitations could arrive on your desk. Don't let flattery win you over; accept only those your heart chooses and start being true to yourself. Study plans may have to be reviewed if you find the extra workload is contributing to stress and interfering with your health.

5. WEDNESDAY. Fruitful. This is one of those days where everything you touch seems to turn to gold. You may feel as though you have a direct line to your higher consciousness and you're getting all the right answers to your questions. An opportunity to earn money for a creative talent might give your confidence the boost you need to branch out with your own business plan. Your partner may be able to give you the support you have been lacking on your own. If you are seeking a loan from a financial institution, you are likely to receive good news. But you must study the fine print diligently to ensure you are not signing up for more than you asked for.

6. THURSDAY. Encouraging. The good fortune from yesterday lingers, but don't exaggerate your potential. Stick to what you know you can achieve and you will get a name for being reliable and competent. Your energy levels are higher now; if you have not been well lately, you are probably well on your way to recovery. If you don't already have a daily exercise routine, this is a good time to start. Go to your local gym and get a personal trainer to put you on the right path for your fitness level. A new love affair could be up and down, causing you to rethink what it is you value in the relationship and whether it is worth the sacrifice of some of your personal pleasures.

7. FRIDAY. Stressful. Problems can be avoided simply by letting another know of your displeasure when it occurs. You don't have to be nasty or rude, just speak the truth. If you bottle things up, then there is likely to be an explosion which could turn nasty or rude quite easily. Today's lesson is to be honest in each moment and you will be amazed at how wonderful the day can turn out to be. Change is in the air, and with a positive attitude you can manifest one of your lifelong dreams. An opportunity to study overseas might stretch your budget but will amply make up for any hardship you might experience now with future benefits. Your biggest problem might be convincing your family to go along with the idea.

8. SATURDAY. Influential. Many varied personal exchanges can give you new ideas for business opportunities or travel, or you might combine both. You will get out and about a lot today, as a sense of boredom may follow at your footsteps. One positive outcome to this is that you are likely to end up doing something you normally would avoid and discover that you are having fun. New horizons can open up, and as you run into new acquaintances, don't let your preconceived ideas get in the way of you learning something new. The possibility that you can meet someone you are attracted to and who feels the same might make this day special. One thing is for certain: this day's end will be quite different to its beginning.

9. SUNDAY. Interactive. Family celebrations for this year's festivities might demand that you spend long hours on the telephone or Internet trying to synchronize the plans of many into a well-oiled symphony that comes together on Christmas Day. Don't give up, even if you start worrying about your phone bill; it will be worth it. Family plans for an outing may have to get shelved when surprise visitors turn up from out of town. Some of you may play matchmaker and have all sorts of deceptions going on just to bring two people together unexpectedly, on purpose! Any deception that you indulge in that isn't honest fun could backfire on you.

10. MONDAY. Karmic. The Moon joins Mercury, Venus, and Saturn in Scorpio and your solar fourth house of home and family today. Try not to avoid a chance for a deep and meaningful conversation with one of your close family members or a distant relative. Either way there is something you need to learn. Give your mother a call, especially if you haven't heard from her for a while, as she may not be well and you wouldn't want to let her down. On the other hand, some of you might start psychotherapy to work on childhood complexes stemming from your mother's parenting. Don't play the blame game, as this will only make you a victim. Practice forgiveness and compassion and begin a spiritual journey.

11. TUESDAY. Intellectual. You can entertain others with your ideas and conversation today. Mercury is in Sagittarius and your sector of self-expression. You have a powerful mental connection to your creativity, so much so that this is a perfect time to start a new creative business venture, learn a new art or craft, or even start teaching. Your ability to communicate with children is better than normal, as is your talent for storytelling. This transit also brings out the prankster in you, and you might need to think twice before you play a practical joke on some people. Don't be surprised if you start researching speculative ventures that you wouldn't normally waste the time on.

12. WEDNESDAY. Playful. Regardless of what's on your agenda, you are looking for fun and adventure. Even the most serious business discussion can end up in shrieks of laughter. People will warm to your winning ways, and your ability to sell your ideas now suggests that's what you should be doing. A freewheeling potential lover could capture your attention. Perhaps you should make the first move and get it back again! Plan to go out somewhere different this evening and add adventure to your daily life. Instead of leaving the country to experience foreign flavors, have dinner at an Asian or Indian restaurant and spice up your life.

13. THURSDAY. Vital. This morning's New Moon in Sagittarius highlights your sector of self-expression and creativity. It also hints at the beginning of a love relationship or the birth of a child. Dedicate this lunar month to discovering your inner talents and letting out the inner you. Decide to do something you have always dreamed about doing, but never had the guts to do. Go skydiving, or bungee jumping and live life to the fullest. If you have secretly desired to study meditation at an Indian ashram or walk the Incan trail, book your tickets and start saving. It might not happen today, but you can set the wheels in motion and change your life forever. Freedom is knowing that fear is only an idea.

14. FRIDAY. Diligent. Your eye for detail and a perfectionist streak will aid you in doing a good job. Some of you might apply for a new position and now you can be sure you will have all the relevant skills. You intuitively know when enough is enough and what other people want. If you have the day off and are stuck at home, get all your chores out of the way to prepare for a weekend of fun. If you haven't sent out your holiday cards, this is the perfect time. You might want to go through your address book to ensure you don't leave out anybody important. Clean out your cupboards and get rid of the junk; in your present frame of mind you can do it.

15. SATURDAY. Nurturing. All sorts of difficulties can be overcome with a loving attitude. People are likely to try to rub you the wrong way and could use underhanded and manipulative tactics. These will all go to waste though, if you can turn a blind eye and concentrate on what's good in the person. This might sound second only to saintly behavior, but give it a go; you might be up to the task today. A shopping trip is likely to be very satisfying as you discover some great bargains that save you the cost of next week's groceries as well. Gift shopping will also be successful, and you might be able to finalize your list well in advance.

16. SUNDAY. Delightful. Invitations to all sorts of entertaining outings could be hard to choose from. Enjoy the delights that the festive season offers, but don't go overboard and wear yourself out. It is so easy to overdo celebrations and forget the things you say and do, with fun events turning into a blur. Be selective and enjoy the clarity of mind that comes with this approach. You may get the opportunity to do a good deed for a neighbor or friend, and this will add to your enjoyment. Venus, the planet of love and harmony, moves into Sagittarius and adds her delights to your self-expression and romantic prospects, so you appear to be set to enjoy the next few weeks. Plan a romantic dinner with your lover.

17. MONDAY. Stimulating. Be prepared to give a little in today's stressful climate. Business negotiations can become heated as differences of perspective seem irreconcilable. It might be wise to defer making a decision until both parties have had some time to think about it, that way you might still salvage the deal. Don't push the point with a legal matter; at this time of year you don't need the extra hassle and it is likely to drag on for months of miserable legalities and make you wish you had never started anyway. A desire to break free of restrictions might instigate thoughts of quitting your job and heading overseas. You do need to talk this through with your family first.

18. TUESDAY. Testing. Any attempt to be somebody you are not will backfire. Be honest and humble and reap the rewards. You will be surprised at the results you receive when you simply do what is in front of you to the best of your ability. Holiday plans might be set back by a fee hike. This often happens during a holiday break; see if you can postpone your holiday until the peak season is over and save some money. If you must go, research different lending facilities and get a loan that you can afford, without hidden costs. Be clear when it comes to the sharing of joint resources and make sure you respect your partner's views as much as your own, otherwise you might wonder why you have joint resources.

19. WEDNESDAY. Rewarding. Take time out for communication with your significant other this morning. Worries and fears can be alleviated when shared, and two heads are always better than one when it comes to solving a problem. Just knowing you have each other's support will make all the difference. Dedication to a cause can bring favorable results also. Your reliance on a powerful ally can pay dividends and renew your faith in humanity. Some of you might need to speak to your parents about a possible loan and give them the opportunity to see you advance in life. Be clear about rights and responsibilities for smooth sailing. Watch out for a rival in love; don't let your lover use them against you.

20. THURSDAY. Exciting. Good vibes are in the air and as long as you stick with your friends you will be on the right track. Your schedule is likely to be hectic, so stay focused on where you are going and who you are with. If you must go shopping, get out and about early, visiting small markets and out-of-the-way shopping spots for more unique and personalized wares. You will enjoy the unusual today and can find yourself doing things that you hadn't planned, so you must keep your eye on the clock. An experience can change your life in some way now. You might gain a new perspective on life or learn something revolutionary, or a chance encounter could introduce you to the love of your life.

21. FRIDAY. Challenging. Normally very competent, you might find yourself out of your depth in a meeting with foreigners, big business people, or just a bunch of people from a different walk of life. The lesson might be to be humble and open to what you can learn rather than feel upset and confused because you can't stay on top of things. Community work could be on your agenda, helping out in poorer areas or with the ill and disabled. Adapting to whatever challenges come your way might be demanding but you can learn a new and positive use for your talents that makes any difficulties you encounter worthwhile. Publishing and teaching are on the agenda, as is travel and spiritual endeavors.

22. SATURDAY. Fulfilling. With the Sun now in Capricorn, shining its loving light on your sector of work and service, and the Moon in Taurus, highlighting career and ambition, your ability to work hard to achieve your goals should be high. There is also indication of extravagance, and you might go overboard in your preparations to make this year's celebrations better than ever before. If you are trying to prove you are better than another, then stop. This is not the point of your life and energy; rather, do your best to be the person you are and enjoy whatever you are doing for the sake of doing it. That way you will not be dependent on another person.

23. SUNDAY. Rewarding. A public performance might take all your willpower and nerves but the wonderful relief and the compliments that follow can make you eager to do it again. Whether you are supporting your children at a school play, or an emcee at a family celebration, your organizing abilities and talent at entertaining are likely to come to the fore. Stay calm if one of your loved ones tries to pick a fight with you early in the day; they are probably just reacting to the pressure of coming festive events. Even if they are just being plain cranky, having a fight won't be any better. Singles may receive a romantic invitation that conflicts with another engagement. Don't worry; follow your heart!

24. MONDAY. Cheerful. It may seem as if everybody wants a piece of you today. You might get stuck minding everyone else's kids so they can get their chores done, while yours have to wait. Throw yourself into whatever comes your way. If you do have lots of children to entertain, take them to a learning center and fill them in on cultural traditions. For older youngsters, expand on the experience by adding ancient mysteries to the mix. On this Christmas Eve, many will want to join a choral or carols group.Double-check your guest lists for tomorrow and call the people you might not see. You are likely to get a surprise invitation that keeps you out late, so your early preparations will allow you to relax later.

25. TUESDAY. Merry Christmas! Today's Moon joins gregarious Jupiter in Gemini, suggesting a wonderful energy for socializing with large amounts of people. Wherever you find yourself, you should be surrounded by interesting people from all different backgrounds. Some of you may be traveling and spend half the day on the Internet talking to people in many different countries. For those playing host to family and friends, you may need to delegate tasks and ensure you get to mingle, as there is a touch of the martyr hanging around. You are a great entertainer at the moment and might have everyone splitting their sides. Love and romance are part of the mix to make this a great day for all.

26. WEDNESDAY. Variable. Irritable aspects in the heavens suggest tiredness might mar your progress. Don't feel you have to tidy up or get going early, but take some quiet time for yourself and your loved ones to unwind after the last couple of weeks. Mars, the planet of energy and action, moves into Aquarius and your sector of partnerships which may contribute a level of tension to this aspect of your life. Cooperation can be harder to achieve, as everyone thinks only about themselves. On a positive note, it is a great time to put energy into resolving partnership difficulties. Working through the sticking points can give you both a lot of reasons to laugh and reminisce about each other's idiosyncracies.

27. THURSDAY. Distracting. Many conflicting interests come into play and can put you at cross purposes. Stay on track to achieve your goals and be seen as a team player. Your work and career are important to you, and a meeting with an influential friend could be on the top of your agenda. However, if they invite you to go elsewhere, ensure that you let your partner and family know where you are. You may feel as if you are juggling all the separate parts of yourself and wonder when you can feel integrated and whole. This is an important point to discuss with your friends and loved ones, as you might learn something that will be very useful to you in the future. You could be the life of the party tonight.

28. FRIDAY. Reflective. This morning's Full Moon in Cancer highlights your sector of unconscious complexes and desires and suggests this is the perfect time to experience transformation through psychotherapy, holistic bodywork, diet, or personal ritual. Circumstances may be such that you have an overwhelming desire to be alone. This is a normal reaction, given your depth of involvement in the festive season as well as your dedication to those you care about and to your career. Even if you have promised somebody that you would do something with them, cancel the engagement and claim some necessary rest and recuperation time for yourself. A secret may be revealed and solve a personal mystery.

29. SATURDAY. Reminiscent. A visit to see an elderly relative can stir up memories from the past, affecting your mood in an unexpected way. Make sure you take the time to write these thoughts and feelings down so that you can review them at a later date. If you don't already do so, now is a perfect time to start a journal and take a trip into your unconscious aspect of life. This type of reflection can add a spiritual dimension and lead to all sorts of enjoyable creative pursuits in the future. Your partner may surprise you with some pretty crazy plans; don't write them off without giving them a thought. Let your inner child out to play.

30. SUNDAY. Emotional. Watch out for your emotional reaction to what others say and do, otherwise you might find yourself in conflict over stupid little things. Instead, give thought to what is going on inside your head and your heart and express your feelings before they become too big to contain in any sane manner. You may feel that somebody is pushing you to do something you don't want to do; it is okay to say no. Leo people are very likely packing for a travel adventure and may have a large bon voyage party to attend in your honor. Enjoy the popularity, as you may be the name on many people's lips. But be selective about who you give your energy to; save some for your lover.

31. MONDAY. Loving. Beautiful vibes contribute to a wonderful day full of friends and fun. A new romance might put you on top of the world and send you out for a shopping spree to find clothes to make you even more attractive. Mercury, the planet of communication, moves into Capricorn and your sector of health and work and highlights mental work. You are much more attentive to detail now and can learn new techniques and get things done properly. If anybody criticizes you, you are likely to jump down their throat, so think before you react emotionally. Your New Year's resolutions list is likely to get quite long as you meticulously note all the things you would like to change.

AMAZING LOCAL PARTY LINE!

Ladies Talk FREE!

**Who needs to type when you can talk!
Make new friends, meet new people!
It's fun and exciting........
Call Now...**

512-400-4374

18+ Ent. Only

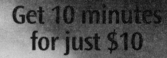